PHYSICIAN'S GUIDE TO DRGs

EDITED BY
- **Robert J. Shakno, M.H.A.**

CONTRIBUTORS
- **Michael J. Kalison, Esq.**
- **Joel May, M.B.A.**
- **Cosmo Mongiello, M.B.A.**
- **Lelio Passaglia, M.D.**
- **Frank J. Primich, M.D.**
- **Robert J. Shakno, M.H.A.**
- **Barbara Shaw, A.R.T.**
- **Mendel Silverman, M.D.**
- **James S. Todd, M.D.**

pluribus press inc.

11-30-83

© 1984 by Pluribus Press, Inc., Division of Teach'em, Inc.
All Rights Reserved

Except for appropriate use in critical reviews or works of scholarship, the reproduction or use of this work in any form or by any electronic, mechanical or other means now known or hereafter invented, including photocopying and recording, and in any information storage and retrieval system is forbidden without the written permission of the publishers.

Library of Congress Catalog Card Number:
83-62695

International Standard Book Number:
0-931028-41-8

Pluribus Press, Inc., Division of Teach'em, Inc.
160 East Illinois Street
Chicago, Illinois 60611

Printed in the United States of America

Acknowledgments

Putting together a book was a new experience for me, and it proved much more difficult and time-consuming than I had imagined. There were a thousand details and questions, and I can say with all sincerity that there would be no book were it not for the cheerful cooperation and assistance of dozens of people both within and outside Hackensack Medical Center.

Making a list of those to be thanked always involves the risk of leaving out someone. Nevertheless, I feel that certain people are to be thanked. So, saying in advance that this list of contributors isn't comprehensive, and apologizing in advance to those I leave out, I wish to acknowledge the following:

* The 400 members of the medical staff of Hackensack Medical Center for making the DRG system work here, and specifically the dozen or so physicians who contributed either by writing for the book, reading it and offering criticism, or participating in the initial planning. From our staff, I want particularly to thank Dr. Alfred A. Alessi, who has become a nationally recognized expert on DRGs, Dr. Ralph J. Fioretti, Dr. Bernard Gardner, Dr. Lelio Passaglia, Dr. Mendel Silverman, Dr. Milton Wiener, and Dr. Michael D. Yablonski.

* From the Medical Record Department, Barbara Shaw, the Director, who contributed what I consider an excellent chapter. She has become a real asset to the medical staff with her extensive DRG knowledge. Her Assistant Director, Michelle Elliott, also deserves credit for providing a hundred technical answers.

* From our Finance Department, Gus Mongiello, our Vice President for Finance, an extraordinarily well-versed executive whose financial advice has kept us a step ahead; and to his team

of financial specialists, especially Robert Cavotto, Joe Samples, Jeff Hart, and Janet Turso-Ahad.

* Lauren Giani, my Executive Assistant, for living with my mood shifts and my sometimes unreasonable demands as the book was being written.

* Duressa Pujat, our Medical Librarian, for locating all of the necessary research material; Mariann Boettcher, Executive Secretary in the Development Office, for putting all of this on a word processor; and James Musto, one of our 600 excellent volunteers, for the many hours spent on the copying machine.

* Edward J. Gorin, Director of Consumer Affairs and Public Information, who understood from past book writing experience what it takes, and became "staff disciplinarian," keeping us working nights and weekends to finish the book on time; and for making us believe we could do it, even at the worst moments.

* Barbara Trecker of our Consumer affairs staff, for putting together the pieces and making this book happen, doing far more work than she had originally agreed to, and more than any of us thought was possible.

* My wife Linda and children Deborah and Steven, for their usual understanding and their willingness to sacrifice family time so I could work on this project.

* The Officers of the Board of Governors of Hackensack Medical Center, not only for allowing us to write this book, but for their active encouragment.

From outside the organization, many friends, old and new, including Jeff Warren, Executive Director of the New Jersey Rate-setting Commission; Maureen Guttenstein of the Bergen County PSRO; Judy Boyd of the New Jersey Hospital Association; Richard Bagger of the U.S. House Select Committee on Aging, and, of course, all of those who donated sections to the book.

And a very special thanks to Joanne E. Finley, M.D., M.P.H., the Commissioner of Health in New Jersey from 1974 to 1982, who developed the DRG system in New Jersey as the inpatient care reimbursement system of the future. Dr. Finley, now Assistant Secretary of Health and Mental Hygiene in Maryland, took time from her busy schedule to review this book and to help with technical clarifications. I know that she would have preferred that this book provide more detailed information in some of the chapters, but she appreciates that this book was written as a quick reference manual for physicians, rather than as a technical resource.

As a physician, it was one of Dr. Finley's main goals that the DRG system would provide meaningful clinical data that physicians could use to analyze how they and their hospitals were caring for their patients, the implications on the quality of care and its costs. As of this writing, physicians and hospitals in New Jersey are just beginning to appreciate these possibilities.

Robert J. Shakno
Hackensack, N.J.
October 1983

Editor:

Robert J. Shakno, President, Hackensack Medical Center, Hackensack, N.J.

Contributors:

Michael J. Kalison, partner in the law firm of Manger, Kalison, Murphy and McBride, Morristown, N.J.

Joel May, President, Health Research and Educational Trust of New Jersey, Princeton, N.J.

Cosmo Mongiello, M.B.A., Vice President—Finance, Hackensack Medical Center, Hackensack, N.J.

Lelio Passaglia, M.D., Department of Internal Medicine, Hackensack Medical Center; Chairman, Utilization Review Committee and Chairman, Quality Assurance Committee, Hackensack Medical Center, Hackensack, N.J.

Frank J. Primich, M.D., Co-Chairman, DRG Committee of the Medical Society of New Jersey; Department of Obstetrics and Gynecology and President of the Medical Staff, Riverside General Hospital, Secaucus, N.J.

Barbara Shaw, A.R.T., Director of Medical Records, Hackensack Medical Center, Hackensack, N.J.

Mendel Silverman, M.D., Department of Family Practice, Hackensack Medical Center, Hackensack, N.J.; member of the Association for Professional Health Care Review, DRG Appeals Panel.

James S. Todd, M.D., Trustee, American Medical Association; Department of Surgery, Valley Hospital, Ridgewood, N.J.; Past Chairman of the Board, Medical Society of New Jersey.

Contents

INTRODUCTION xi

1. HOW DRGs ARE SUPPOSED TO WORK 1

2. DOCTORS AND HOSPITALS—A NEW ERA OF
   COOPERATION 17
   Physicians—Victims of Their Own Success 17
   Lack of Understanding Is the Big Threat 24
   Questions Doctors Ask Administrators 29

3. YOU HAVE A FRIEND IN MEDICAL RECORDS . . . 57
   Questions Doctors Ask Medical Records 61

4. FINANCIAL CONSIDERATIONS THAT WON'T
   GO AWAY 94
   Questions Doctors Ask Hospital Controllers 98

5. QUESTIONS PATIENTS ASK THEIR DOCTORS . . 111

6. THE NEW JERSEY EXPERIENCE 127
   Excerpts from the U.S. House of Representatives
     Hearings on New Jersey's DRG System 138
   Horror Stories 154
   How New Jersey's Practicing Physicians Feel
     About DRGs 163

vii

7. USING DRG DATA 171
   A Look at the Data 176
   Technology Appeals: A Case Study 196

8. LOOKING AHEAD 206

APPENDIX A
   I. Twenty-Seven Suggestions for a
   Smooth Transition 212
   II. Thirteen Dangers to Avoid 218
   III. Fourteen Suggestions to Improve Efficiency 221

APPENDIX B
   How to Speak the DRG Language 228

INDEX 231

EXHIBITS
   3.1   Medical Records Quality Control for DRG
         Assignment 65
   3.2   DRG Assignment Flow Chart 66
   3.3   Medical Records Quality Control 68
   3.4   Medical Records and Billing—Per Diem
         Reimbursement 69
   3.5   Informational Requirements for
         DRG Assignments 70

3.6	Medical Record Department Technical Analysis for Secondary Diagnoses—Its Impact on Reimbursement	76
3.7	DRG Network	92
3.8	Documentation in the Medical Record	93

TABLES

4.1	102
7.1	180
7.2	182
7.3	184
7.4	188
7.5	190
7.6	194
7.7	202
7.8	203
7.9	204

Introduction

On Oct. 1, 1983, a nationwide prospective payment system for Medicare, based on diagnosis related groups, went into effect. This new system marks a very significant change in the delivery of health care in this country, a change with far-reaching effects for everyone—patients, physicians, hospitals, and third party payers.

Physicians all over the country are greatly concerned about this new system of payment for hospital care. They question how it will affect their practice of medicine within the hospital; what it will do to their relationship with the hospital and with their patients; and what it bodes for the future.

It is hoped that this book will familiarize physicians with the new system and why it was instituted, and with the problems that it creates as well as the possibilities that it holds for delivering quality care at a reasonable cost. We are not experts in DRGs, but we *are* experts in living with them, and so we have attempted to give others the advantage of our experience. Perhaps most important, therefore, this book can help physicians learn how to cope with DRGs on a day-to-day basis, from the smallest details (How do I write my diagnoses? How long do I have to finish my charts?) to the larger, more basic issues (How do I preserve quality of care amidst a "bottom line" mentality? How will this affect my relationship with the hospital?).

Hackensack Medical Center, a 500-bed community teaching hospital, was among the first 26 hospitals in New Jersey to come under a DRG system. We have been living with DRGs since 1980, and here in New Jersey, the DRG system applies to all payers—

Blue Cross, Medicaid, private insurance, and self pay patients, as well as Medicare.

As a hospital that has historically operated at or near capacity, we had always experienced pressure toward shorter lengths of stay and greater efficiency because of the demand for beds. In a sense, we had operated all along in a "DRG-like" atmosphere. The DRG system served to give us a greater impetus in the direction we already were headed. Nevertheless, implemeting DRGs was an interesting and at times difficult experience, involving the medical staff, the administration, and the board of governors as well as finance, medical records, nursing, and many ancillary departments.

As chief executive officer of Hackensack Medical Center, I have had the opportunity during the past three years to discuss the DRG system at regional forums and hospitals throughout the country, sharing information with my colleagues, with physicians, and with boards of trustees. I was struck with how well-prepared hospitals and doctors were for the new system. Nevertheless, it became apparent that there was a need for information, especially the day-to-day workings of the system and how it affected physicians, and it is to this purpose that the book was written.

In talking with these various groups, it became clear to me that if the system was properly explained to physicians, and if physicians were brought into the decision-making process at the time DRGs were implemented, they would find DRGs a workable system, even given their very legitimate concerns about the possible negative impact on the quality of care.

Specifically, I became convinced that doctors are as concerned about the rising cost of health care as are administrators, trustees, businessmen and the general public, and that, if properly used, the DRG system could become a very useful tool for physicians in helping to hold down health care costs.

After three years' experience with DRGs here in New Jersey, I fully believe that if hospital management develops a positive climate for physicians in using DRGs, then doctors can become the hospital's greatest ally in its efforts for financial survival under this incentive-based system of reimbursement.

INTRODUCTION

Furthermore, if a hospital expects its medical staff to cooperate by using hospital resources in a way that will help to hold down hospital costs, then the hospital might make provisions for and encourage physicians to participate actively in many of the hospital's management and planning functions.

One of the most important aspects of the new system is the need for medical staffs and hospitals to develop mechanisms for implementing DRGs that retain the medical staff's autonomy in implementing and monitoring the DRG system while still conforming to the economic mandates of the institution. We have dealt with this issue throughout the book because I feel it is essential for the medical profession to monitor its own performance through peer review systems, instead of having hospital administrators and boards dictate to doctors how to practice medicine. We have described how hospitals can provide their medical staffs with the statistical data to monitor the cost of care ordered by physicians on an individual basis, by peer groups, by clinical specialties, and by diagnoses.

We have also addressed, based on our experience, concerns regarding physician autonomy and quality of care, and how quality of care can be protected and enhanced through the appropriate application of the DRG system. The issue of quality care versus cost efficiency is a real one, of concern to hospital administrators as well as physicians. While we cannot be certain what impact DRGs will have on quality of care, we hope we have shown that cost consciousness and quality need not be opposing goals, but rather can be brought together for the good of our patients—quality care at an *appropriate cost.*

Despite three years of living with DRGs at this hospital and in this state, many of us who have contributed to this book believe it is still too early to determine whether the system will ultimately prove to be good or bad for health care. We are still learning about the DRG system, about its idiosyncracies, its strengths, and its weaknesses. There is still much to be learned and there are many unanswered questions. However, I do believe that our experience has shown that there are some very positive aspects to this program, and that hospitals and physicians together can make it work. This bias will no doubt be apparent throughout the book.

However, not everyone involved in health care in New Jersey agrees with this assessment, and, in an effort to provide a balanced, representative view of DRGs, we have included material in the book from contributors who take a different point of view, and who raise concerns and issues which need to be voiced.

Regardless of your point of view about DRGs, it is safe to assume that the delivery of health care in this country, including the role of hospitals and physicians, has been radically altered by DRGs. The basic concepts of prospective pricing and competition we are now beginning to exprience will have a profound effect on health care in the future. It is because of our strong conviction about these matters that we felt compelled to share our experiences, in the hope that we may all have an impact on shaping it and improving it in the years ahead. Indeed, there are many changes that need to be made and we intend to urge their adoption. Although as of this writing DRGs apply only to Medicare in most states, it is reasonable to expect that all payers will soon be covered. We have dealt with that expectation throughout this book, in an effort to make the material relevant in the future.

It is necessary to remember the important differences between the Medicare system and the New Jersey system—differences that we will be alluding to throughout this book. For instance, the information systems available in New Jersey serve as a stimulus for physician involvement, while the information available under the federal system will be more limited. The completeness of the New Jersey system begun by Dr. Joanne E. Finley, Commissioner of Health in New Jersey at the time, makes it an approach that seems to work to the advantage of physicians, hospitals and the public.

If there is one lesson to be learned from DRGs, it is that the physician is the key in determining whether the system works, and, beyond that, in ensuring the financial survival of hospitals while protecting the quality of patient care.

The DRG system represents a very important challenge, one that demands our involvement, our patience, our understanding, our diligence, and our ingenuity. I hope that, after reading this book, you will be left with the message that this challenge can best be met with the active involvement of you and your colleagues as we strive together to improve the care of your patients.

>Robert J. Shakno
>President
>Hackensack Medical Center
>Hackensack, NJ
>Oct. 2, 1983

Chapter One
How DRGs Are Supposed to Work

Before learning how to live with DRGs you should know, at the very least, a few basic facts about the system. DRGs will undoubtedly have a very important impact on the way you practice medicine in a hospital setting, and you ought to know exactly what they are, who dreamed them up, why they're being instituted all across the country, and what they're supposed to cure.

The following questions and answers are your DRG primer—a quickie course in Diagnosis Related Groups for those new to the system.

Here, then, is the theory of DRGs and prospective payment, the way DRGs are supposed to work. Take it from those of us who have lived with the system for three years: things don't always work out the way they're supposed to. But that comes later in the book. For now—DRGs explained.*

WHAT IS A PROSPECTIVE PAYMENT SYSTEM?

A prospective payment system, or PPS, is what we in New Jersey

---

This section written by Robert J. Shakno, President, Hackensack Medical Center, Hackensack, NJ. All other portions of this book not otherwise credited were written by Mr. Shakno.
*At the time of this writing many of the Medicare regulations were still being determined and/or were subject to change. Remember, though, that the specifics of the system are not as important as the concept, and its impact on your practice of medicine.

PHYSICIAN'S GUIDE TO DRGs

have been living with since 1980 and what you must now face for all Medicare patients.

Prospective as opposed to *retrospective* payment sets in advance the revenue the hospital will be reimbursed for treating patients. Under the present system, the hospital in effect treated a patient, added up its charges to care for that patient, and then sent in the bill—and for the most part got reimbursed for the actual amount. Under this system, hospitals have been virtually assured of getting back at least whatever they spent. Thus, there was no incentive to contain costs.

Under PPS, the hospital knows in advance how much money it will receive for each case. There is a set fee that does not depend on how long the patient remains in the hospital or how much it costs the hospital to care for that patient. In a sense, prospectively determined prices put the hospital "at risk" financially and give the hospital a very real stake in ensuring efficient care.

In New Jersey we have been under a prospective payment system for all payers—Medicare, Medicaid, Blue Cross, commercial insurance and self pay. Virtually all hospital reimbursement for inpatient care has been under this prospective payment system, beginning in 1980. The federal government has made a decision to try a national prospective payment system, modeled on New Jersey's, for all Medicare inpatient services.

Now, once the decision has been made to go with prospective payment, how is the amount of the actual payment determined? The mechanism used in New Jersey, and the one adopted for Medicare, is DRGs.

WHAT ARE DRGs?

DRG stands for Diagnosis Related Groups, which are the basis of payment for Medicare's new prospective payment system. DRGs represent a new system of billing for hospital care, based on a patient's diagnosis rather than on the actual services consumed or length of stay in the hospital.

DRGs are basically a classification system[1] which distributes all

---

[1]For a complete listing of the 1984 Medicare DRGs and an explanation of Medicare's prospective payment plan, see *DRG Update: Medicare's Prospective Payment Plan* by Paul L. Grimaldi and Julie A. Micheletti. Pluribus Press, Inc., 160 E. Illinois, Chicago, IL.

HOW DRGs ARE SUPPOSED TO WORK

medical diagnoses and procedures into 467 different categories. DRG #45, for instance, is neurological eye disorder, medical; DRG #114 is upper limb and/or toe amputation; DRG #321 is kidney and/or urinary tract infection in patients 18 to 69 years old, without complications or comorbidities (other medical conditions), medical.

The theory is that all hospital patients assigned to the same DRG represent a homogeneous group—they are similar not only in terms of the broad clinical description of their illness, but also in terms of their length of stay in the hospital, the resources they consume, and the cost of their treatment.

Assuming then that all patients in a DRG will cost the hospital, on average, approximately the same amount to care for, hospitals will now be reimbursed one set fee for each Diagnosis Related Group. The fee is determined *prior* to the actual treatment—hence, *prospective* payment.

Another way of looking at this is to say that each DRG represents what a particular hospital should spend, on average, to diagnose and treat a category of illnesses.

Still another way of viewing DRGs is as products in business. Ford produces cars and knows in advance what price it will charge for each model. Nabisco makes crackers and knows how much each variety will cost. Hospitals treat 467 diagnostic categories, and now they know the price tag for each one—and so do the people paying the bills.

WHAT IS THE PURPOSE OF DRGs?

The new system was developed in response to health care costs that are rising faster than the nation's inflation rate. A DRG-based prospective payment system is an attempt to give hospitals and their physicians an incentive to treat patients more economically, and thus reduce health care costs. In the past, hospitals were reimbursed for whatever they spent; there was no incentive to try to cut costs. With DRGs, hospitals have an opportunity to make money by saving money rather than spending it.

In effect, the system says to hospitals: We will give you a certain amount of money to treat a certain kind of patient. If you can treat that patient for less money, you get to keep all or some portion of the difference. But if it costs you more to treat the patient, you must make up the difference yourself. No longer can hospitals spend money freely, assured that they will automatically be reimbursed whatever their costs are. From now on the meter is running, and hospitals have to keep an eye on that meter as they care for their patients.

For instance, DRG #6, carpal tunnel release, may carry with it a set rate of $1,485.68.[2] That figure is based on a hospital stay of between two and five days. It also assumes a certain amount of resources will be used—tests, procedures, staff time, etc. Once a patient is assigned to this DRG, the hospital will be reimbursed $1,485.68 for his or her care, no matter how much it *actually* costs the hospital to care for that patient—as long as the stay is within the limits of two to five days.

Now, if Hospital A treats a patient in DRG #6 in two days, and more important, uses fewer resources than the average, its reimbursement should exceed its actual cost. Terrific! Hospital B on the other hand keeps its DRG #6 patient in the hospital five days, and the patient utilizes more tests, more procedures, and more overall resources of the hospital than the average. So Hospital B probably ends up spending more on the patient than it will be reimbursed. Too much of this kind of behavior can lead to real trouble for Hospital B. The idea is that Hospital B will take corrective action and begin to treat its patients more efficiently, and thus more economically.

A prospective payment system based on DRGs will, it is hoped, encourage better hospital management as hospitals "compete" for available health care dollars. PPS provides an incentive to the efficient hospital, in the way of profit, and a penalty to the inefficient hospital, in terms of a negative cash flow—a reimbursement rate that is lower than the cost of the services rendered. The former will prosper and the latter will fail, unless it learns to become more efficient.

For the first time, efficiency and cost-consciousness will be rewarded; inefficiency and waste will be penalized. It's the old stick and carrot theory, this time applied to hospitals.

---

[2]All DRG rates in this book are representative and do not necessarily reflect actual DRG rates at any paritcular hospital.

The government is in effect saying to hospitals (and, by extension, to physicians, who determine the utilization of resources in the hospital): You may no longer go on spending freely; it is essential to begin carefully choosing the use of hospitals' resources with a view toward cost. You are in an era of limited resources now, where financial considerations are an integral part of health care (and, if these resources are used properly, the quality of care need not necessarily be reduced). In effect, hospitals are being told that they have a budget and must stick to it.

It is important to remember, though, that cutting costs at the expense of quality patient care will lead to trouble for any hospital. "Less expensive" doesn't mean "more efficient" unless quality is safeguarded. Indeed, one of the aspects of DRGs that make physicians feel very uncomfortable with the system, as you will see later in the book, is what they perceive as a lack of safeguards to ensure quality care.

WHO ARE DRGs SUPPOSED TO BENEFIT?

Given the fact that health care costs have been skyrocketing and that we are in an era of limited resources, DRGs are designed to benefit everyone by reducing costs or, at least, containing the rate of increase of these health care costs. That is the theory, anyway. Whether or not everyone does actually benefit from this system remains to be seen in the years ahead.

Perhaps the biggest beneficiary of the new system will be (or is supposed to be) the health care system, and by extension the public, by controlling the rise in health care costs. That means each health care dollar will go farther and will buy more health care services because the waste will be eliminated from the system. (However, some physicians fear that DRGs will lead to fewer health care services, as the belt is tightened more and more.) In addition, money that would have gone to health care services will now be able to be diverted to other necessities—food, housing, education, etc.

Specifically, patients should be the direct beneficiaries of a well conceived DRG program because each patient will be charged only the amount related to his or her diagnosis. A patient with a gall bladder operation will be charged only for the amount the system has set for that procedure; a patient admitted for a heart attack will pay a different amount, related only to the cost of caring for a heart attack patient. Patients will be paying what have been determined as fair and just fees to treat their particular illnesses. They will no longer be subsidizing inefficiencies and waste in the health care system.

Hospitals, by being forced to become more efficient, should be able to provide quality care within the new, reduced health care expenditure limits.

Doctors, it is presumed, will benefit too, by streamlining their treatment so that optimum care is provided consistent with limited health care resources. (Not everyone agrees with this positive scenario, as you will see in the pages ahead.)

The obvious exceptions to this rosy picture are hospitals that are currently operating inefficiently and do not improve. Hospitals that waste their resources may not survive under this system. As hospitals fail, as some inevitably will, more efficient hospitals will benefit, because scarce health care resources will be diverted to them.

This school of hard knocks theory is the basis for this country's market-oriented economy—an economy that has always rewarded the efficient at the expense of the inefficient. Rewards for efficiency have been at work in many other spheres of the economy for some time. Whether this open competition will work when applied to the health care industry is uncertain.

Critics of the system worry that DRGs may indeed work— only too well, and at the expense of availability of new technology to patients. Decisions about diagnostic approaches and treatment plans, they say, will be in the hands of those not directly involved in patient care. While the system is aimed at improving efficiency, critics fear this will occur only by limiting access to services, which will inevitably lead to underutilization for some patients. But federal legislation does mandate a commission to be set up to review new technologies and treatments and to make necessary adjustments.

WHOSE IDEA WAS THIS ANYWAY?

DRGs were originally developed by researchers at Yale University in 1975 as a research tool and were intended, but never used, for improved utilization review. They were developed as a means of improving utilization review. (For more details on how the DRGs were developed, see page 9.)

New Jersey, searching for a way to cope with rising hospital costs, adopted a basic classification of 383 DRGs as a prospective payment mechanism beginning in 1980. The system was developed with a $5.3 million grant from the federal Health Care Financing Administration (HCFA). In 1982 the original 383 DRGs were expanded to 467, which remain the basis for New Jersey's reimbursement system as well as Medicare's.

Another very important reason the system was begun in New Jersey was in an effort to save inner city hospitals, many of which were on the verge of bankruptcy because of inadequate reimbursement for indigent care.

Because of federal and state controls, hospitals were limited in the rates they could charge Medicare, Medicaid and Blue Cross. Therefore, the only way hospitals could make up for losses for indigent care was by charging higher rates to private insurance and self-payers. But inner city hospitals, which generally did not have a favorable mix of patients with private insurance, had no way to shift their substantial losses from indigent care. The DRG system spreads the cost of indigent care among all hospitals in the state. Indeed, after three years of DRGs, many inner city hospitals that had been on the brink of financial ruin are showing healthy profits for the first time in many years.

Hackensack Medical Center was one of the original twenty-six hospitals in New Jersey to participate in DRGs. Today all 100 of New Jersey's acute care hospitals are under a DRG system.

WHAT DOES THIS HAVE TO DO WITH THE REST OF THE COUNTRY?

The federal government, under pressure to contain a $41 billion Medicare budget, took a special interest in New Jersey's DRG experiment with an eye toward extending a similar DRG-based prospective payment system to all Medicare inpatients.

Consider some of the statistics Medicare was faced with and you may begin to understand the need for a change in the system.

- Eleven percent of all Americans are 65 or older; their number is expected to increase to 19 percent by the year 2025.

- Individuals over 65 generally need about four times as much medical care as other members of the population.

- It was projected that the government would be spending $110 billion on Medicare by the year 1987, when, it was predicted, the Medicare Trust Fund would run dry.

- Medicare reimbursements represent one-third of all hospital revenue.

- The cost of hospital care rose 12.6 percent in 1982, compared to a general inflation rate of 3.9 percent.

Under the disparities of the present system, Medicare was paying vastly different amounts for the same medical care, depending on the hospital. For instance, cataract removals could cost Medicare anywhere from $450 to $2,800; treatment for heart attack varied from $1,500 to $9,000. The government, like any other consumer, does not want to pay more money when it can get the same service at a much lower rate elsewhere. What the government is saying now is not that they are cutting funds for Medicare; they are merely slowing the rate of increase. Instead of a projected 17 percent increase in Medicare funds in 1983, the government wants to hold the increase to 14 percent. There will still be more money for Medicare than the previous year, just not quite as *much* more as there might have been.

Given all these factors, and given the need to stem the tide, Congress approved a DRG-based prospective payment system for Medicare on March 24, 1983, as Title VI of the Social Security Amendments of 1983. The new system has been described by the American Hospital Association as the most significant change in the history of Medicare, which began in 1965 in an effort to extend health care services to the elderly, at a time when cost was not a real factor. Now, in an era of retrenchment, cost has become a critical element in the program.

New Jersey's 467 DRGs are the basis for the federal prospective payment system, which was scheduled to go into effect in all hospitals whose fiscal year began on or after Oct. 1, 1983. The

HOW DRGs ARE SUPPOSED TO WORK

federal regulation applies to Medicare reimbursements for inpatient services in all hospitals in the country, with the exception of children's, psychiatric, rehabilitation and long-term hospitals.

Beyond the federal Medicare legislation, some states (Maryland, Massachusetts and New York) have enacted broader prospective payment systems similar to New Jersey's. These states have applied for waivers from federal Medicare regulations on the basis that the state systems are similar to the federal and satisfy certain requirements. It is predicted that at least thirty states will enact some form of all-payer system by the end of 1984.

Whether prospective payment currently applies just to your Medicare patients or to all of your patients, there is no doubt that this new system will have an enormous impact on your practice of medicine in the years ahead.

The details of DRG-based prospective pricing may vary from state to state, and the Medicare system may vary in certain significant details from the one that has been in operation in New Jersey. Nevertheless, the basic theory of the system—shifting hospitals from cost-based retrospective payment to a set-fee prospective payment system—is the same.

Furthermore, it appears likely that if anything, the system will be expanded to cover other elements of the health care system and, despite small differences in the actual programs, the response by physicians and hospitals will have to be basically the same.

HOW WERE THE DRGs FORMED?

The current system of 467 diagnosis related groups represents a modification of the original classification system of 383 diagnosis related groups formulated by researchers at Yale University. The original system defined 83 major diagnostic categories (MDCs) based on cause of disease. Then, using patient records, a computer broke down these 83 major diagnostic categories into 383 DRGs, based on primary diagnosis, secondary diagnosis, primary surgical procedure, secondary surgical procedure, and the age of the patient.

In 1982, a panel of physicians in New Jersey, including Dr. Michael D. Yablonski of Hackensack Medical Center, helped to refine the system into the current 467 DRGs.

The current system used the ICD-9-CM codes to formulate twenty-three major diagnostic categories based on which of the body's organ systems are affected. For instance, there are MDCs for: diseases and disorders of the digestive system; diseases and disorders of the musculoskeletal system and connective tissue; diseases and disorders of the female reproductive system, etc.

Patients are assigned to a major diagnostic category based on an organ system approach. The groups are then further divided into 467 DRGs based on diagnoses and/or surgical procedures. In all, the 467 DRGs take into account six variables: principal diagnosis; principal and other procedures; secondary diagnoses (presence of complications, which are other conditions that arise while a patient is in the hospital, and/or presence of comorbidities, which are other conditions that were present before the patient was admitted to the hospital); age; sex; and discharge status.

These variables were chosen because they were shown to have an important effect on length of stay and cost.

HOW WERE RATES FOR THE DRGs DETERMINED?

In New Jersey, data were collected from hospitals throughout the state so that average costs could be determined. These costs were reviewed and used to calculate rates. The system attempted to collect data from every single patient bill in each hospital in the state. While this was not totally successful, the vast majority of patient cases *were* reviewed. The base year for the 383 DRGs was 1978; the base year for the revised 467 DRGs was 1979.

For the national Medicare system, it appears, at the time of this writing, that base costs will be developed from Medicare cost data for the next-to-the-last twelve month cost reporting period preceding the first cost reporting period subject to prospective payment.[3] This means that, for calendar year hospitals, 1982 will be the base year for 1984 rates. The determination for the rates is based on a 20 percent sample of all Medicare patients at each hospital.

---

[3]*Healthcare Financial Management*, June 1983, Vol. 13, No. 6, page 1.

Regardless of the exact mechanism, the concept is always the same—strike an average within various peer groups[4] and use it as a payment rate. It is very important that each institution review how its individual rates were determined in order to assess the accuracy of the base period rates. If errors are found, they may appeal and request that 100 per cent of base year cases be used.

SURELY THERE MUST BE EXCEPTIONS. WHAT ABOUT CASES THAT JUST DON'T FIT INTO THE 467 DIAGNOSES? OR WHAT IF THEY DO FIT IN, BUT IT TURNS OUT THINGS DON'T WORK THE WAY THEY'RE SUPPOSED TO?

You're right. In New Jersey there are several categories of patients who are considered outliers and are not reimbursed in the same way. The following cases are considered outliers in New Jersey:

1. Unusually long or unusually short lengths of stay.
2. Any patient who dies in the hospital, regardless of length of stay.
3. Patients who leave the hospital against medical advice.
4. Patients admitted and discharged the same day.
5. Patients who are clinically atypical. Certain DRGs display no clinical homogeneity, and all patients in these DRGs are considered clinical outliers. These are patients with a unique combination of diagnoses and surgeries, very rare conditions, etc., which preclude valid comparisons for equitable rate setting. Clinical outliers also include patients having surgery unrelated to the principal diagnosis, and those DRGs without a sufficient number of patients from which to calculate a rate.

In New Jersey it was found that 25 to 40 percent of a hospital's case mix turned out to be outliers. For these cases, the

---

[4]Peer groups under the federal system are urban/rural hospitals and each within nine census regions. Therefore eighteen different average DRG rates have been issued for the three year transition period. In New Jersey, DRG rates were calculated for these peer groups: major teaching hospitals, minor teaching, and non-teaching.

hospital is reimbursed controlled charges (the actual cost of care plus a mark-up factor for indigent care and indirect costs, subject to limitations by the state) rather than the DRG fee.

The national Medicare system also provides for outliers, but the federal regulators have a different definition of (and tolerance for) outliers. Under the federal legislation, outliers are cases with an unusually long length of stay (day outliers) *and* cases which are unusually expensive to treat (cost outliers). These cases are reimbursed differently. Unusually short and inexpensive cases are reimbursed at DRG rates for the present, although this is under study.

Significantly, however, Medicare officials have set a 5.5 percent goal for total outlier payments. In other words, additional payments for outliers must not exceed 5.5 percent of the total amount of Medicare reimbursement for the year. Thus, there will be far fewer outliers under the Medicare system than have been allowed in New Jersey's system.

HOW ARE THE REIMBURSEMENT RATES BEING DETERMINED FOR EACH HOSPITAL?

Recognizing that present charges vary widely among hospitals, the government has considered a number of factors in determining DRG reimbursement rates for individual hospitals: the hospital's own cost performance, regional average rates, national average rates, the hospital's case mix, inflation, labor cost variations, whether or not the hospital is a teaching hospital, etc.

For purposes of DRG reimbursement, the nation has been divided into nine geographical regions, which initially will have different average DRG rates. DRG rates will also differ for rural and for urban hospitals.

There will an initial three-year phase-in period to establish separate urban and rural national DRG price schedules, adjusted for variations in wage levels. During this phase-in period the reimbursement rate for each Medicare discharge will reflect varying compositions of a hospital's own cost-per-case amount (during a base year), the regional rate and the national rate.

In the first year the payment for each Medicare patient will be equal to 75 percent of the hospital's own cost plus 25 percent of the regional average price for the specific DRG; in the second year the payment will equal 50 percent of the hospital's cost, 37.5 percent of the regional average price, and 12.5 percent of the national average price; in the third year, the payment will equal 25 percent of the hospital's own cost, 37.5 percent of the regional average price, and 37.5 percent of the national average.

In the fourth year, and thereafter, the payment will be based totally on the urban or rural national average price for each DRG, adjusted for differences in area wages. At this point, the hospital's individual cost performance will have no impact on the DRG rate. In effect, the hospital will at this point be matching its own cost performance against the national average. Good performance will mean a favorable reimbursement; poor performance could mean a loss.

WHAT DO DRGs HAVE TO DO WITH ME AS A PRIVATE PRACTITIONER?

A great deal. DRG-based prospective payment represents a profound change in our health care delivery system. The change will, sooner or later, begin to have its impact on you and on the way you practice medicine.

Physicians are truly the key players in this new system. It is the physician who decides whether to admit a patient, what tests and procedures are performed, and length of stay in the hospital. In other words, the physician controls the allocation of the hospital's resources, and therefore the hospital's costs in caring for patients.

Doctors will be affected by how well their hospitals do under this new system. If a hospital fares well, it will mean a better setting for the physician to practice medicine. If a hospital does poorly, and begins to cut back on services, it will obviously adversely affect the physician.

Physicians will be affected in a more intimate sense, also, as this new reimbursement system places hospitals and physicians in a new and unique relationship. In a sense, doctors can control how well their hospitals fare in this new era of regulation. But do not expect hospitals to sit idly by while physicians' practices determine their future. Hospitals have a few bargaining chips on their side too.

Because hospitals must now be concerned with cost efficiency, they will be taking a much closer and a much harder look at the practices of their staff physicians, and just how these practices are affecting their institution's financial well-being. As hospitals gather DRG data, they will be able to see how individual physicians' ordering practices affect the income and expenses of their hospital as compared to their peers. (For discussion on the types of DRG data hospitals will have access to, see page 171.)

Consider how a physician will be viewed by the hospital board and by other physicians if he or she consistently has the longest stays and highest costs for admissions, in light of the negative impact this will have on the hospital's financial status.

In other words, the hospital and its medical staff both have good reason to be in closer partnership to ensure that the hospital has the financial means to function effectively within the DRG system.

ARE MY PATIENTS (AND THE PUBLIC) BEING SHORT-CHANGED BECAUSE OF A DIFFICULT ECONOMY?

The issue goes well beyond a difficult economy. A public policy decision has been made at the highest levels that the inflationary spiral of health care—which far exceeds the inflationary growth of all other sectors of the economy—can no longer be tolerated because the health care system is pricing itself beyond the ability of consumers to pay for it. There is an obvious problem within the health care system, and DRGs are an attempt to deal with the problem.

In 1982, the consumer price index rose 3.9 percent, while the cost of hospital care rose 12.6 percent, according to the Department of Health and Human Services.

The proportion of the gross national product going to health care was 10.5 percent in 1982, marking the first time medical costs have exceeded 10 percent of the nation's total goods and services.

In all, the 1982 health care bill was $322.4 billion. Hospital care accounted for more than 40 percent of this amount—$133.5 billion. Medicare hospital payments rose by 18.8 percent over the previous year. The government, which pays 42 percent of the nation's total health bill, is duly concerned.

The largest payers of health insurance premiums—employers who include group health insurance as employee benefits—are also deeply concerned that premiums for health care are their fastest growing costs. Their other cost increases are moderating, but health care premiums continue to increase, currently at rates of 20 percent annually.

Many reasons have been suggested for the rise in health care costs, from new technology to an aging population to waste in the system. One of the most important factors that must ultimately be addressed is the medical-legal question—the multi-million dollar medical malpractice claim settlements. Defensive medicine is pervasive, and is a big contributor to the rise in health care costs.

Regardless of where the blame is placed, it has been known for some time that choices will have to be made in an effort to moderate these costs or at least reduce their rate of increase. We have truly reached the point in health care where we can no longer afford the services that are offered. That is the reality. DRGs are the current method for dealing with this problem. The aim is not to shortchange the public, but rather to enhance health care so that patients are receiving the most for their money, as in other sectors of the economy.

WON'T THE DRG SYSTEM CAUSE HOSPITALS TO LOWER THE QUALITY OF CARE?

Probably the biggest concern with the DRG system is that hospitals may be tempted to provide fewer services for each admission and to shorten lengths of stay in order to remain within the amount of income that each DRG provides. Proponents of the system say this won't happen because physicians still have the major responsibility for ensuring that the care delivered in each hospital meets the proper standards. No physician will release a patient early, or fail to order a test, if such behavior is not in the patient's best medical interest. And no hospital would pressure a physician to cut back on care or service that is needed. Hospitals would not survive long if the quality of care they offer begins to be affected adversely by DRGs. It is not the goal of DRGs to sacrifice the quality of care; rather, it is the goal of the new system to enhance it by making it more cost-efficient. (Indeed, we have seen situations where physicians, when given specific cost data relating to the care of their patients, have responded in a very positive fashion by considering other, more cost effective, alternatives.) And, of course, the quality of care will continue to be monitored through a hospital's various medical staff committees and through outside review organizations.

That's the theory at least. But, after three years of living with DRGs in New Jersey, many physicians and others remain unconvinced, and you will see these concerns expressed throughout the book. (For a discussion on the controversy over DRGs in New Jersey, see page 127.)

Chapter Two
Doctors and Hospitals—A New Era of Cooperation

Physicians—Victims of Their Own Success

DRGs are upon us, and as we attempt an understanding of how this situation came about, it is important to realize that, to a large measure, the medical profession is the victim of its own success. By virtue of an unprecedented growth in science, technology, and patient care, abetted by governmental subsidy and population shifts, we are now doing more things for more people and they are the better for it. There is virtually no limit to our ability to care for the sick. But this has produced many unanticipated problems, the most acute of which is the realization that our resources are not unlimited, and very rapidly cost has become the number one problem in health care.

This increase in cost really shouldn't surprise anyone. If the composition and age of the population are changing, and if we are doing more things for more people, and if life span and its infirmities are increasing, of course it is going to cost more for medical

---

This section written by James S. Todd, M.D., Trustee, American Medical Association; Department of Surgery, Valley Hospital, Ridgewood, NJ; Past Chairman of the Board, Medical Society of New Jersey. Based on a presentation made before the Texas Medical Association, Texas Hospital Association, Texas Hospital Governing Boards Association, Houston, TX, May 1983.

care. But suddenly, those who have promised so much—the government, industry, the insurance companies—find they can no longer comfortably bear the cost, and, facing a shaky economy, need to do something about it. Make no mistake, they *will* do something, and what we need to fear most is a "bottom line mentality" that ignores quality and access all for the sake of reducing total cost.

To some degree the medical profession has contributed to this problem and surely the profession must participate in the solution. While we must stand fast on issues of quality and access, we must also get our house in order cost-wise. No patient should get more or less care than is needed, nor should that care cost any more or less than is appropriate. The medical profession is not Simon pure as demonstrated by the rather dramatic reductions effected during the height of the "voluntary effort," and by the current cost effectiveness programs involving doctors and hospitals. There is fat in the system and we need to recognize and deal with that fact.

We cannot, and probably should not, do everything scientifically possible for everybody, everywhere, all the time. Our responsibility is to develop a cautious and thoughtful use of resources. This responsibility is clear. Seventy percent of health care costs are generated as the result of physicians' decisions about what our patients need. Furthermore, the greatest percentage of these costs comes from what physicians do in hospitals. If HMOs have proven nothing else, it is that cost can be reduced by reducing hospitalization. Inescapable, then, is the realization that if we are to avoid a collision of economic interests, hospitals and physicians can no longer go their separate ways. Hospitals need physicians, physicians need hospitals, and patients need both. By going separate ways, hospitals and physicians often do terrible things to each other, compete in many ways, and appear to have different objectives, when in reality our goal should be the same—effective, efficient, economical patient care. Now the economic security of our profession, and the quality of the care we provide depends on cooperation.

Three people, all deeply involved in health care, have summed it up:

David Kinzer, President, Massachusetts Hospital Association:

The changes wrought in hospitals' incentives will certainly create new problems in hospital-medical staff relations. Now the incentives in our fee for service medical payment system that reward physicians for doing more are clearly in conflict with those of the hospital. The need for physician understanding, cooperation, and support is critical if the hospital is to survive.

Joseph F. Boyle, M.D., Chairman of the Board of the American Medical Association:

As the hospital continues to evolve as a significant provider of health care, the degree of physician involvement will continue to increase as well. Physicians can no longer be concerned solely with issues that affect their individual practices, but must involve themselves with the collective concerns of the hospital medical staff, and must seek out the most effective channels to deal with these concerns.

John Iglehart, journalist and observer of the medical scene:

Tensions have always existed between hospitals and their attending physicians, and they probably always will, given the reality that their interests are not the same. As the medical care system moves to implement a system of prospective reimbursement the need for a closer relationship between hospitals and doctors will be even more critical as they strive to achieve the appropriate balance between the delivery of high quality care and the judicious use of society's limited resources.

And so, prospective pricing according to diagnosis related groups is here. The mechanisms are well described elsewhere in this book. (Suffice to say, nothing in this world is useless; if nothing else, it can be used as a bad example). After three years' experience with this program in New Jersey, I cannot tell whether it is a good program or a bad program; whether it saves money, whether it has any effect on the quality of care. The answers are just not yet available. This is clearly the reason that the American Medical Association in its testimony to Congress has consistently urged a go slow approach and the gathering of some hard data before embracing what is clearly an unknown quantity.

Despite the absence of a bottom line, the system has already had in New Jersey a profound effect on the way hospitals now do business, and on the relationship between the medical staff and the administration, at least in those hospitals which realize that their entire economic future rests on how well they implement the system. Unfortunately, not all hospitals and medical staffs have reached this realization yet.

Probably there is no system that is all good or all bad. If nothing else, prospective pricing is going to force hospitals and physicians to look at what they are doing and how they are doing it. For the first time, hospitals need to look at their true cost centers and bring them into line, no longer able to rob Peter to pay Paul. Certainly, cost accountability is not all bad. Also, for the first time under this system, data are available to show physicians how they individually contribute to a hospital's cost and efficiency on a per case basis. Most basically, this all becomes a measure of resource consumption and affords comparisons among physicians and hospitals. Viewed in this fashion, the system really can tell us what we are doing, how much we are doing, and how much it really costs individually and collectively.

It would be difficult to argue with the usefulness of this information, but when applied as a reimbursement mechanism, there is the opportunity to adversely manipulate the system resulting in unconscionable cuts in payments, in undue and potentially damaging influences in the way physicians practice and in their reputations, to say nothing of depriving patients of needed care by reducing payments to a level where a hospital may not be able to continue a needed service. A hint of this has been occurring in New Jersey, where it is known as the "ratcheting" process, by which payments are reduced to a level where hospitals, for purely economic reasons, are shifting the focus of their care and activities —at best an invidious influence.

From a very practical point of view, the DRG system requires much of hospitals and physicians. To survive in this program a hospital must have an automated data system and computer capabilities. Extensive additions are required in the Medical Record Department since all reimbursement rests on the final diagnosis and the manner and timeliness with which it is recorded. The accuracy and completeness of the records are a necessary preliminary to being paid. Finally, the financial department needs to be sophisticated and prevent the slipping of accounts receivable with resulting problems in cash flow.

For the individual physician, the system means increased scrutiny in relation to cost as well as quality. There now can be individual and departmental performance review as to the use of resources. Individual data can be and are being used to demonstrate how physicians deviate from the norms in their own hospitals and both moral and other pressures are being brought to bear. Fortunately, when physicians are shown individual departures from the norm, there is a tendency for behavior modification toward more judicious use of resources. This has been demonstrated in those hospitals using the system effectively. Without coercion, relying solely on objective data, physician practices have changed, and mostly for the better. Certainly, there is going to be increased pressure from hospital administrators to stay within the DRG allowances, yet at the same time to keep the occupancy up and to move cases. Capital budgets will be tighter, and marginal services may well be eliminated or perhaps regionalized with the attendant danger that some needed services will no longer be available.

The potential for abuse or circumnavigation by providers trying to beat the system (and of course that's how one survives under regulation) raises great cause for concern. Articles have been written on DRG "creep" where diagnoses are manipulated to give the greatest reimbursement. There is the potential for skimming the "good" cases and either referring or refusing to care for the "costly" cases. While not possible in New Jersey, since all payers are obligated to DRGs, at the national level the potential for cost shifting to nongovernmental payers is virtually assured. Physical plants and equipment may be ignored or deferred in attempts to meet the reimbursement schedule. Education and research that are expensive and provide very little tangible return may well be reduced or eliminated. Pressure for early discharge may result in a higher rate of readmission to capitalize on another DRG. Accommodations suddenly becoming unavailable for patients of heavy utilizers of resources, and ostracism of physicians based on their cost to the hospital are not inconceivable consequences of the system. And these are only the more blatant abuses.

Probably the thing to be feared most is the merchandising of health care for purely economic reasons. It may well be that the cost per case will decline, and the length of stay may shorten, but to what advantage if by increasing the demand through merchandising (perhaps a euphemism for competition) the number of cases treated increases, and health care costs continue to rise in the aggregate? The new Health Commissioner in New Jersey said soon after his appointment that if DRGs fail, the only thing left will be socialized medicine. He may be right!

While prospective pricing has some ominous overtones, it does have the potential for increasing quality accountability as well as cost accountability. By becoming more selective in choosing tests and procedures for patients, physicians might well find that they need not do every conceivable test on every patient. By the same token, it is our responsibility to be sure that this is not a tool to strangle our ability to care for patients all for the sake of economy.

By moving to "cap" hospital revenues on a per discharge basis, and by capping ancillary service utilization, the new Medicare regulations virtually demand that physicians and hospitals work together to restrain patient length of stay and reduce ancillary utilization. They are encouraged to do this, not by changes in incentives to physicians, although this may be the next step, but by penalizing the hospital if the physician fails to cooperate. Hospitals are now locked in a tightening regulatory grip that penalizes the traditional hospital for innovation and for developing many of the new services their communities may need. Administrators and hospital boards are struggling to reshape and reorganize their institutions, not primarily to compete with physicians, but because they will not survive otherwise. Administrators should recognize the increased importance of supporting the private practice of medicine, not because doctors like it that way, but because it is in the hospital's best interest to do so. A competitive, well organized medical staff is the key to the survival of the hospital.

How physicians respond to the changing role of the hospital will also be critical to the future of the health care system. Medical staffs are understandably anxious about actions the hospital may take that could damage their practices. Yet, the hospital offers the physician a number of potential advantages in a tightening market. All of the governance structure and mechanisms needed to compete effectively, including quality assurance and utilization review, are already in place. Hospitals have extraordinary technical resources that can reduce the cost and time demands of medical practice. They have systems and services which they extend to those medical staff members who want them.

Hospitals can help develop and finance, without necessarily owning or controlling, some of the forms of ambulatory care physicians are interested in providing. They can help physicians in organizing or marketing their own professional corporations to compete, as in PIAs or PPOs, for patient business. In the appropriate spirit of cooperation, hospitals can reinforce the private practices of their medical staffs without needing to control them.

The premium is now on cooperation, at all levels. Together state and local medical and hospital associations can work to broaden the understanding of the changing economic pressures affecting each other. Don't underestimate the enormous power of these two groups when used cooperatively to alleviate inequities and loss of access to care affecting our nation's citizens. Seeking to develop a productive economic partnership between hospital medical staffs and administration is probably the most urgent task before us.

Hospitals and physicians must work together to capitalize on the strength each has. The opportunities for leadership have never been greater. If physicians and hospitals can learn to work cooperatively in a period that seems to push them toward conflict, a better health care system might result. With this cooperation can come a sense of restraint and responsibility that will allow the continued translation of technical progress into human progress at a cost all can afford.

Lack of Understanding Is the Big Threat

In a climate of great concern over the rapidly increasing cost of health care, thoughtful physicians have felt for some time that hospital reimbursement by cost was not conducive to the efficient use of a medical facility. Therefore, when the DRG system was introduced, it was regarded with a mixture of apprehension and interest because it presented the possibility of a tool for improving both the efficiency and effectiveness of medical care delivery.

The concept behind the DRG system is relatively simple. A significant number of patients admitted for a particular diagnosis are averaged out as to the cost and length of stay. The average is applied to determine reimbursement for that particular diagnosis and the process is repeated to determine reimbursement for many groups. For example, pneumonia is given a certain amount, gallbladder surgery another set amount, and total hip replacement yet another amount. The patient is the consumer; the hospital is the provider; the product is health care.

However, the individual who is the central player in the health care drama—the physician—remains wary. First, DRGs represent a change in a system of health care that has changed very little since the beginning of civilization, and this in itself is a cause for concern among doctors. Second, the changes occurring in medicine are in an unknown direction—no one has a clear idea as to what type of medical system will emerge from the present turmoil. The new system is perceived by physicians as inevitably causing loss of both financial and judgmental independence as well as moral commitment. Individuality could become lost in this highly organized setting.

Physicians are concerned about the diversionary forces imposed upon the focus of their activities. The practice of medicine requires a high degree of focusing by each individual practitioner

---

This section written by Lelio Passaglia, M.D., Department of Internal Medicine, Hackensack Medical Center; Chairman, Utilization Review Committee; and Chairman, Quality Assurance Committee, Hackensack Medical Center, Hackensack, NJ.

on scientific and practice endeavors. The specter of having to devote increasing amounts of time to social-political efforts at the expense of medical knowledge and practice activities, including perhaps participation in strike activities as seen in other countries, is dreadful.

Physicians are concerned about the preservation of the intimate patient-physician relationship as well as constrictions that may be placed on their choice of both diagnostic and therapeutic procedures. They see this as inevitable as cost threatens to become the basic concern of this new system.

The changes threaten to remove the physician's autonomy. Traditionally, physicians have been in charge, with all others in the health care system, such as administrators, nursing staff, financial officers, support personnel and others, deferring to physician judgment. Officially, physicians do not run the hospital, but there is no denying that they are the heart and soul of the hospital. Doctors control the use of hospital resources and thus have great power over the direction a hospital takes.

In spite of the demystification of medicine in recent years, when people become ill they turn to their doctor, investing him or her with an emotional importance unparalleled in any other relationship. Physicians have thus inherited an unchallenged tradition of doing things their own way. The deep feeling that they are the custodians of human freedom and initiative and the guardians of interhuman relationships cannot easily be dismissed, since dehumanization is generally feared as an inevitable byproduct of increasingly complex social structuring.

However, physicians in general have become acutely aware that the traditional system cannot survive, and in this they are in agreement with the government regulators. The health care system will simply work itself out of the reach of the people it is supposed to serve. Here, however, it must be stated emphatically, that by no means are all increasing medical care costs due to inefficiency in the system. The real advances in our diagnostic and therapeutic abilities as well as education, an emphasis on developing a self-treating population, the introduction of proven and unproven technological and therapeutic modalities—made popular by parties interested in stimulating patient demands—legal pressures and moral dilemmas have all had an enormous impact on rising medical costs.

Many of us in New Jersey who have been living with the system believe that it is a workable effort to force both hospital and physician into more efficient and effective ways. The DRG system in its present form, or a modified one, is here to stay. Placing the providers at financial risk is the only way to force efficiency.

At Hackensack Medical Center we have looked at statistics in our obstetrics/gynecology department and reduced our length of stay without adversely affecting the quality of care. We have begun an intense effort to educate physicians about the cost-effectiveness of antibiotics and have started to see significant savings in the pharmacy.

We recently instituted a new policy whereby we waive fees for certain outpatient procedures if that means we can free up a hospital bed sooner. In other words, if a patient's hospital stay is being prolonged only because of the need for certain tests, we send the patient home and have the procedures done on an outpatient basis with the fees waived. The patient, no longer worried that his or her insurance does not cover the outpatient tests, is usually happy to return home. The hospital finds that getting the patient out sooner and freeing the bed for another DRG more than makes up for the cost of the outpatient tests.

Although I have cited examples of shortened lengths of stay, they represent only one of many opportunities to work with the hospital in containing cost. At Hackensack Medical Center we have viewed DRGs as a challenge encompassing the entire spectrum of utilization of hospital resources and I believe the DRG system has enhanced patient care and made physicians realize that we are bound together in one common goal—the best possible patient care delivered in the most cost-effective manner. Quality and efficiency are synonymous. It is a well-known fact that those physicians with the best knowledge and experience practice in the most cost-effective manner.

Specific concerns relating to DRGs are felt very deeply. One is that hospitals, in order to survive, will be forced to compete with physicians for ambulatory care. But perhaps the major fear is that lowering the reimbursement below the level of maximal quality and efficiency will result in curtailment of optimal patient care.

There is no question that the DRG system, introducing a sophisticated mechanism for scrutinizing physician behavior, is understandably disconcerting. Patterns of illness and therapy, levels of care, utilization of resources, cost, etc.—all of these will be scrutinized and classified.

In recent years we have seen more and more of our profession give way to the speed, accuracy and high technology of computers. The CAT scanner has replaced the neurologist's intuitive diagnosis about the workings of the brain with immediate anatomical views. The location of tumors, which could only be guessed at ten years ago, can now be pinpointed with amazing accuracy. Computers are now reading electrocardiograms, visualizing the vascular system and determining which antibiotic is most effective against a specific infection.

But a computer that tells a physician how long to keep a patient in the hospital, what the course of treatment should cost and, by extension, what tests and procedures should be ordered would be difficult to accept. Physicians are ultimately responsible for their patients' care, and they worry that future medical care may have to conform to predetermined formulas.

However, we can also begin to perceive some ways that computers may facilitate the setting of new patterns; perhaps the fragmentation that we have witnessed in organized medicine can be corrected or modified; perhaps the use of computers will allow the profession to focus on areas that organized medicine has neglected, leaving a vacuum to be filled by practitioners with lesser preparation. The process of integrating scientific knowledge with human needs will certainly be facilitated.

There is no doubt that DRGs were introduced as a response to economic concerns rather than medical concerns, and that, in itself, is difficult for physicians, steeped in the ethic of saving lives at all costs, to accept.

The challenges and opportunities for physicians, although requiring at times painful decisions, are great. But it is essential that physicians educate themselves to the workings of DRGs and that they participate in their implementation. There is no doubt that for the system to work not only cooperation but also direction by the profession will be necessary. It is imperative that they assume leadership in developing the new system as the alternative would be far more distasteful to them. For this, the medical staff will have to maintain a close working relationship with both the hospital administration and governing bodies. Sometimes the relationship will be one of agreement and sometimes it will be an adversary relationship, but with the ultimate goal of creating a system that is workable for the benefit of all and especially for the benefit of the people they serve. Of course, not all physicians at present are able or willing to pursue the new directions in a realistic manner, but I am confident that much of the present suspicion and resentment will decline with time, and physician participation will become increasingly active and secure. I am confident of this because I have worked with DRGs for some time now, and have observed changes in this direction taking place in our hospital.

I would like to close by quoting a statement by the past president of the New Jersey Medical Society and delegate from the New Jersey Medical Society to the American Medical Association. He states: "We must join with hospital and financial experts, representatives of the Department of Health and the consumer to create an alliance for the good of the public. By explaining, by being one of rather than one against, and by becoming a physician advisor rather than an antagonist, we will fulfill an essential role which falls only to us. Let us point out that the system cannot work without physician help. The government decision makers need our constructive input. Let us identify problems and offer solutions which will benefit the patient, the public and medicine."[1]

Although we have had three years of experience with DRGs in New Jersey, the system is still very new. There is not nearly enough information to decide whether DRGs will ultimately work or not. But we as physicians have a responsibility, at the very least, to try to understand the system. It is up to us to monitor

---

[1]Alfred A. Alessi, M.D., *The Journal of the Medical Society of New Jersey*, Vol. 78, No. 4, April 1981.

DRGs and to see that the controls do not go too far, that the regulators do not indeed squelch the imagination, the creativity and the blossoming of ideas that is at the heart of medical care.

Questions Doctors Ask Administrators

WHAT DO DRGs HAVE TO DO WITH ME? THIS SOUNDS LIKE THE HOSPITAL'S PROBLEM, WHY SHOULD I CARE?

There are a number of reasons why you should take a very great interest in the DRG system, and in the outcome of this fascinating experiment.

Let us start with the obvious connection: your hospital. If your hospital is important to you, then you have a very large stake indeed in cooperating under the DRG system and helping to save health care costs. By your actions, you can help assure the financial survival of your hospital and its availability to provide services. Naturally it is to your advantage if your hospital provides the best facilities, equipment and staff, all of which translate to better care for your patients.

The future of your hospital—just what kinds of services it can provide—is now directly related to how well it fares under DRGs. And how well it fares under DRGs is directly related to you and how well informed you are about the new system and how willing you are to cooperate. This gives you both an enormous power and an enormous responsibility. If you have an interest in your hospital and in its success, you have an obligation and an opportunity to work together with the hospital administration for your mutual benefit under DRGs.

Perhaps a more basic reason for you to care about DRGs is the reality that they are here, at least for the present. You may not love them or welcome the change, but they are a fact of life, and it seems to make more sense learning to live with them than spending your time and energy fretting over them.

DRGs represent something bigger than physicians and bigger than hospitals. They were instituted by the political leadership of this country out of a determination to deal with an alarming increase in health care costs. Health care costs, remember, are increasing at a rate that far exceeds the rate of inflation. This is a national concern that is viewed by those in power as a lot more important than the fears or concerns of individual health care practitioners. So the message is, you had better get on the bandwagon and live with the system and learn to make it work better. There is really no advantage in fighting it.

Although at this time the federal system applies only to Medicare patients, there is a very real possibility that the same system or a similar one will be instituted to cover all payers and all patients receiving health care in this country. If you learn to live with the system now, you will have an easier time farther down the road.

And, as we look down the road, there is an indication that physicians may, at some point, be even more directly affected by DRGs. The Federal Government is presently studying the possibility of regulating physicians' fees for Medicare through DRG rates, also.

Critics of the current prospective payment system say that to make hospital adhere to DRGs while physicians still receive fee for service is to put them in antagonistic roles. Further, since physicians determine the resources hospitals must spend on their patients, is it fair to make hospitals accountable for the behavior of their physicians?

Since physicians play a very important role is controlling costs, many people believe they too must ultimately be brought under DRGs if the system is to work.

If anything, the DRG system highlights the interdependence of physicians, the hospital, and the board that represents the community. DRGs point up the fact that the physician is the key player on the health care team, not only from a medical viewpoint, but from an economic viewpoint as well. And now, more than ever, the ball is in your court.

WHAT IS EXPECTED OF ME UNDER THE DRG SYSTEM?

Very simply, to give careful consideration to costs when ordering services for your patients. No one is asking you to skimp on patient care or to cut corners. It is certainly not the intention of this system or of your hospital to have physicians save money at the expense of quality medical care. But you are expected now to be more sensitive to the costs involved in this care. Higher costs don't always mean better care. Since the well-being of your hospital will now be directly related to how carefully and how wisely you dispense health care services, you will be expected to consider the cost factor at all times.

Previously, hospitals were assured of being reimbursed for any and all expenditures associated with the care of your patients. Now there is a direct link between your professional decisions and the hospital's financial well-being. You are being asked to keep this in mind when ordering tests, selecting medications and otherwise caring for your patients.

HOW WILL DRGs AFFECT MY RELATIONSHIP WITH THE HOSPITAL?

Probably in a very dramatic way and a very real way. If the hospital's existence depends upon how you practice medicine, you can be sure the hospital will be carefully scrutinizing your actions. And, with the hospital looking so closely over your shoulder, you have good reason to wonder exactly what this will do to your relationship. But it is counterproductive for hospital administrators and physicians to view each other as antagonists in this new drama. Both groups should view the DRG system as a challenge and an opportunity to work together to improve health care in general and their hospital's efficiency in particular.

But there are some changes in attitude which you will have to accept. Up until now, no questions were asked about the doctors' orders and procedures, with the exception of certain peer review mechanisms such as Utilization Review, Tissue Committee, Transfusion Committee, etc. A new dimension will now be added as hospitals begin to monitor much more carefully the physician costs incurred in the practice of medicine, comparing you with other physicians, seeing what impact your practices have on the hospital's financial status within the DRG system.

Cost-effective delivery of care will become the byword. Hospitals will look to the medical leadership to monitor not only the quality of care, as in the past, but also the cost of care as another measure of quality. You will be given a great deal of information about costs and encouraged to consider alternative ways of rendering care. Cost will be a matter of concern to department and section leaders, as well as to the Quality Assurance Committee, the Patient Care Committee, the Utilization Review Committee and others. You will be asked to account for your cost performance relative to that of your peers and to participate actively in finding ways to deliver quality care in a cost-efficient manner.

WILL HOSPITALS BEGIN TO PRESSURE PHYSICIANS IN TERMS OF TESTS ORDERED OR GETTING PATIENTS OUT OF THE HOSPITAL SOONER?

Hospital officials should not, and must not, interfere directly in determining how physicians care for their patients. Rather than pressuring doctors, hospitals would be wise to educate them with the expectation that once doctors understand the importance of their actions for the hospital's well-being, they will begin to behave in ways that benefit their patients and the hospital as well since these two goals can and should coincide.

It is reasonable to expect that the hospital administration will require the medical staff to monitor its own performance regarding DRGs. Existing mechanisms such as quality assurance and utilization review will become even more important in assuring that the hospital is operating in a manner most beneficial to its patients within the constraints of the new cost-consciousness necessitated by DRGs.

Dr. Mendel Silverman, a Hackensack internist who sits on a DRG appeals panel for the Association for Professional Health Care Review, said the number of DRG appeals the panel hears from patients at a particular hospital is directly related to the strength or weakness of the utilization review system at that hospital. Such systems vary greatly among hospitals, he said, and those with poor utilization review mechanisms consistently have the greatest number of complaints about DRGs.

But, since utilization review is coordinated by physicians, it should not be viewed as interference by hospital administration in the way the doctor conducts his or her practice and treats patients.

When the DRG system began in New Jersey, the possibility of pressure from hospital administrators to influence the way physicians treated their patients was one of the great concerns of doctors in the state. But things have not shaped up that way.

A Bergen County gynecologist said he does detect, at times, subtle pressures. "Occasionally someone comes around to review charts on the floor and will point out to me that my patient has been in the hospital four days and the norm is two or three. But if I believe that the continued admission is medically necessary, I simply ignore the query. There is no way the hospital can possibly influence me to release a patient who I feel needs to be hospitalized."

Hospital administrators should realize that direct, overt pressure on doctors to change their ways would be counterproductive. They should see their role as one of educating physicians to the DRG way of life. Once physicians fully comprehend the need for operating in a cost-efficient manner, they will, it is hoped, become willing participants in a team effort.

As hospitals begin to gather computer information about physician performance (how the hospital is handling one type of case as compared to another and how various physicians compare to their peers in terms of the use of hospital resources), it is believed that physicians will begin to recognize the financial consequences of their behavior. (See page 171.)

Hospitals should not pressure doctors to find shortcuts in caring for patients. They must simply try to show that, as members of a health care team, physicians must begin to be aware of what it means for the hospital's well-being when they order the most expensive antibiotic rather than a less expensive one that will do the job as well; what it means when they keep their ob-gyn patients in a day longer out of convenience rather than medical necessity; what it means when they order a battery of tests rather than the specific test they really need.

Education, not pressure, is the wisest course for hospitals in enlisting the co-operation of physicians.

WHAT DO I HAVE TO GAIN BY COOPERATING WITH THE HOSPITAL?

Quite a bit. You will be helping to ensure the financial well being of your hospital, and that will translate into better care for your patients. Cooperating with the hospital really means you will be helping to make sure your hospital can provide the services and technology you require. So, if you are interested in the well-being of your hospital, you have a lot to gain by offering your assistance with DRGs.

WHAT WILL HAPPEN TO ME IF I DON'T COOPERATE?

This question has to be asked, but the answer is probably more hypothetical than real. Therefore, consider this scenario. You are consistently out of step with your peers in terms of the length of stay of your patients, or in terms of the amount of tests and procedures you order. In either case, you are costing the hospital a great deal more money than your peers. And it is determined that the care you offer is no better than the care of your peers who are cooperating with the hospital by operating in a cost-efficient manner.

As the hospital begins to gather DRG data comparing physicians in this manner, any doctor whose behavior is a liability to the hospital's well-being will become quite obvious. This information will be made available to you either through the chief of your department or a panel of physicans or through any of a number of other physician peer review mechanisms. The facts will be presented to you so that you can understand the impact of your behavior on the hospital's financial picture.

Hopefully, once a physician realizes this connection, and that his or her colleagues may be treating the same kinds of patients, with the same results, in a more cost-efficient manner, he or she will consider the changes needed. This assumes, of course, that the physician feels these changes won't compromise the patient's care.

But perhaps the physician refuses to cooperate and remains insistent on treating patients in this less cost-efficient way, keeping them in the hospital as long as he or she likes. This physician becomes an unacceptable liability to the hospital.

Now it is time for the board of governors to consider your reappointment to the medical staff. As you well know, in most cases reappointments are usually a formality. When physicians fail to be reappointed, it generally has to do with serious questions about impaired ability to practice medicine.

Now, under the DRG constraints, your hospital may be faced reluctantly with the need to consider your financial performance as part of the reappointment process.

For your part, you may feel that cost considerations have no business being a part of deciding whether or not you are reappointed. It may not be fair but could be a fact of life.

If you were denied reappointment, you would have two choices: fight the decision or apply for privileges elsewhere.

But your cost performance will be available to the prospective hospital in the form of a wealth of data. They have merely to examine the "bottom line" to make a determination. If you were costing the original hospital money, why should the other one take you on?

The scenario may seem to you a bit unrealistic. But, as DRG computer systems start buzzing along, and as more and more data about physicians become available, this scenario becomes less and less far-fetched. It is definitely something to consider.

But, if everyone assumes a more positive attitude, then the situation need not develop to the point where it is detrimental to both the hospital and the medical staff. Surely, by working together, hospitals and doctors can form a partnership working toward a common goal.

WHAT WILL HAPPEN TO THE HOSPITAL IF I DON'T COOPERATE?

In many ways, hospitals are at the mercy of you and your colleagues under this new system. It is your behavior that determines how things go under DRGs while the hospital pays the consequences. Here's one way things could go: Because of lack of cooperation by the medical staff, the hospital does not do well under DRGs; its reimbursements continually lag behind its actual costs. Year in and year out, the hospital finds itself in a deficit financial situation. Like any other business, there comes a time when the hospital will have to reduce its expenditures, cutting back on services and equipment that perhaps you had come to take for granted and which you consider essential for proper care of your patients. Ultimately the hospital's long-term existence could be threatened. At the very worst, your hospital could go out of business. The reality of this new system is that not all hospitals will survive; some of the more inefficient ones will fall by the wayside.

Now no one is saying that such a dire scenario could result from your being a little bit tardy about filling out patient charts or cavalier about ordering tests and antibiotics. But multiply these actions by the numbers of physicians on staff and you may begin to understand how your behavior could be the crucial factor in determining the long-term health of your hospital.

Consider the opposite case: Hospitals that perform well under DRGs may actually flourish and be able to increase services, equipment and facilities. All this will have a very positive bearing on the physicians who practice there and on their patients.

Which setting would you prefer to be a part of?

IT STILL SOUNDS LIKE COST IS MORE IMPORTANT THAN MY BEST MEDICAL JUDGEMENT UNDER DRGs.

That is simply not so. Cost is not, and never will be, more important than quality medical care.

But, with all the talk about trim points and DRG fees and cost containment, it is understandable why physicians may initially feel put upon by hospital administrators who may, at times, seem overly concerned with costs.

New Jersey's experience with DRGs has shown that considering costs doesn't automatically lead to a deterioration of services. No hospital administrator or board chairman would want its doctors to put cost ahead of quality medical care—such a hospital wouldn't be around very long if it operated that way. What is being sought is a greater balance—an attempt to deliver high quality care within certain financial realities. Costs are not all-important but they must be given more consideration now than they have been given in the past.

If you think about it, this is no different from the way any successful industry operates—businesslike, efficient, and financially aware to the best of its ability.

I'M A PEDIATRICIAN. I AM NOT GOING TO BE AFFECTED BY ALL THIS. WHY SHOULD I WORRY ABOUT DRGs?

You can worry now or worry later.

True, at this time the new federal system applies only to Medicare patients, and as a pediatrician you won't be affected . . . for the time being. But you can be pretty sure that there are changes lurking around the corner which will affect you. Medicare today, Blue Cross and private insurance tomorrow.

It is inconceivable that these other payers will tolerate for very long the inevitable cost-shifting that will occur as hospitals attempt to make up any Medicare losses by charging more to Blue Cross, private insurance, etc. In all likelihood, states will enact all-payer systems similar to New Jersey's, and then all your hospital cases will be subject to DRGs. And, as a pediatrician, you *will* be directly affected.

Common sense dictates that you and your colleagues should begin to understand the system now and prepare yourselves to function within its constraints. Start learning now how to operate in a DRG-like atmosphere. Why not take advantage of the fact that your patients are not yet covered by DRGs and learn to deliver care as though they were? It will make it much easier for you when DRGs do cover your patients, as they inevitably will.

DRGs make it necessary for physicians to act in a cost-conscious manner, to bring an element of financial responsibility to their care of patients in the hospital. That's not an unreasonable goal to aim for, with or without DRGs.

SURELY THE HOSPITAL'S SUCCESS UNDER DRGs DOESN'T DEPEND SOLELY UPON PHYSICIANS. WHAT ARE YOU GOING TO DO TO MINIMIZE INEFFICIENCES? HOW MUCH COOPERATION CAN I EXPECT FROM LABORATORY AND X-RAY SO THAT I CAN GET MY PATIENTS OUT MORE QUICKLY?

You are perfectly justified in expecting the hospital to improve its own efficiency, not only in lab and x-ray, but in other services as well. Efficient scheduling of the operating room, efficient admission procedures, timely reports when they are needed, coordination of services among departments, proper staffing of nursing around the clock and a myriad of other improvements will probably have to be made in various other services if hospitals are going to lower costs without sacrificing quality care.

Hospital management, nursing and physicians will have to work closely to find more expeditious ways of caring for patients.

For instance, hospitals may find that they must work a full seven-day schedule to assure that a maximum number of patients may be admitted each day of the week and that the facilities can be used more productively each day of the week. Hospitals will no longer be able to limit their schedules to the hours that are convenient for physicians and hospital staff; they will need to consider the same productivity issues that industry continually faces.

Doctors will be affected as they will now be expected to use the hospital during times which heretofore were inconvenient for their own personal and professional schedules.

That is just one of the examples of the kinds of ways—some of them quite radical—in which doctors and hospitals will have to change their ways in the years ahead. (See Appendix A, Page 221)

I'M A STAFF PHYSICIAN AND I'M ALSO A MEMBER OF THE BOARD OF GOVERNORS. WHAT DOES THIS SYSTEM MEAN FOR ME?

You have a double responsibility in ensuring that the new system works. As a staff physician, you want the best for your hospital. As a board member, you have a special responsibility to the community in ensuring quality care and the efficient operation of the hospital.

Your input as a physician on the board will be valuable in helping ensure that a proper balance is reached between cost-effectiveness and service to the community. You are in a unique position to make sure your hospital is operating efficiently, while also safeguarding the health care needs of the community.

I'M PRESIDENT OF THE MEDICAL STAFF. WHAT IS THE HOSPITAL GOING TO EXPECT OF ME NOW?

As president of the medical staff, you are in a very important position, keeping the physicians fully informed of the important changes taking place in hospital reimbursement and representing the concerns of the physicians about quality care to the board and management of the hospital. You can play a crucial role in enhancing meaningful communication between the medical staff and board and management.

Don't forget, the hospital administration is not going to be imposing arbitrary edicts on you. They will be eager for your input. They will need to know the concerns of the medical staff and they will be open to your suggestions. Neither the hospital administration nor its physicians can cope successfully with this new system alone. DRGs require an open exchange of ideas, a period of trial and error, and a relationship marked by cooperation, understanding and trust. As president of the medical staff, you can help foster that relationship.

I'M A VOLUNTARY CHIEF OF MEDICINE. MY ADMINISTRATOR IS GIVING ME ALL OF THIS INFORMATION ABOUT DRGs. WHAT DO I DO NOW?

As chief, it is your responsibility to see that members of your department learn about and respond to the DRG system. But you need not take on this responsibility alone. One sensible approach is to create a DRG advisory committee made up of physicians in your department. This committee would receive data on the performance of individual physicians in the hospital—how their length of stay and costs compare with other physicians in the department and also to regional and national averages.

Under DRGs, it is important for the hospital to obtain this data. It is important also for each physician to be able to compare his performance to that of his or her peers. It would be the responsibility of the committee to share the pertinent information with the doctors.

Thus, physicians will be dealing with physicians on sensitive matters, and at the same time, the members of your department would be learning how the system works and how best to respond to it. This committee would provide a vehicle for involving different physicians each year and thereby educating more of the doctors about how the members of your department are practicing medicine as compared to the standards for the hospital, the norms of practice within the hospital, and how the hospital is faring compared to other similar institutions.

There are certainly other ways that this might be approached, but the key point is to involve other members of the department in the education about and the monitoring of the DRG system.

(See Appendix A, Page 212, for other ways of involving Medical Staff)

WHAT IS THE ROLE OF THE PROFESSIONAL STANDARDS REVIEW ORGANIZATIONS (PSRO) IN DRGs?

PSROs will continue, as they have in the past, monitoring unnecessary admissions and reasons for continued stay. (These organizations may be called by different names in different parts of the country.) Now, since the hospitals are directly at risk, they will be doing much of the work themselves. But these outside review organizations will continue to audit the appropriateness of DRG assignments. In New Jersey they are also responsible for hearing DRG appeals from patients and third party payers.

I UNDERSTAND THE HOSPITAL IS PUTTING EVERYTHING I DO ON A COMPUTER. WHAT ARE YOU LOOKING FOR?

True, hospitals will now be entering all DRG-related information onto a computer. This information is a natural by-product of the DRG billing system, essential to the hospital and to its medical staff in understanding how the hospital is functioning under DRGs and also essential for planning.

DRG information offers the hospital an opportunity to understand a great deal about how the hospital is functioning. It is essential that the hospital generate reports so that management can better understand the use of hospital resources. This data is computerized in several different ways: by diagnosis, by physician, and by department.

It can compare physicians and departments within the hospital, and it can also compare how well the hospital is doing with respect to other hospitals. However, there will not be the wealth of information that is available under the New Jersey system unless, as former New Jersey Commissioner of Health, Dr. Joanne Finley suggests, Congress enacts a feedback system or unless hospital associations voluntarily set up infomation input and feedback.

Obviously this information is essential in helping the hospital understand how its resources are being allocated and in helping to plan for the future—which programs to continue, expand, etc. This information will help the hospital understand both physician and patient utilization of the hospital and how various groups are using specific services.

While strictly maintaining confidentiality, the hospital must share this information with physicians so that they can better understand how they are utilizing the hospital's resources. The data will show physicians how they are, individually and collectively, affecting the hospital's income and expenses. Physicians will be able to compare their length of stay data and costs with others in their department and with regional and national averages.

This information can also be extremely valuable to such medical staff committees as the Quality Assurance Committee, the Credentials Committee, the Patient Care Committee, the Tissue Committee, the Utilization Review Committee and others.

It is hoped that physicians will view these DRG reports as a source of useful information rather than as an attempt by the hospital to pressure doctors into conforming to unrealistic standards.

Hospital management realizes that different doctors treat patients differently, and that two cases are seldom alike. Yet, if one doctor consistently keeps patients in the hospital much longer than those of other doctors, and if this physician's costs are consistently much higher than those of other doctors, the hospital will no doubt bring this fact to his or her attention and expect some changes. (See Sample Management Reports, Page 176.)

YOU CAN'T JUDGE THE LENGTH OF STAY OF MY PATIENTS COMPARED TO ANOTHER DOCTOR'S. WE DON'T TREAT OUR PATIENTS THE SAME WAY.

This is true in the very narrowest sense, and hospitals do not intend to measure your exact mode of treatment compared to your colleagues. The key issue is that the hospital will measure you against the overall norm for physicians who are admitting similar patients. And you will be compared not only with physicians in your own hospital, but also with physicians in your region and nationwide. There is just no getting around this.

You have always been measured and judged against your colleagues on a variety of other standards. Like it or not, cost must now be a factor as you select the services you wish to use.

SUPPOSE TWO OR THREE DOCTORS IN THE HOSPITAL CONSISTENTLY KEEP THEIR PATIENTS LONGER THAN OTHERS IN THEIR DEPARTMENT, AND THEIR COSTS ARE HIGHER. WHAT REMEDIES ARE THERE? WHAT CAN THE ADMINISTRATION DO TO THEM?

Hospitals will establish review mechanisms, probably on a departmental basis, to evaluate the performance of each physician as compared to others in that department. The specific remedies developed to deal with physicians whose performance does not conform will no doubt vary in different hospitals. Possibilities, however, include a restriction of privileges, a suspension of admitting privileges, and even the possibility of denying a physician reappointment to the medical staff.

It will be up to the medical staff leadership to monitor and enforce such review procedures, possibly assisted by staff assigned by the administration.

It is important that these reviews are managed by the medical staff rather than by administration, since it is only appropriate that physicians review physicians, rather than administration interfering into areas that are the proper concern of physicians.

I KNOW MY COSTS ARE HIGHER THAN THE RATE FOR THIS PARTICULAR DRG. ARE YOU GOING TO HAVE MY PATIENTS REVIEWED BY QUALITY ASSURANCE AND PATIENT CARE?

Possibly. The hospital will want to know why any doctor's costs are consistently higher than the average.

But the answer lies in the specific mechanism that your hospital develops for evaluating the appropriateness of patient care costs for each physician. In all likelihood the hospital will make the DRG data available to the medical staff leadership and it in turn will be up to them to handle these cases. Find out what your hospital plans to do for such a review mechanism. Better yet, get on the committee and give them your ideas for an equitable system.

WHAT CAN THE HOSPITAL DO TO ME IF THEY FEEL I AM BEING INEFFICIENT? WILL THEY EMBARRASS ME? WILL THEY TAKE AWAY MY PRIVILEGES? WILL THE REST OF THE STAFF KNOW ABOUT ME? WILL MY PATIENTS KNOW ABOUT ME? WILL THE NEWSPAPER RUN A STORY ON ME?

You need not worry about the hospital watching over you each time you admit a patient and counting the number of days that patient stays in the hospital. However, the hospital will be quite interested in watching the *pattern* of admissions of each physician as this is crucial to the hospital's understanding of the medical staff's case mix and how it affects the hospital's expenses. The hospital, if it is to survive and do well under this new system, must have an appropriate patient mix, one that maximizes use of the hospital. The hospital must also be certain that its physicians are concerned with the cost of care.

It is to no one's advantage to bring embarrassment to physicians. Obviously, administration would prefer to work with physicians in assuring that services are provided in a cost-efficient manner.

Each hospital will undoubtedly use its own mechanisms to deal with physicians who they feel are not working toward the best interest of the hospital under DRGs. In some hospitals this might be done by the director of your clinical department; in others there may be a physician specially designated to oversee the DRG program to whom you would be accountable should your pattern of length of stay and costs deviate substantially from the norm.

Certainly if your performance is dramatically different from that of your colleagues, you can expect your hospital's management to confront you and ask you to find ways to become more efficient.

But, remember, this is a matter between you and the hospital administration. There is no reason to believe the hospital could gain anything by embarrassing you before your patients or the public. The most damaging impact for you would be a loss of admitting privileges, which would become obvious to your patients.

As for the PSRO, their review will continue as it has in the past. Of course, their knowledge of your performance is limited to the use of code numbers rather than to your identity by name.

IF THE HOSPITAL IS GOING TO BE LITERALLY BREATHING DOWN MY BACK, WHAT IS THAT GOING TO DO TO OUR RELATIONSHIP?

That's a concern of hospital administrators at least as much as it is of physicians. While administrators have a very serious responsibility to ensure the financial viability of their hospitals, they do not want to be accused of practicing medicine or of telling physicians how to care for their patients. The relationship is that of partners in a very complex health care delivery system. To guard against unnecessary influence in your care of patients, administrators should work with the medical staff leadership, including the officers of the staff, department directors and committee chairmen in developing a system of self-review in matters of DRG reimbursment.

This is no different from the relationship we've had over many years in the past when physicians have been asked to monitor the quality of care. Hopefully these same mechanisms will now be employed to monitor cost of care as well.

WHAT ARRANGEMENTS ARE MADE IF WE SUDDENLY START SEEING PATIENTS WITH MORE CRITICAL ILLNESSES, PATIENTS AT HIGHER RISK, IN THE SAME DIAGNOSTIC CATEGORY?

The care of the more critical cases and those with higher risk obviously requires the use of more resources, more time in the hospital, and greater costs. Refinements in the DRG system take such things into consideration, and if physicians record all the appropriate primary and secondary diagnoses and primary and secondary procedures, then a correct DRG assignment will be made, assuring a DRG reimbursement that accurately reflects the cost of care for these patients.

That is why DRGs take into account such things as comorbidities (previously existing conditions which have an effect on the patient during hospitalization) and complications (other medical conditions that arise while the patient is in the hospital) as well as the age of the patient. For most DRGs, patients over the age of 70 are grouped separately because they are expected to be sicker and have more problems, thus utilizing more hospital resources than younger patients.

Once again, though, if it costs more to care for these patients in your hospital than in similar hospitals caring for the same types of patients, your hospital will indeed be penalized. The rationale is, if other hospitals can care for these very sick persons at a certain level of cost, why can't your hospital do so also?

IF MY PATIENTS LEAVE EARLY CONSISTENTLY, DOES IT MEAN THE WHOLE DRG SYSTEM WILL HAVE TO BE REEVALUATED? WILL THEY REDUCE THE NUMBER OF DAYS AND THE FEE FOR THAT DRG?

Not necessarily. It might mean that you and your hospital are doing a better than average job in holding down the cost of care for patients assigned to various DRGs.

If, however, the entire physician population is able to care for patients in a DRG classification in a shorter amount of time than the designated length of stay, that DRG rate may indeed be reduced. Since cost containment and increased efficiency are the stated goals of the DRG system, such a reduction in average length of stay would appear to be a positive goal of the system provided, of course, the levels are not reduced below the point necessary to ensure adequate care.

In the short-term, however, it is likely that if your hospital can reduce the length of stay compared to the average, it will work greatly to the hospital's benefit.

SOME OF MY PATIENTS HAVE MALNUTRITION. WHAT AM I SUPPOSED TO DO ABOUT THEM?

Are you assuming that malnutrition can be resolved only through prolonging the hospital stay? What about having these patients enrolled in clinic programs offered either by the hospital or other agencies? Have you offered all the available non-hospital services which may help them, without resorting to hospital admission? By providing nutritional support in an outpatient setting you may be helping to ensure a shorter hospital stay when the patient is admitted. Obviously, if the patient's malnutrition has reached a point where it becomes a valid criterion for admission to the hospital, then you are justified in doing so. Participate with your colleagues in establishing appropriate criteria for this type of admission as well as others, and it will make your decisions a lot easier.

This question points up the importance of relying more heavily on all kinds of outpatient services. Clinics, home health aides, and better coordination with social service are just some of the ways in which you can function more effectively under DRGs. (See page 221 for a list of suggestions to improve efficiency.)

WHAT ABOUT THE 73-YEAR OLD CORONARY WHO REALLY NEEDS TO BE ADMITTED, BUT I TRY TO KEEP HIM OR HER HOME A FEW MORE DAYS BECAUSE I AM CONCERNED ABOUT DRGSs?

As always, your judgement as a physician and the policies adopted by your medical staff regarding criteria for admission must determine how this will be handled.

Again you have an important stake in participating in discussions establishing admissions criteria not only to ensure that quality care is not compromised, but also to prevent the hospital's resources from being used inappropriately for cases that can be handled just as well in a non-hospital setting.

Of course, in each individual case, the final decision is yours. If the patient needs to be admitted you should use your best medical judgement and admit him or her. Do not be intimidated.

WHAT ABOUT ELDERLY PATIENTS WHO ARE DISCHARGED TO A HOME WHERE THERE IS INADEQUATE HOME HEALTH CARE?

Perhaps your hospital should consider developing a contract with a home health care agency to provide services to patients. Or perhaps your hospital might develop its own home health program. It has been demonstrated that those hospitals with home health programs are able to reduce their length of stay and provide necessary care in a less expensive setting. You and your colleagues can now have a very important voice in urging the hospital to undertake the development of these programs and, in fact, you should be directly involved in assisting the hospital in doing so.

With the graying of America, this is a significant problem—under the old system as well as under DRGs. A greater effort by the government and by community hospitals for extended care facilities is an absolute necessity.

But, regardless of the availability of nursing home beds, it must be stressed that hospitals are not, and cannot continue to operate as, convalescent care units. Other less costly arrangements must be made for patients who no longer need the acute medical care hospitals provide.

WHAT ABOUT UNDERUTILIZATION? ARE WE SENDING PATIENTS HOME TOO EARLY, ONLY TO HAVE THEM READMITTED IN 48 HOURS?

This has been a very real concern among physicians and others in New Jersey right from the start. The issue gained headlines in the state when Dr. George Triebenbacher, a Long Beach Island physician and an assistant medical examiner in Ocean County, told the annual meeting of the New Jersey State Medical Society that he believed there was an increase in the number of people who had died soon after release from a hospital. Some of these cases, he said, might be related to DRGs. An investigatory commission has been established to see if there is any truth to Dr. Triebenbacher's charges.

Even before those explosive remarks, the state medical society had charged that DRGs were forcing patients out of hospitals too soon, and that some patients might be dying as a result. The medical society has established a central reporting system to document complaints of this nature.

But New Jersey Health Commissioner Dr. J. Richard Goldstein has said that despite DRGs, doctors remain in charge of when to send patients home. Dr. Goldstein instead blamed any problems on a lack of coordination between physicians and discharge planning. He added that hospital stays could be safely reduced if more attention were given to after care and if, for instance, doctors would start making house calls.

Dr. Robert J. Rubin, Assistant Secretary of Health and Human Services (HHS), also disagreed that DRGs were dangerously shortening patient stays in hospitals. Dr. Rubin said that HHS had very carefully monitored New Jersey's experience, and, after reviewing several hundred thousand Medicare cases, found no evidence of increased mortality or hospital readmissions.

The bottom line is that, so far, there is no evidence of a single case of readmission or death due to a curtailed hospital stay. (See page 127 for a discussion on the controversy in New Jersey.)

As always, utilization review will monitor the amount of time patients spend in the hospital. And, as always, physicians need merely to justify—to other physicians—why the hospital stay is required. But physicians must remember that hospital stays are for acute care only, and not for convalescent care.

If you are concerned about this issue within your own hospital, the best way to resolve this concern is for the Quality Assurance Committee or some other designated committee to review the outcome of selected cases that have been discharged after a shorter stay than in the past. If it can be shown that these cases are being readmitted as a direct function of the pressure of DRGs to shorten the length of stay, then your concerns may be justified, especially if the same thing is happening at other hospitals in your region.

If such is the case, it is possible that the DRG designated length of stay and reimbursement amounts for these cases will be changed. We will all be learning as we live with the new system, and undoubtedly there will be many changes along the way.

YOU TELL ME I'M STILL IN CHARGE AND YOU SAY THE HOSPITAL WON'T BE PRESSURING ME. YET I STILL FEEL UNCOMFORTABLE. I FEEL THE HOSPITAL WOULD RATHER HAVE MY PATIENTS GO HOME SOONER.

As a physician you have a responsibility to assure that your patients are receiving appropriate care. If you feel you are now being asked to send patients home too soon, you should compare your statistics regarding length of stay to similar cases of your peers. If they share your concern, and if it can be demonstrated that these patients are not recovering properly because of inadequate care, then you must take the matter up for further review by the medical staff. Depending on their findings, you will either realize that a problem does not in fact exist, or on the other hand, that changes must be made in the system to ensure that patients remain in the hospital the appropriate length of time. The issue of the DRG payment will then be dealt with by the hospital and by those who regulate the system.

In all likelihood, the hospital will need to compare its length of stay for the DRG in question with similar hospitals and their statistics for that DRG. There are certainly mechanisms for changing the reimbursement for DRG length of stay limitations and thus the reimbursement for DRGs, but the need for this must be demonstrated by many hospitals within a similar region delivering care to similar patients.

Remember that designated lengths of stay and other attributes of DRGs have been carefully arrived at by gathering data from a great many physicians and hospitals. They were not arbitrarily set by some fiendish regulator trying to play havoc with hospitals and physicians (although it may appear that way at times). DRGs are based on actual cases and records. The aim was to arrive at reasonable figures that would be meaningful and workable. Obviously adjustments will have to be made as the system evolves. But you'd better be able to justify very carefully any requests for change.

In your own dealings with the hospital the best advice for you is: learn the system. A simple progress note on a patient's chart could justify the extended stay. Remember, the doctor controls the stay, not the hospital administrator, the board of governors, the medical record clerk or the chief financial officer. Historically, in cases that have come before PSROs or other panels, the doctor's decision is upheld. You should be educated, aware and cooperative in dealing with DRGs, but you should not be intimidated. The more you know about the system, the better you will be able to handle it.

WILL DRGs ENCOURAGE HOSPITALS TO EXPAND CERTAIN SERVICES AT THE EXPENSE OF OTHERS? WILL CERTAIN TYPES OF PATIENTS BE DISCOURAGED FROM BEING ADMITTED?

As hospitals begin to operate under DRGs, it may become apparent that they can offer certain types of services more efficiently than other types. It is only realistic to believe that one hospital may offer better and more efficient care in a certain type of service because of staff, equipment, experience, patient volume or any other factor. Thus we are likely now to see hospitals making choices about the services they offer. Just the way other businesses do, hospitals may now have to determine the services that they provide best and then concentrate on providing those as opposed to others.

Regionalization of services has always been a goal of the regulators. It may well turn out that DRGs result in regionalization of service in a more meaningful manner than could ever have been arbitrarily imposed.

Physicians will then automatically direct their patients to those hospitals which can best serve their particular needs. Inappropriate admissions will not only be detrimental to the patient's care but also affect the physician's performance in the hospital as monitored by various review mechanisms dictated by DRGs.

This does not mean that hospitals will automatically eliminate the most expensive services. If expensive departments can be efficiently managed within appropriate cost levels and high volume, they will be maintained.

WON'T DRGs BE AN INVASION OF MY RIGHT TO PRACTICE MEDICINE THE WAY I THINK IS BEST?

Physicians treat patients; hospital administrators run hospitals. DRGs will do nothing to alter that very important distinction. Physicians are ultimately and solely responsible for decisions about how to practice medicine, when to admit and discharge patients and what the diagnosis should be. Hospitals, on the other hand, are responsible for the well-being of their institutions.

Hopefully, these two areas are both directed toward the same end —the very best patient care in the most cost-efficient manner.

Just as physicians expect cooperation from the hospital in the form of proper equipment, services and support staff, the hospital has a right to demand cooperation in terms of efficient use of resources.

Rather than an attempt to invade the domain of the physician, DRGs are an effort to make physicians aware of the financial consequences of their medical decisions. It is an attempt to show physicians that they and their patients are not acting in a vacuum, but rather as part of an intricate and delicately balanced health care system that must make some very important changes that cannot be made without the full cooperation and support of physicians.

If they are to survive, hospitals must concern themselves with those physicians who are obviously not performing at a level comparable to their peers. You have always been asked to practice medicine at a qualitative level that is generally comparable to other physicians. DRGs merely add a financial component to this review. In other words, you are continuing to be measured among and by your peers just as has been true in years past, when the measures were those non-cost items of quality care. One more dimension has now been added in your overall performance monitoring—cost-effectiveness—which will now be considered an integral factor in quality of care.

Spending more money doesn't always mean better care, just as treating a patient more inexpensively doesn't necessarily mean that he or she received less than quality care. What is being attempted now is to find a reasonable match between quality and cost. Can you deliver the appropriate quality of care at the appropriate cost as measured against your peers?

Some professionals believe, in fact, that a concern about cost can ultimately improve the quality of care. Careful spending entails questioning whether funds are being allocated for those services which are truly important rather than simply "throwing money" at services or equipment simply because they are available.

There will undoubtedly come some point at which cost and

quality must be balanced so that the overall quality of medical care does not drop to a level that is unacceptable to the public, the patients, the physicians and the hospital. Remember that the hospital is just as concerned as you are about the risk of allowing the level of care to drop because of a concern about spending money.

Just as hospitals need to remain competitive financially, they must also remain competitive in terms of their product—health care. The patients and the public would not tolerate for very long an institution it perceived as delivering low cost care at the expense of quality care.

Quality of care is the cornerstone of medical practice, but it is a difficult thing to measure. Just as length of stay has never been a measure of quality, so too the DRG system does not measure quality.

As long as physicians remain in charge of measuring quality of care, it is a pretty safe bet that quality medical care will never be sacrificed to cost-efficiency.

I UNDERSTAND THE THEORY OF DRGs. BUT I STILL HAVE A FEELING MY PATIENTS ARE GOING TO SUFFER. ARE THEY?

You don't have to be concerned about this.

This system now affects physicians, patients and hospitals all over the country as well as all taxpayers. If DRGs do not function properly, rest assured that changes will be made. Of course, it's probably true that the changes will be slow in coming.

Just remember that this new system is not directed solely at you and your patients. We are dealing here with an issue of public policy that affects all physicians, all patients and all hospitals in the same way. No one has singled out you or your hospital for special treatment. If the system truly doesn't work, you won't be the only one who notices it.

DRGs have been in effect in New Jersey since 1980, and there is no evidence that patients are being harmed in any way. Dr. Joanne Finley, who introduced DRGs in New Jersey, formed a physician advisory committee that worked with her to extract a series of quality measures for DRGs. Such quality studies and comparisons were to be a regular activity of the New Jersey system.

HOW CAN I BE AN ASSET TO THE SYSTEM? HOW CAN I AVOID BEING A LIABILITY?

By keeping an open mind to the changes that you and your hospital must face. The key word here is flexibility. Remember, there are no hard and fast rules. Judging by the experience of hospitals in New Jersey, new regulations will be promulgated just as soon as you get used to the old ones. The situation will undoubtedly remain very fluid in the next few years, so be prepared to roll with the punches. Direct your energies to accommodating the new system rather than fighting it.

Learn as much as you can about DRGs and be prepared to become actively involved in implementing and reviewing the DRG system as it relates to you and your colleagues. Be open and willing to discuss issues that will be raised.

Don't be afraid of change because, above all, you will be asked to change some longstanding habits and practices if this is going to work.

In general, give careful consideration to how you can minimize the cost of care for each one of your patients by considering alternatives that might be available during the course of your patient's hospitalization. Just as you work for your patients' medical well-being, work for the financial well-being of your hospital, too.

Become informed; demand information of your medical leadership and hospital management so that you can understand how your actions influence the hospital's costs.

And by all means explain the system to your patients, who will look to you for guidance through the confusion of the new regulations.

In some ways, the DRG system presents a very positive challenge, but that is only possible if we are willing—all of us—to discard old practices and old habits that no longer benefit the health care system.

There are, of course, many specific ways in which you can be an asset; some of these will be discussed in other sections of the book. For starters, consider this representative list of some ways you can be helpful:

1. Complete your patient charts on time.

2. Be careful in writing your final diagnosis; be sure to include all pertinent secondary diagnoses and procedures.
3. Order the least expensive test or product (antibiotics, for instance) that will do the job.
4. Be knowledgeable about home health care services, nursing homes, Meals on Wheels, etc. so that you won't be tempted to keep patients in the hospital when they no longer need acute care.
5. Familiarize yourself with your hospital's list of same-day surgery procedures and other outpatient services. Encourage patients to utilize outpatient services whenever possible.
6. Become informed about DRGs and offer to serve on DRG-related committees.
7. Order diagnostic tests in an orderly fashion so that there will be no conflict of tests and no unnecessary waiting period between tests.
8. Order only tests that are necessary.
9. Talk to your patient about the fact that he or she will be going home as soon as the acute phase of the illness is controlled, and tell the patient that you will continue treatment at home. Do your best to get your patients accustomed to the new realities of DRGs.
10. Utilize pre-admission testing which helps the patient get into the mainstream quicker and helps ancillary departments schedule their operation.
11. Participate in pre-discharge planning which helps the organization better prepare for and expedite the discharge.

WHAT IS THE RISK THAT DRGs WILL BE EXTENDED TO PRIVATE PHYSICIANS' FEES?

Clearly, this is a very real possibility that physicians must face down the road. The Medicare legislation talks about extending prospective payment to physicians' fees and the subject is currently under study.

Many people believe that in the long run prospective payment will not work unless physicians' fees are made a part of the system. In a sense, prospective payment for hospitals can be viewed as a first step toward bringing physicians directly into the system. Hospitals are being held accountable for physicians' behavior now; ultimately physicians may be held directly accountable. As long as hospitals are given an incentive to cut costs, while physicians, receiving a fee for service, are given no incentive to cut costs, the two are placed in antagonistic roles. The ultimate solution, it would seem, would be to bring physicians directly into the system.

This may not be as frightening a prospect as you imagine. In a sense, surgeons have always been paid on a DRG basis, as they charge a certain amount for a given procedure performed in the hospital.

It is quite likely that in the future all physicians will be competing for patients under a prospective payment system where, for instance, employers, who pay most of the insurance premiums for health care, will contract with groups of physicians and certain hospitals for the care of their employees, for whom they will pay 100 percent of all care. Physicians will be keenly aware that this type of competition will impact on patients' decisions about which physicians to see.

IS THIS JUST THE TIP OF THE ICEBERG? IS THERE MORE OUT THERE?

Medicare's prospective payment system could very well be the first step in an evolutionary process that will turn on its ear the reimbursement system we have been living with for 17 years with Medicare and longer with Blue Cross.

It's a pretty good guess that prospective payment is the way of the future and DRGs seem to be the best available payment mechanism under this system. As with all new ventures, there is a great deal to be learned, and there will probably be many changes along the way.

Physicians, because they control the allocation of resources in hospitals, have a central role to play in determining just how well this system will work. Thus, they will be directly involved in deciding what changes are incorporated into the system.

Right now, the system of prospective pricing applies only to Medicare inpatients. But, incorporated into the federal legislation is a mandate to study its applicability to outpatients, physicians' fees, and to other health care settings such as nursing homes.

There is also every indication that prospective pricing will not long be confined to Medicare. Blue Cross and private insurance will not want to put up with the inevitable cost shifting that will occur. Representatives of these other health care insurers have demanded that the system be extended, and some states have already done so.

The changes you are being asked to cope with now are indeed the tip of the iceberg, and the sooner you begin preparing for the future, the better off you will be.

Chapter Three
You Have a Friend in Medical Records

Now you have come to the part of the book that tells you what you really need to know—the nuts and bolts of DRGs. You may hate them or you may love them, but what you may not do, if your hospital is to survive and if you are to remain a functioning member of the staff, is to be indifferent to them.

In Medical Records the philosophical and political discussions are set aside. Our sole concern is to ensure that the hospital receives the maximum reimbursement under DRGs while ensuring that the system is adhered to properly. DRGs are serious business to us. As you will see in the stories and examples that follow, very small details can make very big differences for your hospital. Omitted diagnoses or procedures on a patient chart and coding errors in Medical Records can lead to losses of many thousands of dollars for the hospital.

Under DRGs, as never before, we are extremely, dependent on you, the physician. Very simply, here is how you, DRGs and your Medical Record Department interact.

Just as you have always done, you complete your patient's medical record, which is sent to the Medical Record Department,

---

This chapter written by Barbara Shaw, A.R.T., Director of Medical Records, Hackensack Medical Center, Hackensack, NJ. Ms. Shaw also has recorded an audio cassette program, *DRGs: The Medical Record Dimension*, produced by Teach 'em, Inc., 160 E. Illinois, Chicago, IL.

where specially trained personnel extract from that record the pertinent information needed to determine the patient's DRG classification.

With the help of a computer system, we translate your diagnoses and procedures into one of 467 diagnosis related groups. Your 21-year old with a urinary tract infection becomes DRG No. 321. Your cancer patient hospitalized for intensive chemotherapy becomes DRG No. 410. Your myocardial infarction patient becomes DRG No. 122.

Once the DRG assignment is made, the DRG summary is sent to the billing department, which prepares the patient bill. The quicker and more efficiently this process is completed, the better for the hospital in terms of the timeliness and amount of reimbursement. Delays and errors can result in postponed reimbursement and serious cash flow problems.

Surely, you can understand the importance of our function if you compare the hospital's needs to your own business needs in your private practice.

Many doctors, when confronted with the system, wonder how they will be able to cope with 467 diagnostic groupings. The answer is, you don't have to. DRG assignments are our problem, and, fortunately, we have a computer that does a great deal of the work for us. What you must do is just what has been expected of you all along: you must complete your patients' charts fully and in a timely manner. Your hospital will no doubt set certain time limits about completion of charts, based on the individual needs of your own medical records and billing departments. In our hospital, we set down one very strict rule—the final diagnoses had to be on the patient chart within 72 hours of discharge or the physician's admitting privileges would be withdrawn. This was a policy adopted by the medical board because they understood the necessity of timely documentation. Once they realized we were all serious about this, the medical staff has been very cooperative, although there *have* been occasions when we have had to enforce our 72-hour rule.

In the past you may have been less than meticulous in recording your patients' diagnoses. You possibly recorded them on the chart in the order of severity or in any other order that came to mind at the time. It really didn't matter all that much. But now your listing of diagnoses is crucial in determining what DRG the patient will be placed in.

You must decide what the *principal diagnosis* is—the *reason that explains the patient's admission to the hospital*. Never mind that other problems developed which may have been much more important or which consumed much more of your time and energy and more of the hospital's resources. And never mind that other medical problems may, in fact, have proven a lot more serious for the patient. The principal diagnosis, which is the key factor in determining the DRG, *must* be the diagnosis which explains the patient's reason for admission to the hospital.

Beyond the principal diagnosis, it is crucial that you list all other medical conditions for which the patient was treated in the hospital as well as all procedures performed on the patient. These factors and others are fed into the computer and all have a bearing on the DRG assignment. Leaving out any aspect of the patient's care and/or treatment while in the hospital can have a serious impact on the hospital's reimbursement.

It is important to remember through all this that the hospital has no intention of charging for or receiving money for care that was not rendered. On the other hand, it should, and must if it is to survive, receive all the reimbursement to which it is entitled.

In determining the DRG, we in Medical Records are totally dependent on the patient record that you complete. Without your information, we have nothing to go on. That is why it is very important for you to complete the record as accurately and fully as possible.

We need you, there is no doubt about it; but we can also be a great resource to you. DRGs are a two-way street for doctors and Medical Records. You will most likely be confused in the beginning about exactly how to operate under DRGs. We all realize that diagnoses may be worded in many different ways and sequences. Your Medical Record Department will be happy to share with you what they have learned about proper recording for DRGs. Do you list alcoholism or cirrhosis of the liver first? It could mean a difference of $1,800 to the hospital. Do you say arteriosclerotic heart disease with cardiac arrhythmia or cardiac arrhythmia with arteriosclerotic heart disease? Believe it or not, that change in wording could make a difference of $532.

Do you say dysfunctional uterine bleeding or fibroid tumor for the principal diagnosis? Ectopic pregnancy ruled out or ovarian cyst? These details are crucial now in determining how your hospital fares under DRGs.

Please keep in mind that the hospital is not asking you to change your diagnosis in a way that does not accurately reflect your treatment of the patient. The doctor is still responsible for making the diagnosis and DRGs do nothing to change that. But we must comply with the imperatives of the law under this new system, and the more fully and accurately you complete the diagnosis, the easier our job will be. Under DRGs, Medical Record personnel are trained to extract pertinent information from the records. If we see that your patient received insulin and there is no mention of diabetes in your diagnosis, we will ask you about it. If your diagnosis for another patient is removal of a breast cyst but there is no report about whether it was benign or malignant, we will track down that information. These details, though important in the past, now translate to dollars, and we simply cannot afford to let you be vague.

Yes, there is added paperwork, and, yes, there is probably more work for you. But DRGs demand nothing more than proper and accurate recordkeeping, which should enhance the care of your patients in general.

Remember that Medical Records will go to great lengths to help you and to cooperate with you as we all get used to this new system. As your hospital gears up for DRGs, you will probably receive a great deal of informational literature, and you will have the opportunity to attend inservices and seminars. But, for the ins and outs of the system, we in Medical Records are the experts, and we are more than happy to share our knowledge with you.

We hope you will not view our input as an infringement on your medical judgement. You are the medical experts and we will always defer to your decisions. But as we all get used to operating in a DRG-like environment, isn't it nice to know you have a friend in Medical Records? Together, we can get through this. You may be surprised to find it's not as bad as you think.

Questions Doctors Ask Medical Records*

WHAT HAPPENS TO MY PATIENT CHARTS ONCE THEY GO TO MEDICAL RECORDS? WHO DOES THE DRG COMPUTATION AND HOW DOES THIS OCCUR?

On the day of or the morning after discharge, Medical Records receives the patient's chart. The file clerk logs receipt of the patient record on a discharge list. If the record is not available, the clerk calls the nursing unit to obtain it.

The technical analyst reviews the medical record to see if all diagnoses are present and substantiated. If not, the secretary sends a notice to the doctor, who in most cases complies and supplies the diagnoses.

The record then goes to an analyst-abstractor-coder who analyzes the record and determines if all the pertinent information is present. Using this information, the coder assigns a code number to the diagnosis, according to the ICD-9-CM, the International Classification of Diseases, 9th revision, Clinical Modifications. You may have heard of the ICD-9, but probably few of you have ever seen it. ICD-9 is a three-volume set of rather large books consisting of a list of all diseases, a list of all operations, and an index, respectively. The coder assigns a code number from this book to each diagnosis and procedure listed on the patient's record. The analyst then takes the clinical information and any coded data and records it on a uniform abstract. Fifty-one separate items are compiled from each patient record. Some of this abstracted information—the diagnoses and procedures, the age of the patient, the sex of the patient, discharge status and length of stay (the number of days the patient was hospitalized for acute care only)—is used for the DRG assignment. The other coded data, such as attending physician, surgeon, number of consults,

---

*The following questions and answers describe the way the DRG classification system is handled at Hackensack Medical Center. In the Medicare system, the final DRG determination is made by intermediaries. But the computer system and the method are the same, and the response by Medical Records and by doctors also should be the same.

and the medical specialty, etc., are used for planning, research and external requirements.

The patient's record and the abstract go to the senior analyst-abstractor for quality control and further verification before they are passed on to the DRG data collector.

Then we go to the computer terminal and access the DRG grouper program. The relevant items are keyed in: the diagnosis and procedure codes, the length of stay (number of acute care days), the patient's discharge status (alive, deceased, or left against medical advice), and the patient's age and sex. Within thirty seconds, the computer tells us the patient's DRG classification and rate, and also whether the patient is an outlier.

The DRG number is recorded on the patient abstract and forwarded to the billing department.

Although a computer is not an absolute necessity in classifying DRGs—the process can be done manually—the computer obviously saves a great deal of time. Most, if not at all, hospitals in New Jersey have computer capability for DRG assignment, and your hospital probably will too. If the DRG assignment is performed manually, using what is known as a "decision tree," it takes about a half hour for each record. (I recall a seminar given by the State Department of Health where they described how to assign DRGs manually using the decision tree, and all the medical record personnel there just about walked out of the meeting.)

The process of extracting DRG data from patient records is crucial. A missed diagnosis or incorrect code can mean a loss of money that the hospital is entitled to. That is why the cooperation of the physician in listing the complete final diagnosis and in fully completing patient charts is so vitally important.

Just as important is the accurate and careful reviewing, abstracting and coding that takes place in the Medical Record Department. Medical record personnel must be carefully trained and extremely skillful in extracting all of the pertinent information from the charts.

Errors or inconsistencies in coding can mean a loss of money to the hospital and/or problems when various government agencies, review organizations and third party payers audit the records.

To decrease our error rate at Hackensack Medical Center, in-service education was held, proficiency tests were given, and retraining was sometimes required. In some cases, coding functions were taken away from personnel until they reached the desired level of proficiency. Although we had to handle such a sensitive matter with extreme care, most of our employees realized that correct treatment of the data in Medical Records was crucial to the hospital's well-being.

As you can see in the flow charts that follow, the DRG assignment process is a complex operation, requiring the expertise and cooperation of many people. So physicians should not think, when and if they get a call from Medical Records with a question about the diagnosis, that "some clerk" in Medical Records is trying to tell them what diagnosis to write. Medical Records calls to verify or inquire of the physician whenever they have a good reason to believe something has been left out and that the hospital could benefit by clearing up the matter.

HOW SOON AFTER DISCHARGE DO YOU PROCESS THE RECORDS FOR DRG?

Medical Records gets the patient record the day of or after discharge. If the final diagnosis is present on the record, then we begin immediately to process it for the DRG. This data must be forwarded to the Billing Department within five to seven days after the patient's discharge. Incomplete documentation, of course, delays the procedure.

It is extremely important to have a good working relationship among the Nursing Department, Medical Records and the department which transports the patient records to Medical Records. Any missing or late charts could have serious financial implications.

WHAT ARE THE COMPONENTS USED IN DETERMINING DRGs?

1. Principal Diagnosis—the condition which is responsible for the patient's admission to the hospital;

2. Secondary Diagnoses—complications or comorbid conditions that require treatment during the hospital stay;
3. Principal and other Procedures—diagnostic and therapeutic procedures performed during a patient's stay;
4. Age;
5. Sex;
6. Discharge Status—the circumstances under which a patient leaves the hospital: routine discharge to home, discharge against medical advice, transferred, died;
7. Number of acute care days.

DOES THE OPERATIVE PROCEDURE PLAY AN IMPORTANT PART IN DRG?

Yes!

Some diagnostic divisions are broken down into DRGs with and without surgery.

A detailed description of the surgical intervention ensures all the appropriate codes are assigned, adequately reflecting the complexity of the procedure and ensuring correct DRG assignment.

HOW LONG DO I HAVE TO GIVE A FINAL DIAGNOSIS?

Ideally, the final diagnosis should be on the patient's chart when it arrives at Medical Records. With most patients, a complete and accurate final diagnosis can be made prior to the time of discharge and thus can be written on the discharge summary as soon as it is made.

If the final diagnosis is missing, it delays Medical Records from making a DRG assignment and thus delays the hospital's reimbursement. Your hospital will, no doubt, work out a procedure to ensure efficient handling of the medical records, but here is what Hackensack Medical Center did: If a chart is received in Medical Records without the final diagnosis, a medical records clerk contacts the physician by phone. At the time of the telephone call, a note is placed in the physician's box informing him or her the diagnosis must be entered on the medical record within seventy-two hours of discharge. If, after seventy-two hours, the

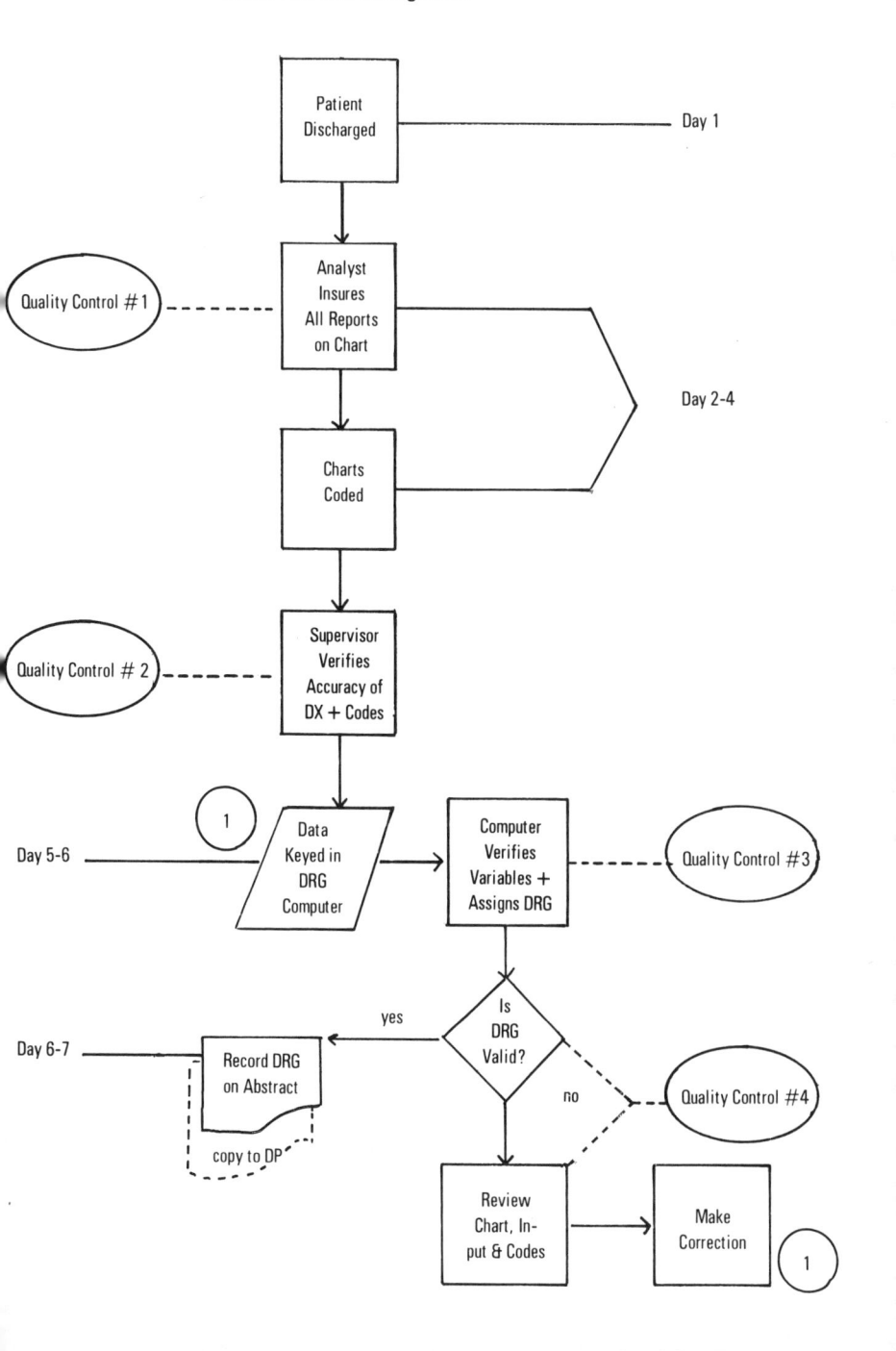

Exhibit 3.1
Medical Records Quality
Control for DRG Assignment

```
                    ┌──────────────┐
                    │   Patient    │
                    │  Discharged  │─────────────────── Day 1
                    └──────┬───────┘
                           │
                           ▼
  ┌──────────────┐  ┌──────────────┐
  │   Quality    │──│   Analyst    │
  │  Control #1  │  │   Insures    │
  └──────────────┘  │ All Reports  │╲
                    │   on Chart   │ ╲
                    └──────┬───────┘  ╲
                           │           ╲  Day 2-4
                           ▼           ╱
                    ┌──────────────┐  ╱
                    │    Charts    │ ╱
                    │    Coded     │╱
                    └──────┬───────┘
                           │
                           ▼
  ┌──────────────┐  ┌──────────────┐
  │   Quality    │──│  Supervisor  │
  │  Control #2  │  │   Verifies   │
  └──────────────┘  │  Accuracy of │
                    │   DX + Codes │
                    └──────┬───────┘
                           │
              ①            ▼                    ┌──────────────┐
  Day 5-6 ──────────┬──────────────┐──▶│  Computer    │  ┌──────────────┐
                    │   Data       │   │  Verifies    │──│   Quality    │
                    │  Keyed in    │   │  Variables + │  │  Control #3  │
                    │     DRG      │   │ Assigns DRG  │  └──────────────┘
                    │  Computer    │   └──────┬───────┘
                    └──────────────┘          │
                                              ▼
                    ┌──────────────┐        ╱   ╲
              yes   │              │  Is  ╱      ╲
  Day 6-7 ◀─────────│  Record DRG  │◀────  DRG   
                    │  on Abstract │     ╲ Valid?╱ ─── ┌──────────────┐
                    │              │      ╲    ╱   no  │   Quality    │
                    │ copy to DP   │        ╲╱         │  Control #4  │
                    └──────────────┘         │         └──────────────┘
                                             ▼
                                      ┌──────────────┐  ┌──────────────┐
                                      │   Review     │  │     Make     │
                                      │  Chart, In-  │─▶│  Correction  │ ①
                                      │ put & Codes  │  │              │
                                      └──────────────┘  └──────────────┘
```

Exhibit 3.2
DRG Assignment Flow Chart

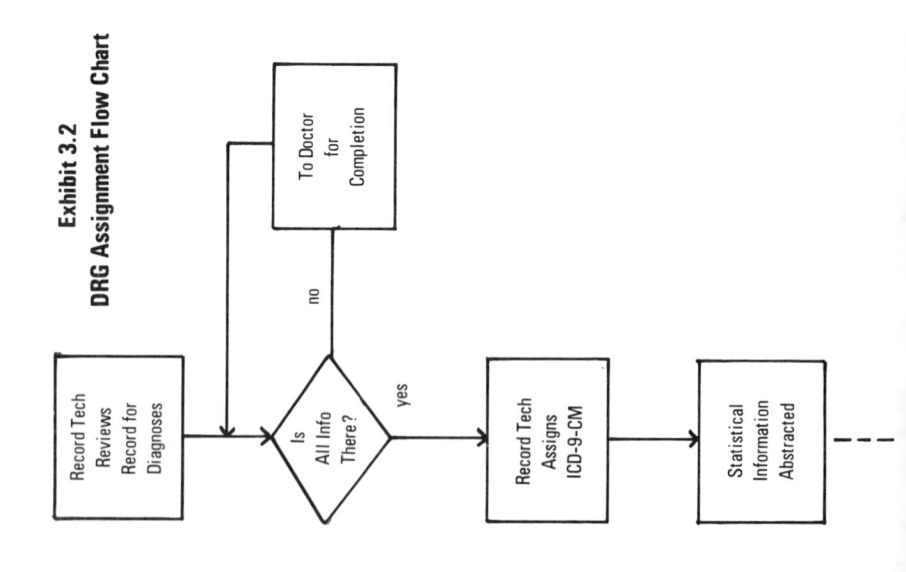

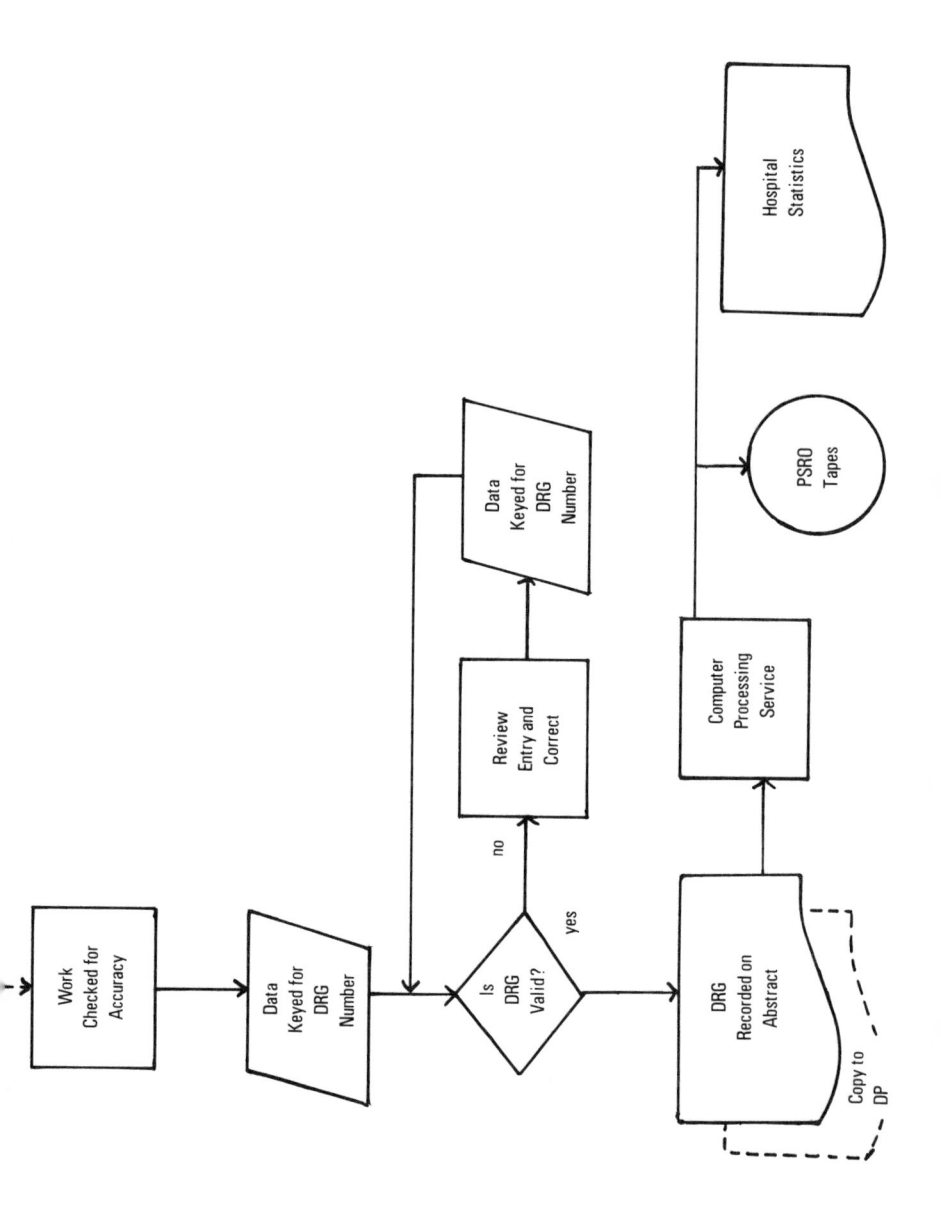

```
Work Checked for Accuracy → Data Keyed for DRG Number → Is DRG Valid?
  ├── no → Review Entry and Correct → Data Keyed for DRG Number ──┐
  │                                                                │
  └── yes → DRG Recorded on Abstract ←──────────────────────────────┘
              ├── Copy to DP
              └── Computer Processing Service
                     ├── PSRO Tapes
                     └── Hospital Statistics
```

**Exhibit 3.3
Medical Records Quality Control**

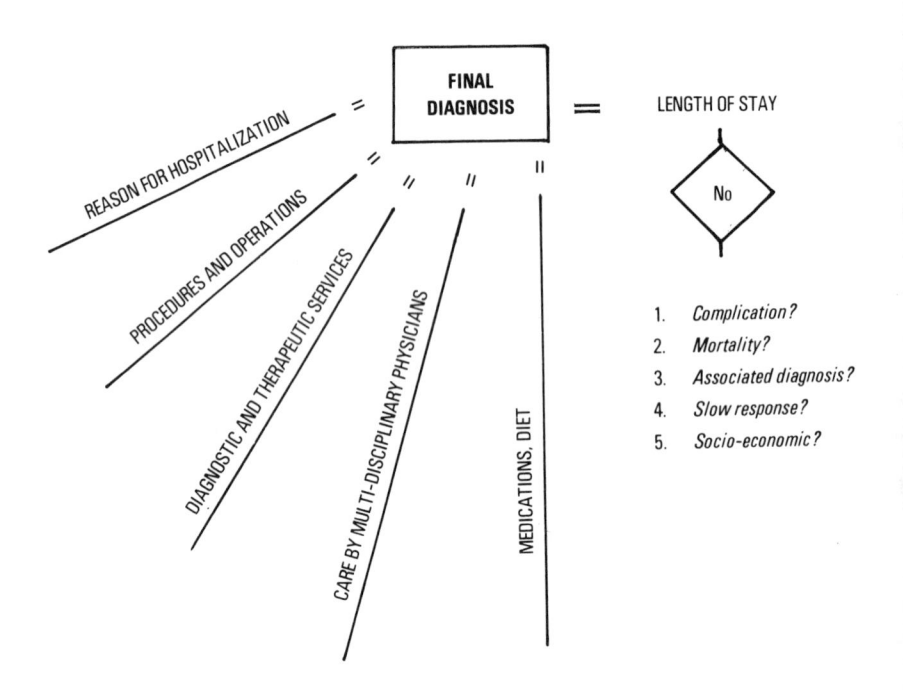

```
REASON FOR HOSPITALIZATION  =  ┌──────────┐
                                │  FINAL   │  =  LENGTH OF STAY
PROCEDURES AND OPERATIONS   =  │DIAGNOSIS │
                                └──────────┘        ◇
DIAGNOSTIC AND THERAPEUTIC SERVICES //              No
CARE BY MULTI-DISCIPLINARY PHYSICIANS //
MEDICATIONS, DIET ||
```

1. *Complication?*
2. *Mortality?*
3. *Associated diagnosis?*
4. *Slow response?*
5. *Socio-economic?*

Exhibit 3.4
Medical Records and Billing — Per Diem Reimbursement

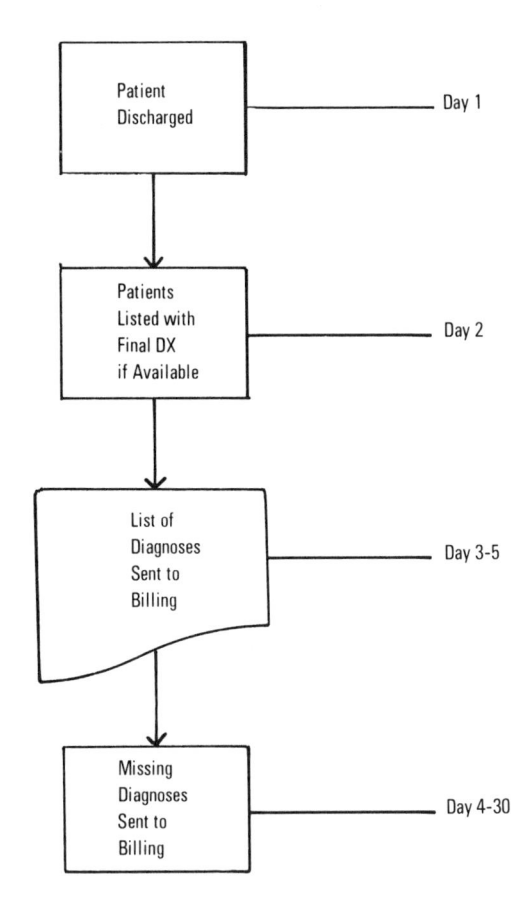

```
┌─────────────┐
│  Patient    │
│  Discharged │─────────────── Day 1
│             │
└─────────────┘
       │
       ▼
┌─────────────┐
│ Patients    │
│ Listed with │
│ Final DX    │─────────────── Day 2
│ if Available│
└─────────────┘
       │
       ▼
┌─────────────┐
│ List of     │
│ Diagnoses   │
│ Sent to     │─────────────── Day 3-5
│ Billing     │
└─────────────┘
       │
       ▼
┌─────────────┐
│ Missing     │
│ Diagnoses   │
│ Sent to     │─────────────── Day 4-30
│ Billing     │
└─────────────┘
```

Exhibit 3.5
Informational Requirements for DRG Assignments

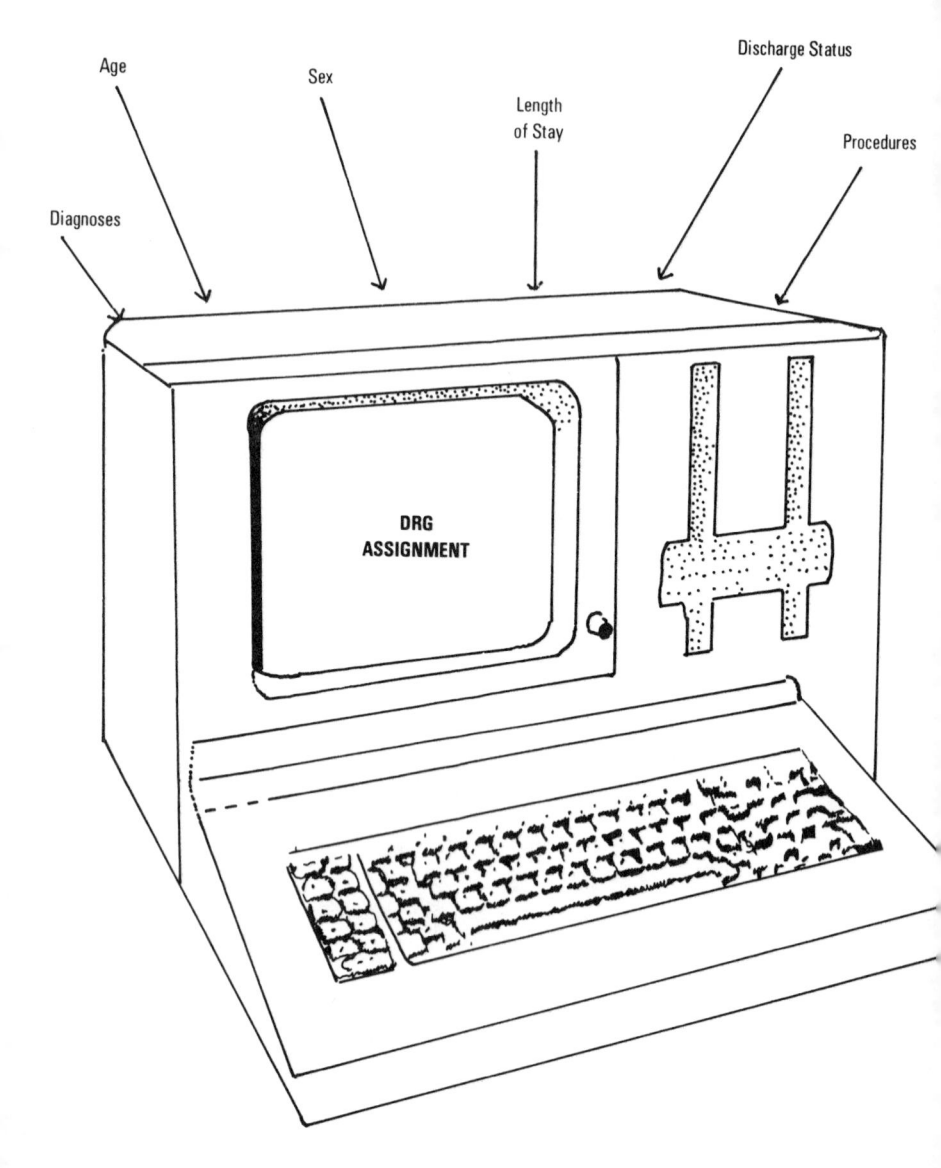

diagnosis has not been received, the physician's admitting privileges are withdrawn until the diagnosis is received. This policy was proposed by the Medical Record Committee and approved by the medical board to ensure efficient and timely DRG classification.

Once we take this action, we receive diagnoses quickly. Physicians may telephone the diagnosis in to qualified medical record personnel and then countersign the diagnosis.

Before DRGs, approximately 60 percent of the patient records were coming to us with final diagnoses missing. That number has been reduced by 25 percent.

WHAT HAPPENS IF A DOCTOR IS DELINQUENT IN GIVING THE DIAGNOSIS?

Without a final diagnosis, it is impossible to assign the patient a DRG classification. Without a DRG assignment, the data cannot be submitted to Data Processing for billing; thus the reimbursement is delayed.

Although most of the medical staff probably will cooperate once they understand the importance of including a final diagnosis, each incomplete chart means extra time and expense for Medical Records and slows down the system.

IF I CANNOT COME IN WITHIN 72 HOURS TO GIVE THE FINAL DIAGNOSIS, WHAT HAPPENS THEN?

You may telephone the final diagnosis to the Medical Record Department within seventy-two hours. Of course, you will have to countersign the diagnosis. If we do not hear from you at all within seventy-two hours, your admitting privileges will be withdrawn.

Most patients are usually discharged in the morning, when you are busy making rounds and getting ready for your office appointments. If you cannot dictate the discharge summary, simply write the final diagnosis on the progress record. The Medical Record Department is anxious to receive it and as one doctor told me, "You're so hopped up about the final diagnosis, I bet you would take it if I wrote it in the parking lot." I replied, "You bet. Simply tell me which lot number."

IF I AM ON VACATION, WHAT SHOULD I DO ABOUT THE FINAL DIAGNOSIS? WILL MY ADMITTING PRIVILEGES BE WITHDRAWN?

If the hospital has been notified that you will be on vacation or away from the hospital for an extended period of time, we will not withdraw your privileges. The physician covering your patients will be asked to give a final diagnosis. If the physician covering your patients does not give us the final diagnosis within seventy-two hours, *his or her* admitting privileges will be withdrawn.

IF THE DIAGNOSIS IS HELD UP AWAITING PATHOLOGY, WHAT DO WE DO?

Notify the Medical Record Department. You can write a provisional diagnosis which we will change when the final is known.

SHOULD I LIST ALL OF THE DIAGNOSES FOR A PARTICULAR PATIENT?

You should. However, Medical Records only indexes existing conditions for which the patient is treated during the hospital stay. For example, if your surgical patient is diabetic and has benign hypertension, but you did not prescribe any treatment for these conditions, these diagnoses will not be reported for a DRG rate. Here's another example: you have a patient with multiple sclerosis who is hospitalized and treated for a fractured arm. The treatment rendered to the patient is not altered by the presence of the multiple sclerosis, but you should list it.

Many doctors prefer to list the diagnoses that were present prior to the current admission so that the information is readily available when needed. The decision to do so is yours. At any rate, the hospital can only classify the "eligible" diagnoses.

IN ADDITION TO THE FINAL DIAGNOSIS, WHAT OTHER DATA DO YOU NEED FOR DRGs?

All elements of the medical record are an integral part of DRGs—radiology, laboratory, pathology, cardiology, physical therapy, medication and pharmacy. These various reports give medical record personnel clues about what other medical problems the patient may have had which are not listed in the final diagnosis. Medical record personnel must make sure that all documented and treated diseases are included. They review the entire medical record, even the nurse's diary.

In one instance, the nurse recorded that the patient had a decubitus ulcer which was being treated by the physician. This was not in the final diagnosis, however. When asked about it, the physician replied, "She sure did. I was so concerned about the primary diagnosis (encephalopathy) and the fact that she improved, I forgot all about the ulcer." The doctor's omission could have meant a loss of $563 for the hospital.

I CAN'T LEARN 467 DRGs. HOW IS THE HOSPITAL GOING TO HELP ME?

Although an overall familiarity with the DRGs and their various rates of reimbursement would be a good idea, no one expects you to learn all 467 DRGs. Nor do you have to. Your diagnosis determines which DRG the patient is assigned to. This classification is done, based upon your diagnosis, by specialists in the Medical Record Department with the help of a computer program. Just to make you feel better, rest assured that your Director of Medical Records has not learned 467 DRGs. Ask him or her what DRG #231 is and he or she probably won't know. (It's local excision and/or removal of internal fixation devices, other than hip, femur.)

Your hospital will provide you with all of the information you need in order to understand the system and what is expected of you in carrying out your responsibilities to your patients. In many hospitals individuals will be assigned to help you; undoubtedly physicians on staff will be responsible for helping acclimate you to the new system. Consultants may come on board, inservices may be of help, and various written materials will be made available to you. In our hospital, the Medical Record Department distributed small, wallet-sized cards printed with thumbnail definitions of principal diagnosis, secondary diagnosis, etc. so that physicians could easily refer to these terms when filling out charts. The definitions, we assume, were of great significance since we do see more accurate sequencing of diagnoses. The card also referred to a

DRG "hot-line" in Medical Records, where all inquiries were handled.

The key thing for you to remember is that you should record all of the pertinent information about your patient's care so that the hospital can bill accurately: what are the principal and secondary diagnoses, procedures, etc.? Complete charts allow the hospital to receive maximum reimbursement. Incomplete charts may mean that the hospital will lose money. Under no circumstances are hospitals interested in billing for services not rendered; on the other hand, they do not want to miss any legitimate opportunities for income.

HOW AM I GOING TO KNOW WHAT DIAGNOSIS WILL BE THE MOST BENEFICIAL TO THE HOSPITAL?

You have no reason to know that. Indeed, if your hospital were to try to get you to record a diagnosis that would benefit the hospital most, it would be an infringement of your right to practice medicine and would also be against Medical Records principles and guidelines.

One young doctor, eager to cooperate, wrote seven diagnoses for a patient, asked us to find out what each was worth, and told us to put the most expensive one first. Of course, we did not comply with his request and explained why.

Your job is to record properly everything that is pertinent to your patient's care. The Medical Record Department will take it from there. You should know, also, that the hospital cannot always use the diagnosis that would be most beneficial, even if it were treated. The principal diagnosis, which is the key element, must explain the reason for admission.

For instance, suppose a patient is admitted for a hernia repair (DRG rate $1,994.86), falls out of the hospital bed fracturing a hip, and then is operated on (DRG rate $7,735.06). The principal diagnosis is the hernia repair, because that explains the reason for the patient's admission to the hospital. The fractured hip is the secondary diagnosis. The reimbursement to the hospital under this set of circumstances is $2,561.84, or $5,173.22 less than if the more expensive procedure (the fractured hip) could have been used as the principal.

Here is how this particular reimbursement is determined:

HERNIA REPAIR without complication	$1,994.86
HERNIA REPAIR with complication (Fractured Hip)	2,561.84
FRACTURED HIP without complication	6,932.95
FRACTURED HIP with complication (Hernia)	7,735.06

Since the principal diagnosis is the key element in determining the DRG rate, it would have been more lucrative to the hospital to list the fractured hip as the principal, since it carries a much larger DRG rate. But the hospital must list the reason for admission to the hospital as the principal diagnosis.

The fractured hip, therefore, is considered a complication of the hernia repair and included in the $2,561.84 rate. No cost consideration is given to the degree of severity of the complication. A complication of post-operative wound infection which would require only the administration of antibiotics (certainly less expensive than repairing a fractured hip) would receive the same reimbursement, depending on acute care length of stay.

I HEAR A LOT OF TALK ABOUT SECONDARY DIAGNOSES. ISN'T THE PRINCIPAL DIAGNOSIS THE ONLY ONE THAT IS USED FOR DRGs?

Absolutely not. DRGs are based on the principal diagnosis *and upon treated secondary diagnoses.* Patients who have secondary diagnoses usually fall into a different DRG. The absence of documentation of secondary diagnoses could result in a lower DRG payment. As a matter of fact, Medical Records screened additional diagnoses with physician approval from nine out of forty-two discharges (see the chart that follows) one weekend day's discharges. An additional $7,300 was reimbursed to the hospital. These were all diseases that were present and treated during the current hospital stay but failed to find their way onto the patients' discharge summaries.

It might be useful here to review some of the definitions of terms used in making the DRG assignment.

Suppose a cardiac is admitted to the hospital for control of

Exhibit 3.6
Medical Record Department Technical Analysis for Secondary Diagnoses
Its Impact on Reimbursement

	Final Diagnosis as Documented by Physicians	Additional Diagnoses Gleaned by Medical Records and Approved by Physicians*	Effect on Reimbursement — Plus (+)
1.	Acute Cholecystitis	Coronary Insufficiency	$1,161
2.	Tachyarrhythmia	Pulmonary Hypertension	757
3.	Carcinoma of Uterus	Uncontrolled Diabetes	820
4.	Benign Prostatic Hypertrophy	Congestive Heart Failure	588
5.	Chronic Cholecystitis	P.O. Wound Infection	1,161
6.	Cellulitis of Hand	Drug Dependence	1,001
7.	Cephalopelvic Disproportion	Postpartum Deep Vein Thrombosis	585
8.	Premature Birth — Living Child — Male	Respiratory Distress Syndrome	794
9.	Peripheral Vascular Disease	Rheumatic Heart Disease	433

A. ADDITIONAL DIAGNOSES WERE ADDED TO 9 OUT OF 42 CHARTS.

B. DRG REIMBURSEMENT WAS INCREASED BY $7,300.00 FOR THESE 9 CASES.

* Physician approval required prior to coding.

arrhythmias. The *principal diagnosis* is atrial fibrillation, because that explains the *reason for admission*.

Now suppose the patient also has gangrene of the right leg, which necessitated amputation, and vascular disease of the left leg, which was treated medically. Both of these then are *secondary diagnoses*, because they both *required treatment while in the hospital*.

Since the amputation for gangrene used the *greatest amount of hospital resources*, that is the *major diagnosis*. The major diagnosis, then, is not necessarily the same as the principal diagnosis.

When DRGs were implemented in 1980, medical record personnel were required to index the principal and major secondary diagnoses in order to determine the DRG assignment. With revisions in the system, Medical Records now classifies the principal diagnosis and lists all the other treated secondary diagnoses and the DRG grouper does the rest, coming up with the appropriate DRG assignment.

HOW DO YOU SCREEN ADDITIONAL DIAGNOSES?

Using preestablished diagnosis-related criteria, data are reviewed for their consistency with the diagnosis. For instance, if your patient had a final diagnosis of acute myocardial infarction and there was evidence on the chart that insulin was received, we would question the absence of a diagnosis of diabetes. Medical Record personnel are trained to notice that certain medications and/or procedures are generally related to specific diagnoses, and if they do not see these diagnoses listed, they should bring the matter to your attention.

Here's another example: the final diagnosis is abdominal aortic aneurysm, but review of the urine culture and sensitivity reports shows a colony count of greater than 100,000, suggesting a secondary diagnosis of urinary tract infection. This would be brought to your attention.

Because Medical Records frequently "discovers" additional diagnoses not listed by the physician, here's one more example: a patient was operated on for intestinal obstruction. A review of the records revealed extensive respiratory therapy orders and atelectasis was reported on the post-operative chest X-ray. We knew something else was going on but we didn't know what, so we asked the physician for the secondary diagnosis. It was a postoperative pleural effusion.

As you can see in this last example, where the diagnosis is not obvious, we defer to the expert, the physician.

DOES THE LISTING OF DIAGNOSES AFFECT DRGs?

Yes! Doctors often say they list diagnoses according to their severity or how they come to mind. But that's not the proper way. The final diagnosis which explains the *acute* reason for admission to the hospital is the principal diagnosis and should be listed first.

For instance, a patient is admitted with chest pains. The discharge summary lists interstitial emphysema, bacterial pneumonia and coronary thrombosis. The coronary thrombosis is the principal diagnosis because a review of the medical record revealed that the chest pain on admission was a symptom of the coronary thrombosis.

Sometimes two or more diagnoses explain the reason for admission. In that case, we list the most important, or major diagnosis, as the principal—the one that consumes the most hospital resources.

Let's look at this example. A 72-year old man was admitted to the hospital after an automobile accident. The diagnoses listed on his record, in no particular order, included cerebral concussion, fracture of the femur, and major chest trauma. Let's say the concussion carries a DRG reimbursement rate of $1,772; the fractured femur has a DRG rate of $5,871 and the major chest trauma has a DRG rate of $3,807.

Remember, now, the principal diagnosis explains the reason for admission. In this case, any one of the diagnoses listed could explain the reason for admission since they all occurred as a result of the car accident.

Medical Records reviewed the record to determine which of the three diagnoses consumed the most resources, and we could not tell if it was the fractured femur or the chest trauma. So we went to the doctor for more information. He told us that the patient's stay was extended because of the fractured femur. Due to the patient's age and a history of hypertension and myocardial infarction, the leg was not operated on, but rather treated medically. The patient was placed in traction and received extensive physical therapy. Treatment of the fractured femur consumed the greater amount of resources, so we listed that as the principal diagnosis and received the DRG reimbursement of $5,871, the highest of the three possibilities.

In some instances, however, the principal diagnosis may carry a lower reimbursement than one of the others, but to list another diagnosis as the principal because it gets a higher reimbursement is upcoding, a fraudulent practice. (A new term has been coined to describe this practice of placing patients in more lucrative DRG classifications—"DRG creep.")

Another category that leads to confusion is when doctors list the underlying condition rather than the acute problem as the principal diagnosis. Many cases illustrate this. We sometimes receive charts with a principal diagnosis of "uterine pregnancy undelivered." Since expectant mothers are not routinely admitted to the hospital prior to the expected delivery date, there must have been another reason for admission, such as toxemia, which should therefore be the principal and which carries with it a greater DRG fee.

Another principal diagnosis which doesn't really hold up is "Status post. . . ." If a patient is admitted status post fractured tibia for removal of a Steinman pin, the principal diagnosis should be "Admitted for removal of orthopedic hardware."

It is important for physicians to list the diagnosis that actually precipitated the admission, not the underlying condition that may have gone on without a hospital admission. Another example is a diagnosis of alcohol intoxication or chronic alcoholism versus a diagnosis of cirrhosis of the liver. Since alcoholics are not routinely admitted to the hospital unless there is a need for acute care for some medical problem, the specific problem documented and treated, such as cirrhosis, should be the principal diagnosis.

In some cases, the chronic, underlying condition carries a lower DRG rate than the acute reason for admission. For instance, arteriosclerotic heart disease with acute congestive heart failure, DRG #132, has a lower rate than acute congestive heart failure with arteriosclerotic heart disease, DRG #127.

A PATIENT WAS IN A CAR ACCIDENT AND SUSTAINED MULTIPLE BODY INJURIES. WHICH DIAGNOSIS SHOULD BE LISTED AS THE PRINCIPAL?

When more than one diagnosis explains the reason for admission, the principal diagnosis is determined by the severity of the illness, the one that consumes the most resources.

Suppose a 44-year old female was in a car accident and came to the Emergency Department with fractured ribs, lacerations of her face and arm, cerebral concussion and a ruptured spleen. The lacerations were sutured in the Emergency Room. The patient was immediately taken to the Operating Room where a splenectomy was performed. Rib belts were applied for the fractured ribs. The patient was admitted to the hospital and stayed ten days.

Based on current medical practice, the patient probably would have stayed only overnight for the concussion. If only the lacerations were present, she would have been treated and released from the Emergency Room. The ruptured spleen, which necessitated major surgery, post-operative care and a ten-day stay in the hosptial, is therefore the principal diagnosis. The others are listed and classified as secondary.

WHAT IF THERE ARE TWO DIAGNOSES THAT BOTH SERVE EQUALLY WELL AS THE REASON FOR ADMISSION TO THE HOSPITAL, AND THEY BOTH USE ABOUT THE SAME AMOUNT OF RESOURCES: WHAT DO YOU USE AS THE PRINCIPAL DIAGNOSIS THEN?

Here's an example that may sound bizarre, but it's probably happened in your hospital. A patient is admitted to the hospital from a car accident with multiple injuries. It is also discovered that the patient has had a heart attack.

Which came first—the heart attack or the car accident? If it could be proven that the heart attack had occurred first and caused the accident, then that would be the principal diagnosis. But suppose the accident happened first, setting off the heart attack. Then one of the multiple injuries would be the principal diagnosis. But what if there is no way of telling which came first? This example will probably be familiar to your Medical Record Department as the "chicken or egg" quandary.

If there is no way of determining which came first, and if both use about the same amount of resources, then you are faced with two principal diagnoses. How do you choose between them? In cases like this, the law states that the hospital may choose the diagnosis which brings in the greater amount of reimbursement. So the medical record people do their figuring and decide which diagnosis would benefit the hospital more. And that's not always as obvious as it seems. One DRG may pay more money, but if the patient's length of stay designates an outlier status in the other DRG, then it might be more beneficial to use the latter DRG, call the patient an outlier, and get paid charges rather than the DRG rate.

In any case, this may only be done in those rare cases where there are two equally bona fide principal diagnoses. Most often, there is clearly one principal diagnosis, and it is that which the hospital must use, regardless of the reimbursement considerations.

WHO IS MAKING THE DIAGNOSIS NOW, THE DOCTOR OR THE MEDICAL RECORD DEPARTMENT?

Medical Record personnel do not make diagnoses. The hospital and indeed the law require you to make the diagnosis and to record all of the information which substantiates the conclusions you have reached. Medical record personnel provide assistance.

However, medical record personnel do carefully analyze the records, and if it is determined that the information shows that additional diagnoses are not listed, the Medical Record Department will add those diagnoses for your approval. Additional diagnoses should be known before a DRG assignment is made, because they can mean additional reimbursement for the hospital. So you can expect a few phone calls from your Medical Record Department if your charts are incomplete.

As you know, under DRGs there may be more than one diagnosis or procedure on any given patient admission, and it is important that the hospital have the opportunity to bill for the DRG that has the most likelihood of providing it with the income it has a right to receive. The hospital will expect you to be aware of these various options; you will, on occasion, be asked to confirm your reasons for selecting a certain diagnosis for a patient. Hopefully, you will not view these questions from the Medical Record Department as invasions of your right to practice medicine. They are only an attempt to ensure that the hospital can collect all the funds to which it is entitled.

SINCE WHEN DOES A MEDICAL RECORD CLERK TELL ME WHICH DIAGNOSIS TO USE?

Only highly qualified medical record personnel review medical records for adequate documentation. Job assignments were modified so that "clerks" would not be performing this function. The technical analysis that is done assists the department in assigning DRGs. It is also a tool by which Medical Records can assist you in areas of quality assurance, medico-legal, and, most important, assuring that the medical record is accurate and complete for continuing patient care. It is the hospital's intent to provide you with the necessary means so that your completed medical records will measure up to all requirements.

IF I UNDERSTAND THE SYSTEM, WE WOULD GET MORE REIMBURSEMENT FOR ADMITTING A PATIENT TWICE WHO NEEDED TWO OPERATIONS vs DOING THE TWO OPERATIONS DURING ONE ADMISSION. IS THAT SO?

This may not be the case. In any event, if it is medically appropriate to perform both operations during the same admission, this should be done, as it was prior to DRGs.

For example, if a patient needed cataract surgery on both eyes, it would be medically appropriate to perform the surgeries at different times, so the patient would not be totally without sight while recuperating. In this case, the DRG rate of $1,757 would be billable and reimbursable for each admission.

Suppose, on the other hand, a patient needed a cataract operation and also had a cyst on the same eyelid. It probably would be medically indicated to do the cataract surgery and remove the cyst at the same time. In this case, the DRG reimbursement would be less than if there were two separate admissions. But at all times medical decisions must take precedence over financial considerations.

Here's another example: a doctor admits a patient for an inguinal hernia repair. The DRG rate is $1,994. Suppose a complication occurs during the surgery, such as a laceration of a nerve. The surgeon repairs this laceration. The DRG rate is $2,561.84 because of the presence of the complication.

Now, suppose the inguinal hernia repair patient does not suffer a complication during the hospital stay. The patient goes home, and while recuperating, suffers a post-operative complication such as disruption of the operative wound. The patient is readmitted to the hospital for secondary closure of the wound. In this case, an additional DRG rate would be billed and reimbursed.

These examples point out that the decisions were made on the basis of sound medical judgment, not financial considerations.

MY JOB IS TO TREAT PATIENTS, NOT TO SHUFFLE PAPERS. WHY MUST I BOTHER WITH ALL THIS PAPERWORK?

Early in our experience with DRGs, physicians frequently complained about having to complete their charts in the manner mandated by DRGs. They viewed our questions and comments as a bother.

Here are a few examples of some interaction between the Medical Record Department and the doctors:

- In the beginning, we had to keep contacting one of our high volume physicians frequently. "Why do you keep bugging me?" he asked. We responded that without proper information on the charts, we can't bill and we can't receive reimbursement. He paused, thinking about how important it is to have the hospital, his "place of business," remain financially sound. He got the message and now cooperates fully.

- A member of the surgical department told us, "I don't care. Put down any diagnosis. I don't have time. All you want me to do is complete papers, papers and more papers." Somehow, though, he came in before the deadline and completed his papers.

- Another doctor said, "The bureaucrats wanted it, let them do it.

I treat patients. Every time I turn around it's more documentation. Soon we'll be clerks, and the people down in Trenton (the State Department of Health) can treat the patients."

- A psychiatrist told us that his patient had everything, and that our choice was as good as his. Why were we so picky, he wanted to know. We told him about DRG requirements for adequate documentation so the hospital could receive the maximum amount allowed for the patient stay. When he saw the difference in payment based on each diagnosis he had listed, he replied, "Oh boy, how can we survive like this?" I told him we had to, and we would do all we could to cooperate with the doctors and make sure it was done.

- One of our doctors seemed to sum up the frustration of our medical staff during those early months when he said, "DRGs may mean Diagnosis Related Groups to the regulators, but to me it means the 'Demise, Ruin and Goodbye' to a once well-run industry."

Some of the complaints continue, but by and large the medical staff wants to cooperate. Just as we recognize the pressure the doctors are under, they are beginning to realize that Medical Records has an important role, too, one that just may help them keep their hospital alive and functioning.

MY PATIENT IS IN FOR GALL BLADDER SURGERY. HOW LONG CAN I KEEP HIM IN THE HOSPITAL?

As long as he needs acute hospital care.

The trim points of DRGs are statistical cutoff points, and they were never intended to be used as clinical guidelines. You really have no reason to know about these trim points because they should not affect your medical judgment as to how long your patients remain in the hospital. As always, your patients should stay in the hospital as long as is medically necessary.

When the DRG system was devised, it was recognized that not all patients would fit into the average lengths of stay, and therefore, the concept of outliers was included. If your patient stays an unusually long time in the hospital, he or she will be considered an outlier, and your hospital will be reimbursed controlled charges rather than the DRG rate. (Unusually short lengths of stay are also considered outliers in New Jersey, but not at present under the Medicare system.)

However, it is important that the entire length of stay is for acute care. If you keep your patient in the hospital beyond the trim points, and it turns out the hospitalization was not medically necessary, the hospital will be reimbursed the DRG rate only. Any costs beyond the DRG rate, no matter how long the patient was hospitalized, will be at the hospital's expense.

For instance, suppose you know what the high trim point is for your patient's diagnosis, and you suspect that the DRG rate will not cover the costs of the patient's stay. You may not arbitrarily extend the patient's stay for the purpose of making him or her an outlier in an attempt to have the hospital reimbursed charges rather than the DRG rate. All outliers are subject to review and if it is determined that the entire length of stay was not medically necessary, the hospital is reimbursed only at the DRG rate.

To illustrate: A twenty-eight year old woman is admitted for a repeat cesarean section. You know that the high trim point is twelve days. After the patient has been in the hospital eleven days, all medical indications are that she may be discharged—her wound is healing, she has no fever, she is out of bed and ambulatory. She is totally ready to go home.

Now, you happen to know that the DRG rate for this patient is $2,949. Her costs to date are exceeding that amount. You are tempted to keep her in the hospital an additional two days so that she becomes an outlier. Without adequate documentation in her medical record to justify the extended stay, the hospital would be reimbursed only the DRG rate of $2,949. Only if the stay were extended for medical reasons would the hospital receive actual charges.

At Hackensack Medical Center, this problem does not occur, since the trim points are not known to medical staff members. As I told one member of our medical staff, we do not want to beat the system, we simply want to be able to live within it. We want to survive and show very few scars from having done so.

IF A REPORT DOES NOT SUBSTANTIATE MY FINAL DIAGNOSIS, WHAT THEN?

If your written diagnosis is a benign cyst of the lip and the pathology report reveals a malignant melanoma, we will flag the record for your review.

Or, if the diagnosis is acute myocardial infarction but this is not demonstrated on the EKG and the laboratory report shows that serial enzymes were not elevated, this will be brought to your attention. If it is your medical judgment, nevertheless, that the patient did have an acute myocardial infarction, the diagnosis would stand.

You could equate our role to that of your accountant. We audit—but our deadline isn't always April 15th.

ARE THE ANCILLARY DEPARTMENTS NOTIFIED WHEN THEIR REPORTS ARE NOT AVAILABLE?

Definitely. The chart cannot be coded and a DRG assignment cannot be made unless all the information is available. The vital missing reports are logged and are requested from the departments. At Hackensack Medical Center we implemented communication flow sheets with our departments, and they are notified stat about missing reports.

One department manager said, "It used to be the doctors yelling at us to get the reports in. Now the medical record people are yelling, too." We keep on top because we have to. Without timely reports, we would not be able to process records.

The importance of developing good communications with these other departments cannot be overstated. An example of underpayment due to missing information is the coding of an infectious disease without final reports from the laboratory. Infection without principal diagnosis of viral meningitis is DRG #20 ($4,226.35). Infection with viral meningitis is DRG #21, $2,023.96. Knowing the exact organism is crucial in this case as well as many others for proper indexing.

Another example is coding circulatory disorder without an EKG from cardiology or an enzyme report from the laboratory.

YOU HAVE A FRIEND IN MEDICAL RECORDS

Documented acute myocardial infarction has a DRG rate of $6,188.53. Circulatory disorder without acute myocardial infarction has a DRG rate of $1,903.61. If these reports are not available to Medical Records but the doctor is aware of the results, he or she should document them on the record so the proper diagnosis may be made.

Similarly, without clinical information to document a diagnosis of cellulitis (DRG reimbursement of $2,171) the patient falls into DRG #28 which deals with minor skin disorder and has a rate of $1,254. It is clearly evident that missing reports and inadequate documentation mean hospitals cannot collect allowable funds.

AM I RESPONSIBLE FOR THE FINAL DIAGNOSIS FOR PATIENTS THAT I TREAT AS A COVERING DOCTOR?

The physician who discharges the patient is usually asked to give the final diagnosis. However, if the majority of the care was rendered by another doctor, you may request that we get the diagnosis from him or her. Since the final diagnosis is so important, we try to cooperate with the medical staff as much as possible to gather our data. Believe it or not, we even make house calls. Well, actually, it's office calls—we make lots of them.

IF I HAVE A PATIENT WHO WANTS AN IDEA OF WHAT THE BILL WILL BE, CAN I GET THAT INFORMATION?

Yes. Simply call the Medical Record Department and give the patient's age, sex, anticipated length of stay, provisional diagnoses and procedures and we will give you the conditional DRG rate. The rate is conditional at that point because much depends what happens during the patient's stay—the final diagnosis, procedure, complications, an unexpected lengthy recovery, etc.

For example, if you plan to admit a twenty-five year old patient with abdominal pain and you suspect acute appendicitis and plan surgical intervention, the conditional DRG will be #167, appendectomy without complicated principal diagnosis in patients under age seventy, rate $2,198.71.

If after admission you discover that the appendix had ruptured and the patient developed a peritonitis, the DRG assignment would be #165, appendectomy with complicated principal diagnosis, rate $4,043.60.

Any DRG information given prior to discharge of the patient is obviously subject to change, depending on the patient's clinical course. It is important that you communicate this to your patient, especially if yours is an all-payer system and he or she is a private pay patient.

WITH DRG, CAN THE RESIDENTS DICTATE THE FINAL DIAGNOSIS ON THE DISCHARGE SUMMARY?

Yes. As in all other matters, the attending physician is responsible for all house staff documentation. If the attending disagrees with the final diagnosis written by a house staff member, the diagnosis is changed and the resident is informed. This, too, is part of their education.

At our hospital, the residents are given detailed orientation to DRGs and what is expected of them when they commence their affiliation with the hospital. They are often surprised at the intricacies and importance of DRGs. Of course, we stress the importance of quality patient care, but we also make them aware of how their behavior affects the hospital's reimbursement. Within their best medical judgment we ask them to be selective rather than ordering every test in the book. We tell them that the hospital receives exactly the same reimbursement for a pneumonia patient whether they order one chest X-ray or five, one week's expensive antibiotic or a two-week course of an inexpensive antibiotic therapy. We ask them to perform necessary tests and go on from there, based on results, rather than a battery of tests all at once.

House staff frequently do a great deal of the charting; they dictate discharge summaries and operative reports. Charting by house staff is generally comprehensive, and for the most part their diagnoses are complete. If there is a question regarding the resident's final diagnosis, we contact the attending physician.

HOW CAN I AVOID BEING PAGED IN THE HOSPITAL OR GETTING CALLS IN MY OFFICE FOR FINAL DIAGNOSES?

When discharging a patient, document at least the principal and secondary diagnoses and procedures performed, if any. Be specific to avoid follow-up calls.

- Don't say "Fracture of the arm." Upper arm fractures are reimbursed for $442.67 more than lower arm fractures.
- Don't just say "diabetes." Not all diabetics are admitted. Was it uncontrolled with ketoacidosis? Were there other complications?
- Don't say "brain tumor" unless you specify benign or malignant.
- Don't say "ectopic pregnancy ruled out." Was it a cyst? Salpingitis?
- If your patient was in the hospital for twenty-one days for a cholecystectomy, received digoxin, and had serial EKGs, where's the medical diagnosis?
- Don't say "multiple trauma." Although there is a code number for multiple injuries, it is very nonspecific and is lumped into a miscellaneous DRG. However, if the traumas are specified and fractures are among them, the reimbursement could be substantially higher.

The more specific and comprehensive you are in filing out your patients' medical records, the fewer calls you'll get from Medical Records.

WHO ELSE IS INVOLVED IN DETERMINING THE DRG ASSIGNMENT?

Many different people at the hospital provide important input for the DRG assignment. Admitting gives basic facts—the admitting diagnosis, patient's age and sex, and admitting date.

Physicians provide diagnoses and procedures. Nursing records vital signs, transfers, dates and other pertinent information about the patient's course. We often pick up very important information from the nurses' notes.

Pharmacy provides a record of medications.

Ancillary departments such as laboratory, cardiology and radiology provide reports which always have an important bearing on the DRG. A radiology report turns a suspected fracture into an actual fracture. A pathology report confirms which specific disease is present. Similarly, suppose a patient has a gall bladder removed and the diagnosis is acute cholecystitis. But the pathology report shows the gall bladder is normal, so the diagnosis is referred to the surgeon for verification.

Utilization review checks the record to monitor the acute care days and proper use of hospital resources.

Medical Records analyzes, codes and comes up with the DRG.

Finance provides the bill, which must be completed before the hospital can be reimbursed.

As you can see, DRGs require a team effort. A breakdown in any one area delays the process and hinders efficient handling of the case.

I WANT TO COOPERATE. BUT WHAT DO I DO?

Do what you've been expected to do all along—only better and more carefully. It's quite simple, really. You must fully document all medical record entries in a timely fashion. In the past, leaving a secondary diagnosis off a patient's chart affected statistics. Now it could mean a loss of hundreds or thousands of dollars to the hospital.

WHAT CAN MEDICAL RECORDS DO FOR ME?

We can help you.

No one ever said it would be easy. Converting from one system to another, especially one that has far reaching effects on hospital administrators and managers, physicians, nurses, medical record personnel, data processing personnel and billing personnel, is bound to be confusing. A prospective payment system based on DRGs requires changes not only in behavior and habits but changes in our way of thinking. We've really got to unlearn attitudes that many of us have come to take for granted.

Your Medical Record Department is largely responsible under this new system for working out new ways of viewing records. They will no doubt be eager to share with you their newly learned expertise. It is hoped they will guide you through some of the confusion that is bound to accompany the transition. They will carefully review your records and discuss any problems or questions with you.

At our hospital, the DRG system has led to an enhanced relationship between physicians and Medical Records. Physicians have a new respect and understanding for what goes on in this department; they are cooperative and willing to learn. For the most part they do not regard participation by Medical Records as an invasion of their right to practice medicine; rather, they are happy to have the help and guidance.

**Exhibit 3.7
DRG Network**

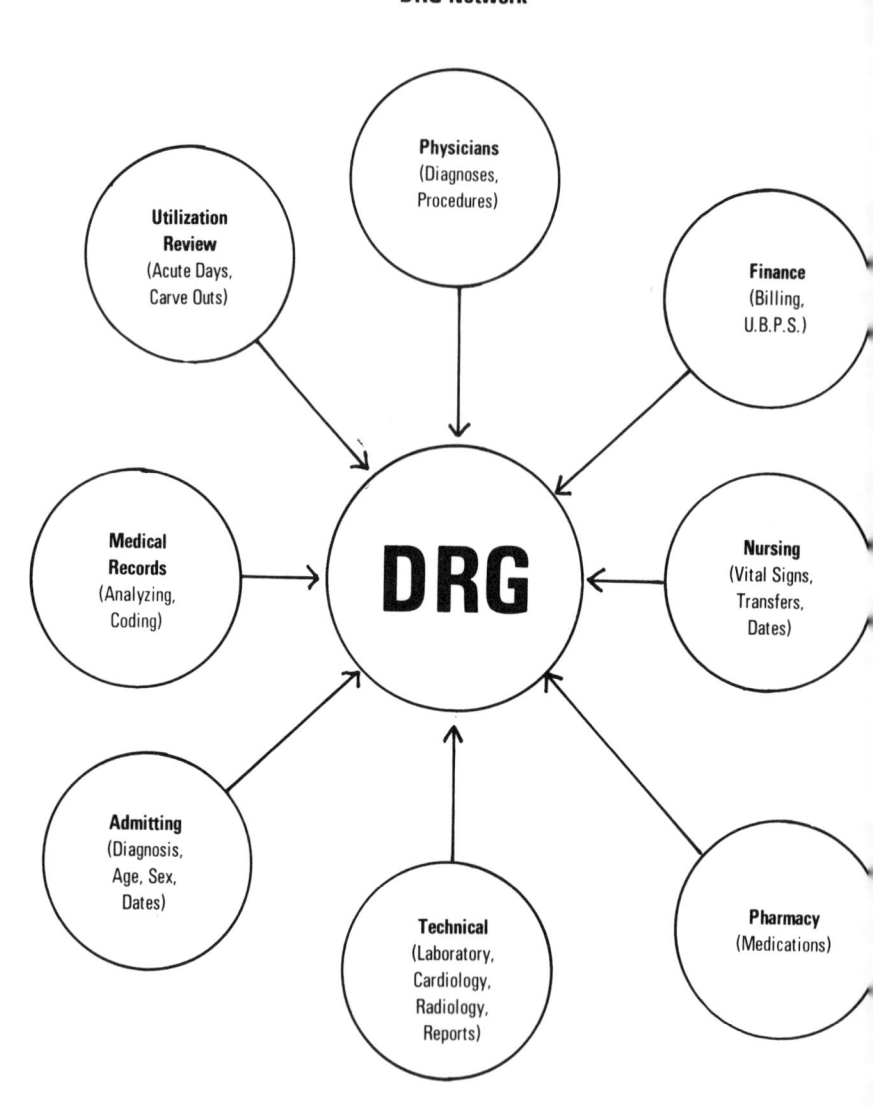

Exhibit 3.8
Documentation in the Medical Record

Together, It Completes the Picture

Chapter Four
Financial Considerations That Won't Go Away

Before dealing with some specific financial aspects of DRGs, let's consider the prospective payment concept in a broader financial and economic setting.

Prospective payment—setting the price for something before the product or service is delivered and then sticking to it—is the way most other businesses operate. From air conditioners to automobiles, toothpaste to tomatoes, products have certain prices. The supplier and the consumer both know the price up front. Most services, too, have set prices. You know what you will pay your gardener to cut your lawn for the summer, and you know the amount it will cost to have your car tuned up. Obviously, the more efficient the tomato seller or gardener is in keeping costs down, the greater the profits will be.

Up until now, hospitals have been largely exempt from this process. Hospital care has been one of the few areas where the consumer does not know what the total cost will be. The way the system worked, hospitals spent whatever they had to (whatever the doctors told them to) to treat the patient. The doctor said a patient needed four blood tests, a CAT scan and a G.I. series, and the hospital complied, with little regard to the cost of those tests.

This chapter written by Cosmo Mongiello, M.B.A., Vice President—Finance, Hackensack Medical Center, Hackensack, N.J.

Afterward, they totalled up their costs and submitted the bill, virtually assured that someone on the other end—the government, Blue Cross, commercial insurance—would pay the tab, few questions asked. Obviously, under this system, there was little incentive for the hospital to think and act in a business-like manner because it knew it would get reimbursed the entire amount. The more it spent, the more it received.

Those who paid for health care, from the government to insurance companies to individuals, accepted this system. After all, health care was somehow "different" from other areas of the economy. Treating sick people was not supposed to be a business. So, in effect, hospital care has been immune from the economic and financial realities that have governed most other sectors of the economy.

But in recent years, problems began to develop. Hospital costs were skyrocketing, increasing at a rate much faster than the inflation rate for all other sectors of the economy. Those who were paying the bills suddenly began squawking. Enough was enough. The government, which pays more than 40 percent of the cost of hospital care in this country, started to think more like a consumer. Employers, who offer hospital insurance as a fringe benefit to employees, saw their insurance premiums increasing at rates of 20 percent a year, faster than all their other costs. And the more money that was spent on health care, the less there was to spend on other areas of the economy. Health care was taking too great a share of the pie and hospital care was pricing itself far beyond the point where consumers could afford it.

Enter prospective payment, a way of making hospitals financially at risk for the cost of care they provide. Diagnosis Related Groups, the particular mechanism for determining prospective prices, tells hospitals they will get a set amount of payment for each type of illness they treat. For the first time, hospitals have a direct stake in operating efficiently and in considering cost as a factor in patient care.

The idea was both simple and outrageous—simple because it was merely applying rules that have governed other sectors of the economy all along, outrageous because it was telling hospitals that they were a business also. Hospitals from now on would be held accountable for their financial dealings. They would have to compete with each other, in a sense, for their share of the available health care dollars.

As one hospital administrator said, "There's going to be a certain amount of health care money out there, and they're going to make us compete like hell to get our share of it."

The change to DRG-based prospective payment will undoubtedly have an enormous effect on the way health care service is delivered in this country, and some of these changes have already begun to happen in New Jersey, where the system was instituted in 1980. The changes will affect everyone in the health care system —patients, physicians, hospitals, insurance companies, employers and the government.

By instituting DRGs, the government has gone after hospitals rather than physicians in attempting to reverse the upward spiral of health care costs. But physicians, who control the use of the hospital resources, will have a lot to say about whether the system works or not. After all, it is the physician who makes the decision to admit and discharge patients; it is the physician who decides how long the patient remains in the hospital; and it is the physician who decides what tests and procedures are to be performed.

In short, it is the physicians who tell the hospital what it must spend. In a sense, the hospital is at the mercy of the doctors. The hospital is being told to become more efficient and think in a cost-effective manner, yet it is the physician who really holds the purse strings.

On the other hand, doctors may also find they are "victims" of the system. In the past, doctors in effect wrote their own ticket in hospitals. Hospitals were there to serve their patients. If physicians felt the hospital should acquire a CAT scanner, the hospital did its best to get it. If the physicians wanted an expanded intensive care unit, an alcohol rehabilitation center, or a new generation linear accelerator, the hospital pursued it. Once the certificates of need were granted, there was virtually a blank check for hospitals and doctors.

But now that hospitals must consider the bottom line, now that they are truly in a struggle for financial survival, doctors may well find hospital boards of governors scrutinizing their requests more carefully. Can the purchase of a CAT scanner be justified

FINANCIAL CONSIDERATIONS

financially? Will more beds in the intensive care unit help or hurt the hospital financially?

The belt is being tightened, there is no doubt about it; and everyone involved in health care will feel the pinch.

The transition to DRGs in New Jersey has not been easy, because no one likes to hear that the free ride is over. How would sales representatives feel if their expense accounts were taken away? How would your children feel if you cut off their spending money while they attended college?

But DRGs were instituted to benefit the health care system as a whole, and if a few hospitals fall by the wayside in the process, that isn't as important as saving the entire system. At least that's the rationale of the regulators.

Doctors say that you cannot put a price tag on health care. "Sure, everyone complains about the cost of health care, but when your mother is in the hospital, you want the best for her," one doctor said. "You want whatever the doctor thinks is necessary to make her well and you don't give a damn about the cost. Cost is important in the abstract, but when the individual is faced with a sick mother or child, cost is forgotten."

Physicians also worry that belt tightening will mean their hospitals will no longer be able to afford the expensive, high technology equipment that has revolutionized health care in the past two decades. What about teaching hospitals, they say, whose costs are so much higher than other hospitals? Will they be jeopardized by a system that is doling out the health care dollars so stintingly? These are serious questions, and indeed it may be too early to tell if health care will be jeopardized by these few financial constraints.

What *is* clear is that health care will be very different in the future than it has been in the past. No more blank checks for health care—no more Cadillac comfort ride. Now that there is a budget, there may be a lot more Toyotas on the road. But that doesn't necessarily mean that patient care will suffer or that health care standards will be lowered.

Few will deny that there was a fair amount of waste, inefficiency, and duplication in the way health care was delivered in this country, and it is this waste in the system that the regulators are attempting to eliminate.

Quality medical care will still be available, but our access to it may not be as convenient as in the past. Every hospital can no longer have everything. In an ideal world, where cost is not a factor, it is great to have every service available close to home, in our community hospital. But that won't be feasible anymore. Your patients may have to travel a greater distance than in the past to have a certain procedure done because your local hospital simply cannot afford to provide that service. Another patient may have to have a procedure done as an outpatient because your hospital cannot afford to tie up a bed. Other patients may have to leave the hospital earlier than they might like, as long as their continued admission is not necessary for acute care.

You and your hospital will both have to be involved in coming up with alternatives to traditional hospital care, alternatives that still ensure quality care but in a more cost-effective manner.

Well, that's the financial rationale of the system—an effort to reverse rising health care costs by treating hospitals as businesses.

The following questions and answers deal with some of the specific concerns doctors have about this new system of financial reimbursement. Although all the answers aren't in yet, our experience in New Jersey has given us some insight into the very complicated financial implications of DRGs.

Questions Doctors Ask Hospital Controllers*

WHAT HAPPENS IF MY HOSPITAL'S COSTS ARE CONSIDERABLY HIGHER THAN THE DRGs? WHAT HAPPENS TO THE HOSPITAL AND WHAT HAPPENS TO ITS PHYSICIANS?

Prospective payment was designed to benefit the health care system and not necessarily the individual hospital. Those hospitals

---

*Specifics on the Medicare program are available in the *Federal Register*, Sept. 1, 1983. Your hospital probably subscribes. If not, check the public library.

that cannot meet the test will either become more efficient, merge with other institutions to share services, or go out of business. In the last five years in New Jersey there has been a sharp increase in the number of hospitals that have either merged or folded, and there is no doubt that this is due to the new cost constraints, most recently DRG's.

The burden has been placed on the hospital to bring its costs into line with the average. The legislators who enacted the system will not take much notice if your hospital has a hard time. However, if a great many hospitals have difficulty with certain aspects of the system, it might be a sign that the regulations need to be modified.

In any case, don't look to the system to change; DRGs may not be the final answer, but the concept of cost containment is here to stay. Work from within to change your hospital so that it comes more into line with the average. If indeed your hospital's costs are consistently higher than the DRGs, it will be faced with some very difficult decisions about the types of services it can provide.

Physicians will have to work closely with hospital management in reaching these decisions. For example, some hospitals may have to turn increasingly to other settings to care for their patients more economically—settings such as nursing homes, extended care facilities, home care, or hospice.

Beyond the financial problems of your individual hospital is the possibility of regionalization of health care once the government begins to collect data about the financial performance of doctors and hospitals relative to other doctors and hospitals. Doctors fear, and it is not an unfounded fear, that there may come a point in time when certain hospitals are allowed to accept only certain types of cases—those they handle in a cost-efficient manner. What happens to the physicians who treat the other kind of cases? Will physicians be penalized because their practices involve cases which cost the hospital more money? Physicians who perform esophageal surgery, with its extremely high rate of complications and, frequently, long stays, may be wondering if their patients will be welcome at hospitals trying to keep costs down in order to survive under DRGs.

Theoretically, DRGs compare apples to apples, so doctors whose patients require more resources and cost the hospital more money will be compared only to doctors with similar types of patients. But there is, nevertheless, the very real possibility that DRGs will bring about a regionalization of health care which will directly affect doctors.

Physicians worry that we may be heading toward a system of health care similar to Great Britain's, where certain procedures are performed only in certain hospitals, and where there are physicians who treat patients out of the hospital and different physicians who care for hospital inpatients.

These are all valid concerns among doctors who worry about what happens when cost becomes such an important factor in health care planning.

However, the best way for physicians to avoid the dire possibilities outlined above is to cooperate to the fullest with their hospitals in making sure that their hospitals, their services, and their individual doctors are the efficient ones, the ones that will be rewarded by the system.

HOW DOES MY HOSPITAL COMPARE TO OTHER HOSPITALS IN THE AREA WITH RESPECT TO PAYMENTS? ARE DRG RATES THE SAME AT OTHER HOSPITALS IN THE AREA?

During the phase-in period, the DRGs will become increasingly similar as the hospital's own costs become less important and the average cost more important. After three years, once the phase-in period is over, all hospitals with the same distinction (rural or urban) should have uniform rates. The national DRG rates, however, will continue to reflect regional wage variations.

IF DRGs APPLY ONLY TO MEDICARE, WON'T HOSPITALS MERELY MAKE UP ANY LOSSES BY CHARGING OTHER PAYERS MORE?

Probably. That's the reason many advocates of prospective payment feel the system should apply to all payers.

Prospective payment for Medicare may save the government money, but many people think it will merely rearrange expenditures rather than cut costs across the board. In other words, what Medicare saves, Blue Cross will have to pay.

It is unlikely that Blue Cross and commercial payers will tolerate this system for very long. What will probably happen is that states, responding to pressure from these other insurers, will adopt all-payer systems. And the federal government will be more than happy to let the states take the problem off their hands this way.

DOES THE REIMBURSEMENT SYSTEM PROVIDE FOR INFLATION?

As of now the system will make a *provision* for inflation; however, this does not mean that it will *provide* for inflation. The difference may be subtle yet it is important to understand the distinction.

The system will most likely use some type of "market basket" approach, which attempts to determine, proportionately, the types of goods and services an institution will use in the course of a business cycle. A provision will thus be made to account for the weighted average increase in the costs of these goods and services by using accepted published proxies (i.e. components of the consumer price index (CPI), the product price index (PPI), etc.) to determine the national or regional inflationary experience for each major category.

In New Jersey, the weighting is hospital-specific. That is, if *Hospital A* spends 3 percent of its total operating expenses on drugs and *Hospital B* spends 5 percent of its total, Hospital B will have a higher weight applied to the inflationary effects of drugs. A less specific method would be to use an average across all hospitals for each expenditure category. In that case, Hospital A and Hospital B would have spent an average of 4 percent on drugs, and the inflation rate for drugs would reflect that average, with each hospital receiving the same percentage increase. (See following example.)

In this way a *provision* for inflation is made based upon a series of averages and indices. But it will probably not provide for the exact inflationary effect that each institution will experience. This also assumes that exactly the same mix of products that were used in the base year will be used in the rate year. If a hospital

Table 4.1

Hosp.	Salaries Base yr.	Salaries Proxy Index Increase	Salaries Hosp. Spec. Rate Yr. Amount	Drugs Base Yr.	Drugs Proxy Index Increase	Drugs Hosp. Spec. Rate Yr. Amount	Rate Yr. Total	Total Role Yr. Total	% Change
A	$70	110%	$77.00	$30	120%	$36.00	$100	$113.00	13%
B	64	110%	70.40	36	120%	43.20	100	113.60	13.6%
AVG.	$67	110%	$73.70	$33	120%	$39.60	$100	$113.30	13.3%

Under a hospital-specific approach Hospital A would get a 13% increase, or $113 per patient, and Hospital B would get a 13.6% increase, or $113.60 per patient. Under universal weighted average approach each hospital would get 13.3% or $113.30 per patient. Clearly, the former approach is more appropriate, albeit more involved, too.

decides to use a more expensive alternate drug, the increase in cost is then not due to inflation but rather management or clinical prerogative.

This application holds true for new technology, also. There may be a 1 percent factor added on for technology, but since it is somewhat subjectively determined, its longevity, if it occurs at all, would be tenuous.

Here's an example: assume two hospitals—A and B—each spend $100 per patient in a base year. For simplicity, assume each hospital provides only labor and drugs. Hospital A spends $70 on labor and $30 on drugs. Hospital B spends $64 on labor and $36 on drugs. If the labor proxy goes up 10 percent, and the drug proxy goes up 20 percent, what will be the difference between a hospital-specific and an overall weighted average approach to inflation adjustment?

WHAT HAPPENS IF A PATIENT IS TRANSFERRED FROM ONE HOSPITAL TO ANOTHER? WHICH HOSPITAL GETS REIMBURSED?

Under Medicare regulations, the final hospital will receive full payment upon discharge. The transferring hospital will be entitled to a per diem payment that will be determined by dividing the full DRG payment rate by the average length of stay for that DRG. This amount times the number of days stay in the transferring hospital would be the entitlement. In New Jersey each hospital assigns the patient to a DRG. But it has been proposed that as of Jan. 1, 1984, the patient will be an outlier in both facilities, which are reimbursed controlled charges rather than the DRG rate.

SUPPOSE MY PATIENT MUST BE SENT FOR A CAT SCAN TO ANOTHER HOSPITAL. WHO PAYS?

Again, the exact details have not been worked out, but the most likely approach in the case will be for the hospital that receives the prospective payment for this patient to remit money to other hospitals for special services rendered to its patient. This is distinct from the case where the patient actually spends his or her stay at two different hospitals.

WHAT HAPPENS IF THE HOSPITAL IS TOO EFFICIENT? WON'T THE DRG RATES GO DOWN IF WE'RE TOO EFFICIENT?

That is a good question that may not have particularly good answer, since the answer is—it depends. It depends on what the system will evolve into or perhaps regress to. If the system evolves into a reasonably competitive one, then a hospital can never become too efficient. Competition should spark increased efficiency, ultimately translating into greater profits for those hospitals who adapt to the system best.

Rate setting under the new prospective payment system will, over the course of four years, reduce the influence of a hospital's own cost performance on its DRG rate from 75 percent in the first year to zero in the fourth year. Thus, the important consideration, ultimately, is going to be a hospital's own performance and efficiency relative to other hospitals in the region and the nation. The more efficient you are, compared to other hospitals, the better for you in terms of favorable reimbursements.

Consider the shortcomings of the old system, where there was no economic incentive to reduce spending, since reduced spending brought with it only reduced reimbursement. The only way for a hospital to generate revenue was to spend. As a result, hospitals learned to spend more since they got reimbursed more. This is essentially the reason why DRGs have been embraced by the regulators. For the first time, a hospital will receive an economic incentive to reduce its cost or at least restrain the spiraling increase in costs.

This incentive is the opportunity to keep the difference between the reimbursement rate and the actual cost. Even though the fixed rate will be reduced over time, as, presumably, all hospitals begin to operate more efficiently, it will still be within a hospital's power to maintain a spread between its costs and the average, because the average will always reflect both the strong and the weak competitors. The trick is to become a strong competitor and stay at least one step ahead of the pack.

Taking this logic further, a point might be reached where all the weaker competitors have been eliminated, and you are left with all strong competitors operating at approximately the same level of efficiency and with similar costs. It is unlikely that we will ever get to this advanced state, yet it is theoretically possible. The greater risk at this point would be for the regulators to reintroduce regulation and impose spending caps to keep costs at the new low levels, rather than to allow normal market equilibrium to keep competitors and costs in check.

No one knows to what extent the system will evolve. But the safest and wisest course of action at present is for each hospital to determine its own position relative to its competition, remain flexible, and experiment to some degree.

Some hospitals may elect to reduce costs as quickly and as deeply as possible in order to generate the greatest profit; others may be more conservative and try to hang on to a break-even operation in order to see which way the wind will blow; still others may dare the system by continuing to spend what they feel is appropriate to maintain the level of quality they choose. Each position has its pros and cons and at this point no one can say which is correct. The best approach, therefore, is to understand the opportunities and threats, the risks and rewards, and act in the manner you feel suits your own needs best.

IF YOU EXPECT ME TO HELP, YOU HAVE TO GIVE ME THE BOTTOM LINE. YOU'VE GOT TO TELL ME WHAT YOU'RE GETTING REIMBURSED. TELL ME EXACTLY WHAT THE RATES ARE UNDER DRGs. CAN YOU DO THAT?

The DRG rates are not a secret and the hospital will no doubt be happy to share this and other DRG information with you. However, the intent of sharing DRG information with physicians is not so that they can put down the most lucrative diagnosis, but rather so that they will begin to see the financial impact of their behavior on the hospital. If a doctor knows that a secondary diagnosis can add hundreds or even thousands of dollars to a hospital's reimbursement, and that the hospital is entitled to the money, the hope is that the doctor will be more assiduous in recording the secondary diagnosis on the patient's chart.

Obviously it is in the hospital's best interest to tell the doctors exactly what is going on regarding the impact of DRGs on the bottom line. There should be a great deal of discussion not only about DRG rates but also about how these rates compare to the actual costs associated with the services that are rendered. The bottom line is reviewed simply in terms of the difference between DRG rates (reimbursement) and the hospital's actual costs.

As your hospital begins to collect DRG data, it will probably share a great deal of information with you. For instance, you will be able to see the bottom line performance of each doctor based upon the DRG rates and the costs of all his or her cases in the hospital. The doctors' performance needs to be discussed, and so does the performance of the hospital as a whole. By reviewing this information, doctors should be able to appreciate how their individual and collective behavior impacts on the hospital's ability to remain financially solvent.

Physicians and hospitals have a symbiotic relationship; each needs the other. If this has not been totally obvious to you in the past, DRGs will bring this very special relationship into sharper focus. Both doctors and hospitals must come to realize that each has a significant influence on the other's ability to market its services and compete effectively. The hospital's role is to provide a reputable high quality service that will enhance the marketability of doctors who are associated with it. The doctors must keep costs to a minimum so that their hospital can utilize its resources more effectively and remain competitive by offering the staff, services and technology that provide the kind of quality care doctors want and need for their patients.

Those hospitals that are truly competitive—those that with the cooperation of their medical staffs make it under the new system in the years ahead—will generate a surplus that will allow further qualitative improvements and enable new programs and services to be established.

The coming years, like it or not, will be marked by diminishing resources and increased competition. There will be a finite number of health care dollars, and hospitals will have to compete for those dollars. The winners in this new environment will be those hospitals that, through sound business practices, manage to get a larger share of the pie. To succeed in this environment physicians and hospitals must work together to achieve the common goal of quality care at affordable prices. If either party is unable or unwilling to fulfill the obligations of this partnership, the venture may well be doomed to failure as the system will exact its price by discouraging utilization at that facility. This need for the exchange of information and cooperation cannot be overstated, and there is no better way to begin than by discussing the "bottom line"—what your behavior means to the hospital's future.

IS THERE ANY EVIDENCE TO SHOW THAT DRGs ACTUALLY WORK TO CONTAIN COSTS? ARE THE RESULTS IN YET ANYWHERE?

The experiment has not really been in operation long enough to gather meaningful statistics.

In the twenty-six hospitals in New Jersey that came under DRGs in 1980, there were some favorable comparisons to national figures. Operating expenses during the first year in these twenty-six hospitals were up an average of 13.8 percent, compared to a national increase of 17 percent. Proponents of the DRG system point to those figures as evidence that the system is indeed working.

But skeptics say that New Jersey hospitals have always shown a slower rate of increase than other hospitals. Indeed, they say, when the figures from those twenty-six hospitals under DRGs are compared with figures from other New Jersey hospitals not yet in the system, the differences are negligible.

While there are subjective impressions on both sides, the truth is that it is too early to tell, and it may be a few years yet before the impact of DRGs on cost containment can be determined.

IS THE ADDED PAPERWORK AND STAFF NEEDED FOR DRGs BYPASS DRGs BY MAKING SEPARATE ARRANGEMENTS WITH THE HOSPITAL?

Since the national system applies to Medicare only, the government will be paying the rates set by the system. Those payers not covered by prospective payment will continue to pay the charges set by the hospital.

In New Jersey, where all payers are covered, rates are determined by the Hospital Rate Setting Commission. Although rates do vary among hospitals, all payers pay the same rates at any given hospital.

DOES THE SYSTEM ALLOW FOR THE PURCHASE OF NEW EQUIPMENT BY A HOSPITAL IN ORDER FOR IT TO KEEP UP WITH NEW TECHNOLOGY? WHAT ABOUT REPAIRING AND UPDATING EQUIPMENT? WHERE DOES THIS MONEY COME FROM?

Under the proposed federal regulations, existing capital expenditures will be considered a pass-through item through October 1986. So those items currently being utilized, and for which a hospital has obligated itself through March 1983, will continue to be reimbursed through 1986.

Any additions approved after March 1983 are still pending further clarification. A number of options are being considered, including one similar to the way this is currently handled in New Jersey.

In New Jersey, all costs associated with major moveable equipment—be they depreciation, principal, interest payments or lease payments—are reimbursed for historical cost-based depreciation as of a base year, along with a "price level factor" allowing for the impact of inflation and purportedly reflecting technological changes that have occurred since the base year.

Non-major moveable capital expenditures are generally treated as a pass-through, providing appropriate certificates of need have been received.

Any costs required for the repair of equipment are considered part of the DRG reimbursement, as this would be an expense item included in the base year.

In theory, then, the system allows for new technology. But, given the technological boom in health care, and given the difficulty in determining a factor for technology, hospitals are probably not being given an appropriate amount for new technology. It is now up to each institution to decide how to spend these limited "discretionary capital dollars."

This means that hospitals will need to evaluate very carefully the purchase of new technology based on whether its cost can be offset by increasing efficiency of care. If a particular piece of equipment offers the possibility of eliminating other, more expensive types of care, or of shortening length of stay, then the hospital might very well make a business decision to purchase the equipment. If, on the other hand, the new machine offers no cost saving but does provide state-of-the art medical care for its patients, the decision might be a tougher one, as it will be made with the expectation that those capital dollars may not be regenerated through the reimbursement system and therefore lost forever.

In other words, hospitals may no longer automatically acquire every new machine or other new piece of technology that comes along. Instead of all hospitals within a radius of thirty miles having the latest CAT scanner, perhaps just one or two will be able to afford it now.

Patients may have to travel thirty or forty miles to have a special procedure or test, and doctors may have to get used to sending their patients to different hospitals depending on their needs. Every hospital may not be able to "have it all" any more. Serious thinking will have to be done and some difficult choices will have to be made. It is not a matter that the latest technology will not be available; rather, access to it, for patients and doctors, will probably not be as convenient.

IS THE ADDED PAPERWORK AND STAFF NEEDED FOR DRGs GOING TO ABSORB THE EXPECTED SAVINGS FROM THIS PROGRAM?

Certainly there will be added paperwork and staff necessary to deal with DRGs—more detailed record-keeping, whole new computer programs, and possibly new staff positions. However, it is believed that any extra clerical work required by DRGs will not offset the expected savings. It will be up to hospitals to review their entire expense budgets and staffing patterns to minimize any increased costs necessitated by instituting DRGs. However, in New Jersey, there was a provision allowing hospital operating costs to increase because of the DRG system, and these costs were included in DRG rates. These were called implementation costs and were allowed for a period of two years, after which time they were eliminated from the rates. There does not appear to be any provision, temporary or permanent, in the federal system for the cost of implementing DRGs.

WHAT ABOUT TEACHING HOSPITALS? DO THEY GET REIMBURSED FOR THE EXTRA EXPENSE OF AN EDUCATIONAL PROGRAM?

Recognizing that teaching hospitals have greater costs, such as salaries and house staff, the regulations currently allow the direct costs for such educational programs to be passed through.

Indirect medical education costs (the extra tests ordered by residents, the need to support research, the greater severity of cases) are also recognized in the federal regulations. But the exact formula for these teaching costs was not yet worked out at the time of this writing.

Under the New Jersey regulations direct medical costs are treated as a pass through. Furthermore, distinctions are made between major teaching, minor teaching and non-teaching hospitals to reflect more accurately the amount of indirect costs involved. In other words, teaching hospitals are compared only to other teaching hospitals, so they are not competing with hospitals that have lower costs.

Chapter Five
Questions Patients Ask Their Doctors

If you've read this far and you still insist you don't care about DRGs, here's one more reason why you should. DRGs weren't your idea, you say; they have nothing to do with you and you couldn't care less about them.

Tell that to your patients.

In the same way that an irate customer takes it out on the sales clerk in the department store or the telephone billing office, you are the point of contact for patients with the health care system. Indeed, to many of your patients, you *are* the system. Your Medicare patients have probably heard something about DRGs by now, and you can be sure they have lots of questions about them, and the person they'll be asking is you.

You know how frequently patients complain to you about things which are out of your control—hospital procedures, hospital charges, etc. Imagine what it will be like when these patients start receiving bills from the hospital which charge them amounts totally different from the actual cost of their care. What will you say when they tell you they want to stay in the hospital longer because their insurance covers a certain amount of days, or because they are willing to pay for the longer stay? Remember, your patients don't always make a distinction between you and the hospital, or you and the government regulators. It will help if you can respond to their basic concerns.

The following questions and answers about DRGs deal with

patient concerns. They are real questions that patients have asked their doctors about the system. Think of the answers as a survival guide in dealing with your patients who may be confused, upset and angry about DRGs. Take the time to learn the answers.

If these answers don't work, then you must, of course, resort to that most useful of all responses: "Ask the hospital."

WHAT'S GOING ON HERE? NO ONE TOLD ME ABOUT DRGs WHEN I WAS ADMITTED.

To save yourself much aggravation, it would be in your best interest to make sure your hospital adequately informs patients about DRG billing both in writing and orally. Even when this is done, patients may not fully understand what is going on. DRGs are a complex system of hospital reimbursement, and patients coming into the hospital, under emotional stress about their illness and about being hospitalized, cannot be expected to comprehend fully the rationale, let alone the intricacies, of DRG billing. Doctors should expect to get many inquiries from their patients about DRGs and DRG billing, even though DRGs apply to hospital costs and not physician charges. As doctors, you are generally the first recourse for patients who are concerned or angry with aspects of the health care system, so it's a good idea to be prepared to answer some basic questions. Beyond that, hospitals must be prepared by having well trained personnel and procedures for handling requests for information and clarification, and for alleviating the confusion that will inevitably result during the early transition period.

Don't forget, you will inevitably share the bad rap if your hospital is inadequately prepared to explain DRGs to your patients.

WILL I BE PAYING MORE OR LESS FOR HEALTH CARE UNDER DRGs?

The large majority of hospital patients have their bills fully or mostly paid by Medicare, Medicaid, Blue Cross or private insurance. Since Medicare (or these other third party payers, in the case of all-payer systems) will be paying the DRG rates, most patients will see little or no difference in their out-of-pocket expenses. Patients will still be subject to the same deductible and coinsurance provisions that were in effect under previous reimbursement systems.

For those patients who pay all or some of their hospital bills out of pocket, DRGs may indeed affect the amount they must pay. Although the theory is that DRGs will lower the cost of health care, some patients may actually end up paying more under DRGs than if they were billed charges by the hospital. That is because DRGs are based on averages. So, some patients are paying more and some less.

Remember that under the DRG system there will still be separate charges to patients for items not covered by the DRG rate such as television, telephone, and private room, for instance. Of course, physicians' fees do not appear on the hospital bill, are not covered by DRGs and will be billed separately as always.

WILL DRGs MAKE A DIFFERENCE IN MY INSURANCE COVERAGE?

DRGs should make absolutely no difference in insurance coverage. An individual's policy, with its deductible and coinsurance stipulations, should remain exactly the same. In the long run, if DRGs do work in bringing down the cost of health care, we may all begin to see a drop in insurance premiums. But, although that is one of the stated goals of the DRG plan, it's probably a long way off.

THE LAST TIME I WAS HOSPITALIZED I SAVED MONEY BY LEAVING THE HOSPITAL EARLY. CAN I DO THIS AGAIN THIS TIME?

Within certain limits, it makes no difference in your charge when you leave the hospital. At any rate, the decision should be based on medical rather than financial considerations.

WILL MY HOSPITALIZATION COST THE SAME NO MATTER WHAT HOSPITAL I GO TO?

Not initially, although uniformity in cost is one of the goals of the DRG-based prospective payment system. During a three-year transition period, the individual hospital's actual costs will be a factor in determining its DRG rate. For instance, during the first year, 75 percent of the hospital's own costs will be reflected in its DRG rate, and 25 percent of the rate of competing hospitals. Therefore if Hospital A's costs are less than Hospital B's, then its DRG rate will also be lower.

The weighting of the hospital's own costs will decrease to 50 percent the second year and 25 percent the third year. By the fourth year, the hospital's own costs will not figure at all, as its DRG rate will be based only on the national rate. Therefore, DRG charges should be basically the same, although they will still take into account regional wage-level variations. DRG rates will also be different for rural and urban hospitals.

WHY CAN'T I HAVE THIS PROCEDURE DONE AS AN INPATIENT? WHY MUST I HAVE IT DONE AS AN OUTPATIENT?

As part of the cost-containment effort, regulators have identified certain procedures that can be done safely on an outpatient basis. Outpatient procedures cost less money and do not needlessly tie up hospital beds.

Most hospitals have same day surgery units where patients may have minor operations and other procedures peformed without having to spend a night in the hospital. At Hackensack Medical Center, more than sixty types of procedures are performed on an outpatient basis, including laparoscopies, chemotherapy, and breast biopsies. Currently at Hackensack, one of every five surgical procedures is performed on an outpatient basis. You should know your hospital's capabilities and statistics.

In most cases, patients prefer this approach because it is less costly and it does not entail the anxiety and inconvenience associated with spending a night in the hospital.

There are probably some patients, however, who prefer to have these procedures done as inpatients. What they must realize is that the government is telling physicians and hospitals to treat patients in the most *economical,* if not always the most *convenient,* manner.

WILL IT COST ME MORE IF I STAY LONGER IN THE HOSPITAL?

Within certain limits (known as trim points in the DRG terminology), you or your insurer will pay the same charge no matter how long you stay in the hospital. If your stay is unusually long and falls outside the trim points set by the DRGs, then your case is considered an "outlier" and you will be billed charges for what you consumed. These charges will most likely be considerably higher than the DRG rate.

However, just as in the past, the only consideration in determining how long you remain in the hospital should be whether you still require acute medical care.

WHY CAN'T I STAY LONGER IF I AM WILLING TO PAY FOR IT?

Once again, the amount of time you stay in the hospital should be determined only by your medical need for hospitalization—not by your willingness to pay for it. No matter how long you stay in the hospital (unless your stay is atypically long and you are classified as an outlier) the DRG rate remains the same regardless of the patient's willingness to pay extra. The hospital can collect only the DRG rate. The rates are established by the system, and "special arrangements" are inconsistent with the intent and requirements of the new regulations.

As always, once the patient is medically able to leave the hospital, he or she should do so.

Even before DRGs were in effect, all hospitals practiced utilization review, to ensure that patients were not staying in the hospital longer than necessary. No matter what the system of reimbursement, resources have been scarce and costs high for some time now, and the system has never encouraged over-utilization of hospital facilities, no matter who pays, nor how much they are willing to pay.

DOES A PRIVATE ROOM AND A TWO-BED ROOM COST THE SAME UNDER DRGs?

No. The DRG rate is based on a semiprivate room, and the hospital is still entitled to charge for a private room in addition to the DRG rate. Insurance companies and other third party payers generally do not pay for private rooms, so you will most likely have to pay the difference yourself. The same holds true for certain other items such as telephone and television, which are considered additional.

IF INSURANCE PAYS FOR 120 DAYS, WHY DO I HAVE TO GET OUT IN 10 DAYS?

An individual's coverage has never determined the necessity or length of hospitalization. Admittedly, in the past, generous coverage has made it convenient for both patient and doctor to be somewhat liberal in deciding when a patient could go home. For instance, if an elderly patient was about to be discharged, but someone was not coming to help care for the patient for a few days, the doctor might decide that the patient should stay in the hospital a day or so longer rather than be discharged to go home alone. Since the patient would not have to pay any additional out-of-pocket expenses, and since the hospital would get reimbursed for the extra time, neither party felt a great responsibility or incentive to be cost conscious.

Imagine if the hospital, the doctor or the patient had to pay for those two extra days out of their own pockets! They would probably, in that case, be much more inclined to find some other, less costly arrangement for the patient—in accordance with good medical practice, of course.

In a sense, this is what the new system will mean. No longer will it be convenient to let that patient stay in the hospital until a family member arrives to care for him or her. Once the system becomes all payer, the post-partum patient will no longer be allowed to stay a day or two longer because her infant must be in the newborn intensive care unit a few extra days. For instance, at one hospital a woman was ready to be discharged after giving birth, but her baby had to remain in the hospital a few more days because of a medical problem. The woman asked to stay in the hospital also, because she was breast-feeding. Instead, the hospital told her she must leave the hospital but could return as often as she liked to breast feed the infant. It would be both medically inappropriate and financially detrimental to the hospital for a healthy woman to remain as an inpatient.

Reasons of health, safety and good medical practice must now be the only determining factors.

What the new system is attempting to do is raise the level of cost awareness among all the players—patients, doctors, nurses, hospital administrators, boards of governors—so that only necessary health care services are provided, and to make sure these services are based on an individual's medical needs rather than what insurance will cover.

Therefore sound medical judgment, not generous insurance benefits or considerations about convenience, must be the determining factor in committing the consumption of scarce health resources.

THE HOSPITAL WANTS TO MAKE MONEY, AND UNDER DRGs, THE WAY HOSPITALS MAKE MONEY IS BY GETTING ME OUT QUICKER. AM I GETTING GOOD HEALTH CARE?

DRGs, if properly implemented, should enhance patient care. Hospitals do not want to get you out "quicker" so much as they want to make sure you stay in the hospital only as long as you are in need of acute hospital care. The hospital wants you to stay just as long as you need to. And, of course, it is your doctor who remains in charge of your care. It is the doctor who must sign the order to admit or to discharge his or her patients. You will stay in the hospital exactly as long as your physician feels you need acute hospital care.

In fact, there is every reason to believe that your hospital care will improve under DRGs. For instance, tests and procedures will be ordered in a more efficient and rational matter, so that you will not have to wait days between procedures because of the sequence in which they are ordered. Since, under DRGs, the hospital will be encouraging ancillary departments to provide faster results, you may find that your hospital stay is handled more efficiently, while the high quality of care you are accustomed to is maintained.

SUPPOSE I AM MOVED FROM THE HOSPITAL TO A NURSING HOME. DOES DRG PAYMENT COVER CONVALESCENT CARE?

DRGs cover only acute care facilities, although the possibility of extending the system to nursing homes is being studied.

In the meantime, services for less than acute care are unaffected.

UNDER DRGs, IS THERE ANY LIMIT ON THE NUMBER OF TIMES I CAN BE A MEDICARE INPATIENT?

The system applies only to the way hospitals get reimbursed for Medicare patients; it does not in any way change your Medicare coverage. Medicare provides a certain amount of full pay days and a certain provision for co-pay days. The individual is also allotted a certain amount of lifetime days. However, once all these benefits are exhausted, the obligation for the bill becomes the individual patient's responsibility and the bill is no longer subject to the federal DRG system. (Of course, the patient may very well have other insurance coverage that will pick up where Medicare leaves off.) So there is and always has been a limit on how many hospital days will be covered by Medicare.

THEY PUT ME IN THE HOSPITAL "FOR TESTS" AS THE SAYING GOES. DESPITE ALL THE TESTS, THEY DO NOT COME UP WITH A CLEAR DIAGNOSIS. THEN WHAT?

There are two ways to handle this. If, despite the inconclusive test results, the doctor writes that the final diagnosis is, for instance, probable myocardial infarction, the hospital can go ahead and code the heart attack and base the DRG assignment on that diagnosis.

But suppose a patient is admitted to the hospital with an admitting diagnosis of chest pains. After study and tests, the doctor can find nothing wrong with the patient, so the final diagnosis remains chest pains. In this case, the chest pains may have been due to a heart problem, a digestive problem, or any of a number of other conditions. The hospital will simply code "chest pains." There is a code for chest pain, just as there is a code for abdominal pain or other symptoms.

I GO INTO THE HOSPITAL FOR A URINARY STONE REMOVAL VIA CYSTOSCOPE WITH BASKET EXTRACTION; ORDINARILY, WITH LUCK, A RELATIVELY SHORT STAY—

SAY THREE TO FIVE DAYS. BUT THE SCOPE WON'T DO THE JOB AND EVENTUALLY I HAVE TO HAVE A URETHRAL LITHOTOMY AND I AM THERE TWO WEEKS. WHAT IS MY DRG CLASSIFICATION?

Your admitting diagnosis is a kidney stone, but your major procedure, which will have a very big impact on your DRG classification, is the urethral lithotomy. The cystoscopy did not work, and it was the more complicated procedure that was needed. Therefore, the urethral lithotomy is the basis for your DRG assignment.

SUPPOSE I AM ADMITTED TO A HOSPITAL, BUT FOR SOME REASON AM UNHAPPY THERE AND MY SPOUSE TAKES ME OUT THAT SAME NIGHT AND ADMITS ME TO ANOTHER HOSPITAL. WHAT HAPPENS ABOUT MY DRG?

Since you would probably be leaving against medical advice, you would be treated as an outlier at the original hospital and be billed charges. It would be up to the hospital to which you transferred to determine a proper DRG assignment for you. At least that's the way the New Jersey system handles these cases. It is not clear yet how federal regulators will deal with this type of situation.

WHEN WILL I AS A PATIENT KNOW WHAT CLASSIFICATION GROUP THEY HAVE PUT ME INTO?

After your discharge, and after the medical record data have been processed and sent to the billing department, a patient bill is prepared and submitted to you. The actual charges are listed along with the DRG assignment and rate. Patients with questions about their DRG assignment or rate may contact the hospital's billing department or the local PSRO in New Jersey. At this time there does not appear to be any mechanism for handling patient complaints in the federal system.

SINCE MEDICAL RECORDS ARE CONFIDENTIAL, WILL ONLY COMPETENT, TRAINED AND DULY AUTHORIZED PEOPLE BE ALLOWED ACCESS TO MY CHART AND THE DECISION MADE BY THE HOSPITAL AS TO MY DRG CLASSIFICATION?

Medical records are always safeguarded from unauthorized use by anyone. Certainly only competent, trained and authorized individuals have access to your medical records and decisions made by the hospital regarding your treatment, your DRG classification, and anything else related to your medical care while in the hospital.

I AM HOSPITALIZED AND MY PRIMARY PHYSICIAN AND I WANT SECOND OR EVEN THIRD OPINIONS FROM SPECIALISTS. HOW DOES THIS AFFECT MY DRG?

If your stay is within the DRG trim points, this will not affect the DRG. However, the number of physicians who consult on your case may have a great impact on the actual hospital costs even though physicians' fees are not covered by the system (yet). And, of course, each physician will probably need to order his or her own tests and procedures in order to further work up your case and aid in making a diagnosis.

For instance, one consulting doctor may order a gall bladder series. Another may want a sonogram. Yet another may ask the laboratory for serial blood tests. Each time a consultant visits you in the hospital, it could involve additional nursing time, more medication, and other types of resources.

WHY DID THEY CHANGE THE WAY HOSPITALS BILL FOR CARE?

Hospitals are charging for the services they render differently now as a result of a new reimbursement system that went into effect on Oct. 1, 1983. This new type of billing applies to all patients covered by Medicare as mandated by federal legislation. Even if you are not a Medicare patient, this new system may apply to you, since some states may have opted to extend this new system of prospective pricing to all payers—Medicare, Medicaid, Blue Cross, and private insurance companies. So the type of bill you are now receiving may be quite different from your hospital bills in the past.

Your bill, if you are covered by the prospective payment system, will show your DRG (Diagnosis Related Group) charge, which has been set by the government as the amount the hospital will be reimbursed for treating you according to your diagnosis rather than according to your length of stay, as in the past.

One way of looking at this new system is that patients are now billed for a complete finished product (one appendectomy, one mitral valve replacement, one urinary tract infection) rather than being billed for the total of the individual goods and services the patient consumed while in the hospital. Because DRG rates are based on averages a specific patient's DRG charge is probably different from the actual cost of treating that particular case. Some patients will be paying less than the actual cost to the hospital, some patients will be paying more.

The system is based on the premise that most times the actual cost will cluster around the average, and that the highs and lows will balance each other out.

In any case, it is important to remember that there is one set charge for each of the 467 Diagnosis Related Groups. If a patient is classified into DRG #10 (nervous system neoplasms in patients aged 70 or over, or with substantial complications and comorbidities, treated medically), for instance, then the charge is $3,791.20, no matter what the length of hospital stay (within certain limits) and no matter how many X-rays, blood tests, angiograms or radiation therapy treatments have been given.

WHY DOES MY BILL SHOW A DIFFERENT AMOUNT THAN WHAT THE DRG IS?

Under New Jersey regulations, which may be similar to those in other parts of the country, your hospital bill must show two different amounts—the DRG charge for your individual case (remember, this charge is set by law and is not up to the discretion of individual hospitals) and the actual charges generated by the hospital for caring for you as long as you were in the hospital. This part of your bill is set by the hospital and covers such things as your room rate, surgery, tests, procedures, medication and supplies, as well as a percentage of the hospital's "unseen" costs, such as capital expenses, salaries, its education program, etc.

Although under the new regulations you will be billed the DRG amount, it is still important for you to know the actual resources committed by the hospital to care for you. Hopefully, the two amounts will differ only slightly.

But since the DRGs are based on averages, there may be a considerable difference between your actual charges and your DRG charge. Admittedly, it may be jarring to see two columns of figures that do not match, especially if you are being asked to pay the greater amount. The theory is that your high charge will be balanced by your neighbor's low charge and it should work out in the end, as far as the system is concerned. Individuals who are asked to pay higher DRG charges may take little consolation in this, however, since they can't "average out" their costs. Fortunately, most individuals are covered by insurance, so they will not have to pay any difference out-of-pocket. But to those who *are* paying their own health care bills, the new system can seem very unfair.

WHY ARE YOU SENDING ME THIS BILL IF IT IS MEANINGLESS?

A hospital bill should never be considered meaningless. Although patients are being asked to pay the DRG set fee for their stay in the hospital, they have a right to know, and should want to know, what their actual charges were.

Each entry on a bill generally relates to either patient/payer information (name, address, coverage, etc.) or what the patient/payer is being billed for. This billing information may be itemized (by test, procedure, etc.), summarized (total laboratory costs, total X-ray costs), or totaled (price per case).

The composition and details of the bill are mandated either by regulation or by the payer. In the absence of these requirements, bills should be tailored to satisfy a patient without being confusing.

In any event, hospital personnel should be able to guide a patient or payer through a bill and key in on the relevant areas. Ideally, the bill should be designed to allow a patients/payers to follow their own way through, but there will always be some who require assistance.

Although you, the doctor, are not responsible for the hospital bill, you would be wise to familiarize yourself with it and be prepared for at least some of the questions which will inevitably come your way as patients grope with their new DRG bills.

HOW COME I HAVE TO PAY $1,500 WHEN I WAS ONLY IN THE HOSPITAL OVERNIGHT?

Under DRGs, your charge depends almost entirely on your diagnosis—what you were in the hospital for. Admittedly, $1,500 sounds like a pretty steep charge for an overnight. There might be an error in calculation or the charge might result from an inequity in the system.

In New Jersey there is an appeals mechanism for both patients and hospitals that feel they have been treated unfairly by the system. Patient complaints go to the State Department of Health, which refers them to the local PSRO for review and recommendations. If the patient is still not satisfied, then a committee of doctors appointed by the PSROs and the state medical society review the records and either affirms or denies the decision. During the first three years under DRGs, approximately 1,500 patients appealed bills they felt were unfair, and half of them won their appeals.

Hospital concerns are generally in the area of inadequacy of the rates. These appeals are handled by an independent, five member Hospital Rate Setting Commission. In 1981, New Jersey hospitals asked for $118 million in rate adjustments, of which $48 million were granted.

Thus far, the Medicare system has no appeal mechanism beyond a provision for appealing errors in calculation, which means the federal system will be a lot less flexible than New Jersey's.

IF THE REIMBURSEMENT TO THE HOSPITAL IS LESS THAN THE COST OF MY CASE, THEN WHO IS MAKING UP THE DIFFERENCE?

Although the hospital may be getting reimbursed less than its actual cost in your case, rest assured that there are other cases in which the reimbursement is greater than the actual cost. The DRG rate is an average. That means sometimes the hospital will receive more and sometimes less, but it should just about even out in the end. If the hospital is repeatedly coming out on the losing end of the reimbursements, that is a sign to the hospital that it is not operating as efficiently as other hospitals, and it's time to make some changes.

Since the national system currently applies only to Medicare, there is the likelihood that hospitals will make up any losses by charging more to their other payees—Blue Cross, commercial insurance, etc.

IT'S ALL VERY CONFUSING. HOW DO I KNOW I'M NOT BEING CHEATED?

You can't blame patients for being not only confused by the bill, but worried that they are somehow being treated unfairly. This is especially true when the traditional billing of charges, based upon actual services used, is less—and in some cases considerably less —than the fixed rate that they are asked to pay under DRGs. Fortunately, most patients' bills are taken care of by a third party payer—Medicare, Medicaid, Blue Cross or private insurance. If these patients are in all-payer systems, they may be confused by their bills, but they will not be greatly affected by DRG rates, since they will see little or no difference in their out-of-pocket expenses, regardless of what their bills say. Furthermore, it can be rationalized for these patients that third party payers will be able to offset the inequities—the highs and the lows—because of the great volume of cases involved.

Unfortunately, there is very little the hospital can do or say to justify or rationalize apparent inequities on the hospital bill for patients who must pay their own bills. The individual patient—dealing with one hospital stay—does not have the ability to offset a bill against a more favorable outcome. For the patient who sees that actual charges are considerably less than the DRG amount being billed, arguments about cost containment, incentives toward efficiency, and the law of averages probably won't hold much water. Fortunately, only a very small percentage of patients are not covered by third party insurance.

Inevitably, inequities will result. Soon you will begin to hear the horror stories: the $6,000 broken finger, the $4,000 charged to a patient who died after four hours of treatment in the Emergency Room. The only way to deal with this type of inequity is through an appeals process. This is how the New Jersey system has chosen to provide some type of relief for those patients who feel—often justifiably—that they have been dealt with unfairly under the system. The reviews are conducted by an independent organization and the objective is to recognize those cases where applying the fixed rate billing just won't work; in other words, those cases where a significant inequity would result from such a billing. In those cases where the fixed rate is indeed found to be inequitable, the actual controlled charges for the patient's stay are substituted. The hospital is then allowed to increase its "markup factor" for all other cases in order to make up for this loss; in other words, it may pass along the costs by increasing rates in general.

At present, the Medicare system allows appeals only in cases of errors in calculations and incorrect application of the methodology. There is no provision in the legislation for appealing inequities that may result despite correct application of the methodology. If New Jersey's experience is an indication, this lack of a broader appeals process may be a serious problem.

I DIDN'T HAVE ALL THESE THINGS DONE TO ME. I DIDN'T HAVE ALL THESE TESTS. I DIDN'T HAVE ALL THESE PILLS! WHAT IS GOING ON HERE?

DRGs are no excuse for charging a patient for services or goods he or she did not consume. The actual charges (not the DRG side of the bill) should reflect the services and supplies the patient actually utilized. At times a hospital may use a per diem or average daily charge for items that are usually high volume, low cost consumables, such as bandages and aspirin. It would be highly impractical, in terms of time and paperwork, if the hospital were to charge separately for each of these items. So either the hospital charges the patient a per diem amount for these items regardless of usage, or the hospital increases the charge for the items that are separately billed to account for those that are not. Each method is acceptable, but the latter method is generally preferred, since patients can more easily accept being charged a high price for something that is received than being charged any price for something not received at all. But it is important to remember that DRGs in no way affect this billing or change this situation. However, since patients may begin to scrutinize their bills more carefully because of the new DRG component, hospitals (and doctors) should expect more questions about every item that appears on the hospital bill.

HOW COME MY NEIGHBOR AND I BOTH WERE HOSPITALIZED FOR THE SAME THING AND WE PAID DIFFERENT AMOUNTS?

There are a number of reasons why this may have happened. Although you and your neighbor both had the same type of illness, a number of other factors also affect your DRG classification. For instance, age, complications, surgery and secondary diagnoses all affect your DRG assignment. So, although you may both have been in for similar ailments, you or your neighbor probably had one or more of the variable factors which affect DRG assignment.

For instance, if you (seventy-two years of age) and your neighbor (thirty-five years old) were admitted for acute appendicitis and you developed a fever after surgery and your doctor treated you with antibiotics for an infection, you would be assigned to a different DRG and the payments would be different. Your ages and your complications affect the DRG assignment here.

Chapter Six
The New Jersey Experience

In the spring and summer of 1983, as hospitals across the country were gearing up for DRGs for Medicare patients, the controversy about New Jersey's three-year experience with the system spilled over into the press. On one side was the Medical Society of New Jersey, the oldest state medical society in the nation, calling the system a "stepping-stone on the road to socialized medicine,"[1] a system "fraught with confusion and spun from an illusion".[2] On the other side, defending the system, was Dr. J. Richard Goldstein, New Jersey State Commissioner of Health, telling physicians that any fault in the delivery of health care lay with themselves rather than with the system.

Everyone was having a say—physicians, nurses, patients, hospital administrators, discharge planners, insurers and taxpayers, and, depending on whom you listened to, DRGs were either the last, best hope to salvage a health care system that had gotten out of financial control or a form of "fiscal euthanasia"[1] and an "abysmally impersonal approach to hospital care."[1]

For some time, physicians in the state had been simmering

---

[1]Frank J. Primich, M.D., co-chairman, DRG Committee, Medical Society of New Jersey, in testimony presented to the health subcommittees of the Senate Committee on Finance and the House Ways and Means Committee, Washington, DC, February, 1983. (See article by Dr. Primich on p. 163.)

[2]New Jersey Medical Society advertisement, The Record, July 20, 1983.

about the concept of DRGs. It reduced the science and art of medicine to a numbers game, they said; it jeopardized the quality of the doctor-patient relationship, they alleged; and it would, they assured, lead to substandard medical care.

Physicians complained and they worried, but, for the most part, they went on practicing medicine in the same way they had always done. If anything, most physicians in the state ignored the imperatives of the new system. Two years into DRGs, *Medical Economics* surveyed physicians in the state and found a surprising reaction: "They find adapting to DRG no great burden—so far,"[3] The fears of added paperwork, pressure from hospital administrators, and an infringement on their right to practice medicine as they saw fit simply hadn't materialized, the magazine article found.

Yet, talk to doctors in the state and you would undoubtedly find a strong philosophical objection to the concept of DRGs.

At the annual convention of the state medical society in May, 1983, an offhand remark by a medical examiner stirred up all the antagonism and concerns that had been lying just below the surface. Dr. George Triebenbacher, an assistant medical examiner in Ocean County, said the number of individuals who had died shortly after being discharged from hospitals had quadrupled. He said he thought DRGs were probably to blame.

Since, under DRGs, hospitals are rewarded for shorter lengths of stay for their patients, physicians and others had always worried whether patients would be sent home too soon so that hospitals could profit financially. When Dr. Triebenbacher voiced those concerns he set off a flurry of reaction.

The state Department of Health said there was no documented evidence of even one case to support that claim, but the department announced that it would begin monitoring hospitals to see if patients were being sent home too soon and then subsequently being readmitted. The state medical society said it would begin its own study, and asked doctors who believed a patient's care had

---

[3]"Payment by Diagnosis: How the Great Experiment is Going," *Medical Economics*, May 10, 1982, pp. 245–257.

been jeopardized by DRGs to write to them so they could begin documenting all incidents.

Previously the Home Health Agency Assembly of New Jersey, which represents fifty-one home nursing agencies in the state, announced plans to begin its own study after some of its nurses complained that patients were being sent home from hospitals too soon.

Faced with the prospect of all Medicare billing going on a DRG system based on New Jersey's, Representative Matthew J. Rinaldo of Union, NJ, called a special session of the House Select Committee on Aging to gather information about how the system was working in New Jersey. The hearings were held in Newark in July.

Dr. Alfred A. Alessi, a Hackensack surgeon, past president of the New Jersey Medical Society, and one of the most outspoken critics of DRGs, testified. He ticked off the faults of the system: it was expensive for hospitals to implement, with any cost savings being eaten up by increased clerical and computer expenses; it encouraged the premature discharge of patients; it discouraged hospitals from adding "innovative improvements"; and it might cause hospitals to turn away expensive-to-treat-cases, while encouraging the types of patients who made money for the hospital.

The state's Commissioner of Health countered that the system was working in that it was limiting health care costs. As for the alleged premature discharges, he said those charges were totally unfounded and undocumented. "I believe that the DRG system is a cost-effective system," he said, "and that we have found no evidence of a decline in the quality of medical care." Dr. Goldstein had said previously that it is doctors who decide when a patient leaves the hospital, and DRGs had done nothing to change that. If there were problems, he said, it was because of poor discharge planning and coordination. He even suggested at one point that some of the problems could be overcome by better after care, such as house calls by doctors.

Louis Scibetta, president of the New Jersey Hospital Association, attributed hospital readmissions to the fact that many patients are chronically ill and are routinely readmitted, regardless of DRGs.

More testimony was offered by Carolyn Smith, representing the Community Nursing Service of Essex and West Hudson County. She blamed other areas of the health care system for readmissions. For instance, she said, chronically ill patients were sometimes readmitted to hospitals because Medicare benefits for home care were extremely limited. Some of the testimony offered at these hearings is in the next section of this chapter.

Venting their disapproval further, the medical society took a full page advertisement (see following page) in twenty-six newspapers in the state, declaring that "Three years into the experiment the Medical Society of New Jersey has been unable to secure any comparative figures despite repeated requests to the State Department of Health. This is surprising in view of the expenditures of millions of dollars in federal funding for the evaluation."

The ad continued: "Physicians are being asked to regulate patient care to conform to an unproven format in which a patient's needs are subjected to the limitations of averages. It's not fair to the patient or the physician responsible for providing the care.

"The expansion of this as yet unproven experiment is forcing physicians to render medical care under the restrictions of unsubstantiated economic standards that may not be in the best interest of the patient. A system that is fraught with confusion and spun from an illusion is not only a disappointment it can also be dangerous."

On the eve of the system's expansion to all Medicare patients in the country, the DRG controversy continued to rage in New Jersey. Doctors remain basically opposed. Hospital administrators and fiscal officers are somewhat more favorably disposed. The state bureaucrats are staunch defenders.

In an effort to pin down opinions about DRGs in New Jersey, in June, 1983, Rep. Rinaldo sent a questionnaire to all 100 acute care hospitals in the state and all 21 county medical societies as well as the state medical society. Half the medical societies responded, along with 68 percent of the hospitals. Results show that although neither expressed an overwhelming vote of confidence in the new system, hospital administrators were more optimistic.

THE NEW JERSEY EXPERIENCE

SOME WOULD HAVE YOU THINK DRGs WERE HANDED DOWN FROM THE MOUNTAIN

Diagnostic Related Groups (DRGs) are a new trend in hospital patient care. DRGs were developed by a national representation of researchers, physicians and hospital executives, and directed by a team from Yale University under a grant from Health Care Financing Administration, in 1980.

The program was supposed to pay hospitals for the health care their patients consumed. The concept is appealing. By grouping patients by diagnosis and then reimbursing the hospital according to the average cost per diagnostic group costs were to be contained. Three years into the experiment the Medical Society of New Jersey has been unable to secure any comparative figures despite repeated requests to the State Department of Health. This is surprising in view of the expenditure of millions of dollars in federal funding for the evaluation.

While the Department of Health struggled with the technical difficulties of starting up the DRG concept, the Legislature was busy drafting laws to standardize payments for hospital care.

Without a proper evaluation of the process, the Department of Health mandated the system statewide. The DRG system of reimbursement still hasn't had a scientific and proper evaluation.

Physicians are being asked to regulate patient care to conform to an unproven format in which a patient's needs are subjected to the limitations of averages. It's not fair to the patient or the physician responsible for providing the care.

The expansion of this, as yet unproven, experiment is forcing physicians to render medical care under the restrictions of unsubstantiated economic standards that may not be in the best interest of the patient. A system that is fraught with confusion, and spun from an illusion, is not only a disappointment but it can be dangerous.

The public should demand a full and open report and accounting of the DRG program.

The Medical Society of New Jersey
2 PRINCESS RD., LAWRENCEVILLE, N.J. 08648

For instance, 44 percent of the hospitals responded that DRGs had improved hospital efficiency, while only 9 percent of the medical societies thought so.

Sixty percent of the hospitals rated DRGs as better, overall, than the previous system, while only 9 percent of the medical societies agreed.

Eighty-two percent of the medical societies agreed that "The DRG system is inherently biased toward formula care and will always present the danger of premature discharge." When that statement was presented to hospital administrators, only 24 percent, by comparison, agreed.

Here are the complete survey results:

QUESTIONNAIRE ON DIAGNOSTIC-RELATED GROUPS

Final Results

	Medical Society Results	Hospital Results

1. The DRG prospective payment system has received much attention, both in New Jersey and across the nation. Listed below are a number of statements about the system. Please check those you feel accurately reflect your experience with the DRG payment methodology.

   Do you feel the DRG system has—

	Medical Society Results	Hospital Results
Made hospital personnel more cost-conscious?	72.7	80.9
Made physicians more cost-conscious?	45.5	54.5
Made patients more cost-conscious?	9.1	8.8
Reduced the average length of stay of patients?	36.4	80.9
Hindered the ability of the hospital to provide newer or better services or technology?	54.5	61.8
Had any effect on readmissions of patients formerly discharged?	45.5	16.2

Promoted greater reliance on outpatient or home health care services?	36.4	11.8
Affected future hospital planning?	63.6	75.0
Improved hospital efficiency?	9.1	44.1
Helped to restrain price increases in health care?	9.1	55.9
Other	36.4	22.1

2. From the point of view of restraining rising costs in health care, how would you rate the system *based on your experience?*

Very successful	0.0	5.9
Somewhat successful	18.2	33.8
Not yet successful, but holds promise	18.2	14.7
Unsuccessful and unpromising	18.2	0.0
Temporarily successful, but does not deal with the underlying cause of health care inflation	27.3	45.6
Other	18.2	—

3. From the point of view of patient care, how would you rate the system *based on your experience?*

Allows for maximum patient care	9.1	11.7
Further safeguards are needed to assure maximum patient care	18.2	33.8
System is inherently cost-oriented and relegates patient care to a secondary consideration	90.1	55.9

4. Overall, how would you rate the DRG system in New Jersey?

Better than the previous system	9.1	60.3
Equal to the previous system	18.2	11.8
Not as good as the previous system	36.4	10.3

5. Recent news reports have cited instances of premature discharge of patients from hospitals and linked these discharges to the DRG system. Listed below are several statements relating to this issue. Please check those you feel most accurately reflect *your experience.*

Premature discharge has not been a problem	18.2	57.4

Premature discharge could present problems and requires close monitoring	45.5	41.2
Premature discharge has occurred	18.2	7.4
The problem is no greater than under the previous system	27.3	19.1
The DRG system provides sufficient flexibility to doctors to avoid premature discharge	9.1	38.2
Doctors do not have sufficient flexibility under DRG without resorting to more costly treatment (i.e., outliers or DRG-creep)	36.4	N/A
The DRG system is inherently biased toward formula care and will always present the danger of premature discharge	81.8	23.5
Modification of the "outlier" criteria could easily remove any danger of premature discharge	9.1	16.2
Other	9.1	—

Additional Questions for Medical Societies

6. Has your organization—

	Response
Issued any statement or taken any position with respect to premature discharge?	45.5
Taken any position on the DRG system as a whole?	36.4

7. In general, how would you characterize the sentiment of physicians in your organizations about the DRG system?

Generally satisfied	0.0
Generally unsatisfied	72.7
Other	9.1

8. Have any physicians cited *specific* instances in which they were "pressured" to get their patients out of hospitals?

Yes	54.5
No	9.1
Don't Know	18.2

Additional Questions for Hospitals

6. Has the DRG system led to any *specific, substantiated* complaints related to patients care (other than premature discharge)?

Yes	35.2
No	67.6

7. In New Jersey, fully one-third of all patients have been classified as outliers and thus reimbursed outside of DRG methodology. Do you think it is realistic to expect this figure can be reduced?

Yes	25.0
No	58.8
Don't Know	16.2

8. The New Jersey DRG plan applies to all payers, while the nationwide system will cover only Medicare patients. Do you think the Medicare-only system will result in cost-shifting to private paying patients in other states?

Yes	95.6
No	1.4
Don't Know	4.4

9. The New Jersey Department of Health will be applying for a waiver from the Health Care Financing Administration at the end of the year to continue the state's DRG system. Do you believe the waiver should be renewed?

Yes	79.4
No	7.4
Don't Know	13.2

While physicians continue to fear the worst, no one, so far, has come up with any real evidence to show that health care has suffered in the state. Nor, on the other hand, has there been any indication that health care costs have been contained. It is simply too early to tell. As a recent *Medical Economics* article concluded after an extensive study, "The fact is that three years into the experiment, no one really knows how New Jersey is doing under DRGs."[4]

Furthermore, although the federal system was modeled after New Jersey's, there are significant differences between the two, so that it may not be meaningful to extrapolate from the state's experience, were it known.

In New Jersey, all payers are covered by DRGs—Medicare, Medicaid, Blue Cross, private insurance and self-payers. Since the national system covers only Medicare, it is possible for hospitals to shift any losses they incur by charging other payers escalated rates. If this cost shifting does occur, as many observers believe it inevitably will, it will mean health care costs are not being contained, but merely shifted around.

The New Jersey rates include allowances for covering the cost of indigent care as well as provisions for hospitals' capital needs and requirements for implementing the DRG system. All these factors are missing, at this point, from the Medicare system.

The New Jersey system includes generous provisions for outliers—those patients with atypically long or short stays, and patients who die in the hospital, are transferred, or leave against medical advice. Up to 30 percent of all patients in the state are classified as outliers, and hospitals are reimbursed charges for these patients rather than the standard DRG rates. The national system, while allowing for the concept of outliers, intends to limit them to 5.5 percent of all Medicare patients, a figure which many think is unrealistic, judging by New Jersey's experience.

In New Jersey there is a mechanism for hospitals, third party payers and patients to appeal DRG rates which they think are unfair. No such appeals are allowed in the federal system.

New Jersey DRG rates vary among hospitals because they take into account the individual hospital's past performance. The

---

[4]"DRG: What It Is, How It Works, and Why It Will Hurt," *Medical Economics*, Sept. 5, 1983.

aim of the national system is to set uniform rates for all hospitals with differences allowed only for rural versus urban hospitals.

Excerpts from the United States House of Representatives Hearings on New Jersey's DRG System*

Representative Matthew J. Rinaldo, Ranking Republican Member, House Select Committee on Aging

Mr. RINALDO. The committee will now come to order. I would like to begin this hearing by stating that we are here this morning to gain information about an issue that touches the lives and health of millions of Americans. Over the last three years, New Jersey has phased in a new method of paying for hospital care. The system is known as DRGs, which stands for diagnostic related groups.

Under this system fee schedules are set in advance and hospitals are paid according to those fees, not according to their actual expenses. The goal of the system is relatively simple, to hold down rising health care costs. Our nation is spending more and more for health care. Expenditures for health now represent 10 percent of our gross national product, and that is a real increase of over 50 percent since 1965.

In 1983 we will spend over $360 billion for health care. And nearly half that amount, about $155 billion, will be spent on care given in hospitals. All the trends point to a continuing rise in health care costs. As a result, the Federal government has been searching for a cure to the inflation that has taken more and more of our national wealth. The last three years in New Jersey have been an experiment. It was begun with the approval of the Health Care Financing Administration, and as of April of this year $4.9 million in Federal funds had been spent to implement the New Jersey program. But we have gone beyond experimenting because starting this fall, every Medicare hospital in the nation will be required to shift to DRGs.

Looking at national statistics one cannot underestimate the profound impact of this change. Sixty-seven hundred hospitals participate in Medicare. Thirty million Americans are enrolled in Medicare. Twenty-seven million of them are over the age of 65. This year alone Medicare will spend over $60 billion and 70 percent of that amount, over $40 billion, will be for hospital care.

---

*The hearings were held in Newark, NJ in July 1983.

THE NEW JERSEY EXPERIENCE

Preliminary statistics indicate that DRGs in New Jersey have been successful in restraining hospital inflation. Dr. Carolyne Davis, Administrator of the Health Care Financing Administration, testified at a hearing we held earlier this year in Princeton that inpatient hospital costs in the nation rose last year by over 17 percent. In New Jersey, on the other hand, they rose only 13 percent. These results are promising, but we also want to ensure that the effort to hold down rising costs does not compromise patient care.

Many of us were disturbed earlier this year when the Newark Star-Ledger ran several stories describing instances of premature discharge of patients under the DRG system. We want to ensure that we do not cut corners on providing health care for the elderly under Medicare. We want to ensure that the New Jersey experiment remains a success, and we want to ensure that the national DRG system benefits from our experience in New Jersey.

Before hearing from our first witness I want to recognize my colleague, Congressman Jim Courter, who was appointed to the Aging Committee at the start of this year. He has brought a tremendous commitment and energy to our committee, and we are pleased to have him working with us.

Dr. J. Richard Goldstein, Commissioner, New Jersey Department of Health

Dr. GOLDSTEIN. Thank you. The testimony is quite short. I think it would probably be easier to go ahead and read it into the record.

The DRG system was implemented in New Jersey acute care hospitals over a three-year phase-in period. Twenty-six hospitals entered the system in 1980, 35 additional hospitals entered in 1981, and the remaining 37 entered in 1982. This gradual phasing was deliberately planned, so that the problems with implementing such an innovative and different payment system could be more easily resolved.

The results for the the first two years of operation (1980 and 1981) are complete, and the hospitals are now submitting their 1982 financial and statistical data to the Department of Health.

While the initial results are favorable, we believe we will see more efficient and effective delivery of health care services. The effects of the DRG system can be illustrated by comparing the statistics from those hospitals which entered the system during 1980 and 1981, in contrast with national averages.

In year one (1980) the DRG hospitals' total operating expenses increased at a rate of 13.8 percent while the national increase for that year was 17.0 percent. During the second year, the 61 hospitals on the system experienced an increase in total operating expenses of 14.0 percent while the national increase was 18.7 percent.

One of the most important characteristics of the DRG system is full payment for the treatment of the medically indigent. This feature provided needed revenue to our inner-city hospitals which previously experienced substantial operating losses. Additionally, payments were made in the years of entry onto the system to account for working capital needs of those hospitals that had cash shortages due to services rendered to the medically indigent. Hospital revenue statistics show a sharp increase in the first year on the system and then drop to the anticipated levels.

For example, in 1980 the DRG hospitals had an increase in total revenues of 20.2 percent while in the second year their revenues rose only 13.2 percent. The second group of hospitals showed a 14.2 percent increase in revenue during 1980 and then an 18.3 percent increase in revenue during 1981 when they first entered the system. We expect the revenue increase for this group to fall in 1982 to a level consistent with the experience of the first group. Parenthetically, I should add that there are no comparable national data on total revenue increases.

The first group of DRG hospitals showed a 1.6 percent decrease in length of stay in 1980 and a 2.6 percent decrease in length of stay in 1981. Nationally, for that time period, length of stay remained essentially constant. These DRG hospitals also experienced a slight increase in admissions. In 1980 there was a 2.6 percent and in 1981 there was a 1.6 percent increase in admissions.

With regard to quality of care, the New Jersey Department of Health has focused major attention on this issue since the inception of the DRG system. In 1980 the Department insisted that utilization review be performed for all patients. Working with the Professional Standards Review Organizations, the Department was able to implement the utilization review system in March of 1981. By 1982, the Department required all review organizations to establish monitoring systems designed to study changes in admission and discharge patterns. To date, the utilization review organizations have not presented to the Department any evidence of premature discharge.

Another major feature of the New Jersey system is the commissioner's Physician Advisory Committee, which provides consultation directly to me regarding the issues of quality and clinical practice under the DRG system. This group of physicians has developed clinical criteria to monitor quality thresholds on an agggregate level. More recently the committee has reviewed with me the issue of readmissions. We have identified those types of cases which should be studied to determine the effect of the DRG system on early discharge and readmission.

Currently, a study is in progress in two PSRO areas to examine all patients discharged during 1982. This study, covering all DRGs, will determine how many cases were readmitted during the ensuing 24-hour period as well as the readmissions occurring within one week. The study will be completed within the next month and will cover half of the State. The Advisory Committee will review these results and then assist the Department and the utilization review organizations in further monitoring activities.

As a side note, last week I was a panelist on a public television broadcast with Mr. Maressa, the Executive Director of the Medical Society of New Jersey. During the show, Mr. Maressa indicated that the Medical Society has not found any evidence, to date, to show that the DRG system has resulted in premature discharge. I am personally committed to working with any responsible group to study this issue. I believe that the DRG system can be cost effective while ensuring quality medical care. The Department will continue its efforts on utilization review and encourage hospitals and physicians to do effective discharge planning.

The New Jersey system incorporates a number of safeguards so that patients with extenuating medical conditions are not arbitrarily assigned to a DRG which is not reflective of their condition and needed treatment. We believe that these patients are atypical and that a flat price cannot be established for their treatment. These atypical patients are called outliers and the hospital is paid on the basis of the itemized charges for actual services rendered to these patients regardless of treatment or length of stay.

We determine outlier status in a number of ways. Patients with either abnormally low or high lengths of stay are called LOS outliers and comprise about 18.5 percent of the approximately 1.2 million yearly admissions. Patients who die (5.5 percent of total) may experience intensive "heroic" efforts or may die shortly after admission and hence are treated as outliers. Patients who leave against medical advice (1.8 percent of total) do not receive a full medical regimen and hence are outliers. The DRG patient classification system was completely refined for 1982 and new groups called clinical outliers (6.3 percent of the total) were established. These patients have either a complication or co-morbidity and hence have atypical resource consumption. Thus, we have found that almost one-third of all patients are not covered by the DRG flat price. These patients represent the most severe and medically difficult cases and since payment for all services is provided, there is no question that our most ill patients will not receive appropriate care.

I think there are several important differences between the New Jersey DRG system and the national system which will take effect on October 1, 1983. These reasons make it imperative that New Jersey's waiver be extended so that we may continue to operate our current and successful system which is required. I think there are several important differences between the New Jersey system and the national system.

First, in New Jersey we have an all payer system so there is no potential for cost shifting since everyone pays the same amount. By contrast, the national system covers only Medicare and there is the danger that costs will be shifted to Blue Cross and commercial insurers.

Second, the New Jersey system incorporates payments for uncompensated care of the indigent, working capital needs, and the maintenance and replacement of the physical plant and equipment. These additional financial elements are not included in the national Medicare system. It is estimated that uncompensated care in New Jersey will cost approximately $170 million during 1983. Medicare shares in approximately $65 million of this burden but will not under the national system.

Third, the sensitivity of the New Jersey DRG system allows for the identification of the outlier or atypical patient. This allows for a more direct and equitable payment for these patients than does the national system.

Fourth, in New Jersey there is an avenue of appeal to a Hospital Rate Setting Commission while the national system will not provide redress opportunities for either hospital reimbursement adjustments or State-level review.

Fifth, the New Jersey system recognizes unique differences which may exist between New Jersey hospitals while the national system will move to a flat price per case for the whole country.

Sixth, through its Health Planning and Certificate of Need process, the Department has the ability to control the development of new services and capital expansion in concert with its rate setting system.

Seventh, New Jersey's current system and its inclusion of uncompensated care has increased the access to care for the most vulnerable segment of our society, the medically indigent. While the national system will result in a restricted access to care for the indigent and the elderly, this is not, nor will be, the case in New Jersey.

Last, and highly important to the operation of a successful program, is the fact that the DRG system in New Jersey is administered at the state level. The health care industry in New Jersey had a great deal of input into the design and implementation of the system. We have a vigorous and responsive health care network in the State that is dedicated to early identification of problems and the assembly of pertinent information, to arrive at fair and equitable solutions. Open and meaningful communication between the regulating agency and all facets of the industry most assuredly encourages cooperation and leads to a better system.

In summary, I have highlighted those issues which are of concern to the committee. I believe that the DRG system is a cost effective system and that we have found no evidence of a decline in the quality of medical care. As a physician, and the State of Commissioner of Health, I am firmly convinced that the New Jersey system has numerous advantages over the national system and it is critically important to extend our Medicare waiver.

Dr. Alfred Alessi, Past President, Medical Society of New Jersey

Dr. ALESSI. I want to thank you for the opportunity of being able to testify today and represent the Medical Society of New Jersey in this committee hearing.

In order to establish my credibility, I have to say that at the time the DRG system was implemented I was President of the Medical Society of New Jersey and we were asked to participate in this program to help develop an innovative, experimental program. We did cooperate fully. Many physicians in the State Medical Society were members of committees, that helped develop the DRG program at the request of the Commissioner of Health prior to Dr. Goldstein.

Dr. Goldstein questioned whether we represented adequately the physicians in the State of New Jersey. I want to tell you that out of 11,000 physicians and osteopaths in the State of New Jersey, we have over 9,000 members. We by far have more than the majority of practicing physicians in the State of New Jersey. Those that are not members of the Medical Society are really physicians who practice out of the State of New Jersey or are a member of certain commercial organizations. So that we feel our testimony does represent by far a majority of the physicians in the State of New Jersey.

The Medical Society of New Jersey is opposed to the concept of the DRG methodology for hospital reimbursement. We advocate a moratorium, as you stated, on further implementation of the program until such time as the experimental involvement of the participating hospitals in the past few years can be evaluated. The DRG program should not be continued at the end of the year. The DRG waiver should not be extended in the State of New Jersey.

I want to make that adequately clear. The Commissioner stated, and you asked the Commissioner, whether the Medical Society had offered any innovative programs to deal with cost. This is probably true that the State Medical Society has not participated in this. But we have cooperated with the AMA in developing a program to control costs. As a matter of fact there is a four volume series in which it accurately delineates what physicians in the United States feel should be done in order to cooperate with costs.

Now, this commission report was not only physicians in the United States, it was members of unions, members of the insurance companies, a hospital association. There was a broad spectrum of people that were involved in developing this program. I certainly would advise that your committee get this volume and study it very, very carefully.

The Medical Society of New Jersey recommends that the first priority for each hospital patient should be quality care. That is what we emphasize. This medical care should not be lowered, just purely for the purpose of making the program successful. Cost saving alone is not the entire answer. It is an important answer but it is not the entire answer. It must be emphasized that as a physician and the Medical Society as physicians, our reimbursement is not based on a DRG methodology. We don't have an axe to grind. The DRG system does not directly influence the level of remuneration a physician receives. Our concern, then, is plainly quality care at a reasonable cost at the hospital level.

THE NEW JERSEY EXPERIENCE

Now, what are our broad concerns with the DRG program? First, the system was designed to lower hospital costs. At the present time there is no evidence—and I emphasize there is no evidence—that this has been accomplished. The organization evaluating the program which the Commissioner told you about is the Hospital Research and Educational Trust—HRET.

Joel May is the President of this trust and he was interviewed and I personally had conversations with him recently and asked him what he thought about the DRG program in regard to costs. He said, "I would have little confidence in any evaluation made from the data that was available to me." This is a direct quote.

When asked specifically whether the system has reduced cost, Joel May said, "To date it is my judgment that it has not."

Now, this is the experimental organization that was designated to delineate what has happened to costs. They are producing a four volume series report which I would suggest you review. As part of its study, the HRET conducted several surveys of New Jersey hospitals. The results of these surveys as reported in the first volume are interesting and problematical. More than 77 percent of the responding hospital finance directors anticipated that the DRG system would cause accounts receivable to climb. A broad consensus exists that the system has increased management, and cost due to management, data processing, medical records, fiscal and patient billing costs, and a need for additional staff at each hospital certainly has occurred.

Finally, in the various surveys, from 66 percent to 86 percent of those responding indicated considerable uncertainty as to the effect of the program on reducing the costs of medical care.

The argument that the New Jersey hospital costs are lower than the national average doesn't hold water. New Jersey has an overview of costs in hospitals since 1972. There has been some type of program in existence since 1972 and I have been a participant in these cost reviews. New Jersey, since 1972, its average cost has always been below the national average so that it is not surprising today if our average is below the national average. I don't think it is due to the DRG system. It is due to things that have occurred in the past.

Why is the DRG system defective? Well, number one, it doesn't take into account social and economic factors—the poor people may require more resources and more complicated care. Now, the DRG system is

145

not responsible for distribution of indigent care in the State of New Jersey. There is legislation that occurred by the House of Representatives before the DRG system was instituted by the Commissioner of Health and that specific legislation made all urban and rural hospitals equally responsible for indigent care.

Types of admission, acute and chronic. The DRG system states that you are paid an average cost. Let's take, for instance, a patient that needs a gall bladder removed. If it is an acute case, the patient is very sick, may have diabetes, heart trouble and hypertension. The costs to the hospital are higher than the elective case. The DRG system does not take this into account. The stage of illness affects consumption. A patient in the terminal stages of cancer requires more resources than a patient in the early stages.

Record room errors. It has been established pretty well there are record room errors of 35 to 40 percent in the record rooms in coding. Now, the minute there is 35 to 40 percent error in our record room coding your hospital is in jeopardy. The DRG system in New Jersey affects the way hospitals operate, the way physicians practice, and the way patients are treated. When hospitals are put in financial constraint, there are certain subtle gray methods by which the hospitals put constraints on the physicians.

Let's talk a bit about the early discharge of patients, especially early discharges that are encouraged and this affects especially Medicare patients, because under the early discharge system, the hospital makes money. Now, the hospital cannot force a physician to discharge a patient. However, physicians are being threatened to tell their patients that they will not have coverage, Medicare coverage if they don't discharge the patient. This has occurred and is occurring.

Now, the problem that the physician is up against is that at the present time there are not enough nursing homes to adequately take care of your discharges so that you are under a certain amount of pressure. When you discuss whether a family at home is capable of taking care of the individual at home, again there are gray areas. The family doesn't always want to take care of the indigent aunt. So we have real serious problems in discharges.

As far as the Ocean County report as to deaths were occurring in that particular county, I personally spoke to the coroner yesterday, and he told me a little bit different than the Commissioner reported to you. He said, "Yes, we have had an additional number of deaths occurring within the county. We don't know the cause of this at the present time, but it is serious enough in our opinion—it increased from one a week to four a week—and we think it is serious enough that it should be considered."

Now, data as to readmissions is not available. Mr. Maressa truthfully told you before that the data were not available for this and that no one has the data. Not only the medical society in New Jersey but no one has the data. And we feel it should be very carefully studied. Some of the data that are going to be presented to you have to be carefully considered because I know at the present time, and you are going to have a report from Union County, and the criteria from their study is very different from the study in Bergen County, where I come from.

For instance, the criteria that I mentioned is that the study should be on readmissions for seven days. Well, in Bergen County, we feel the study should be 30 days because some of the early discharge complications are reflected in a longer period of stay. So they think that the data are not available and we do not know, but this should be very, very carefully studied.

And you have to be very careful of what the bases for the data are, because the PSROs that are investigating it in the State of New Jersey, each has a different criteria. So that there is no uniformity of study. You can make statistics say what you want to say but you have to look at the basis for all these statistics.

As far as starting of innovative programs in the hospitals, when a hospital is under financial constraint, the hospital does have trouble starting innovative programs. The program that is innovative is put on the back burner in subtle ways. They don't say we won't start the program, but the money sometimes isn't there to start the program. Or instead of being in a good, nice facility the program is put into an aircraft hospital where the facility is not nice. The innovative programs are not getting the stimulus that they need in those hospitals that are in financial contraints.

Another problem is that we are beginning to develop standard treatment criteria in order to meet restraints of costs. Now, I have never had a family relative come to me and say, Doctor, I don't want every resource available to treat my ill person. That is the problem the physician is confronted with. We get standards of care in order to not increase costs but every family wants the best available, and I will want the best available for my family.

Hospital and physician profiles as to cost in treating a specific DRG are being utilized to determime what types of cases should be treated. In other words, with the DRG system we are accumulating extensive data on physician profiles as to cost and hospital profiles as to cost as well. I am not saying it is not good to have that data but we are concerned with the way that these data are going to be utilized.

Would regional programs be based on cost or would it be based on the status of what is good for quality care in a particular area?

The proponents of DRG continue to assert that it has contained costs or at least has decreased the rate of escalation of the average hospital costs in New Jersey as compared to the average cost of hospital care in the United States, and I emphasize to you that that is not a fair statistic. The response assumes that the baseline relationship between New Jersey hospital costs and all United States hospital costs was appropriate, and that the amount of "fat" in New Jersey hospital budgets was minimal at the time the baseline parameter was established. Neither assumption has been proved and the evidence in this regard is lacking.

As a matter of fact, it often was asserted by the New Jersey State Department of Health prior to the DRG system that the rate of growth of hospital costs in New Jersey was lower than the national average.

The Medical Society of New Jersey believes it is imperative, therefore, that a prompt and independent evaluation of the DRG system and its impact on health care costs not only as far as costs, but as far as quality, should be made by the State Legislature and the results made public.

We will continue to question the department regarding its inability or unwillingness to publish data. At the present time the Medical Society has not had the data and it is a problem. On the bills each patient gets there is an itemized statement of what the costs were and what is being given under the DRG program. We think that it would be very, very simple with the computers we have available to come out with the statistics and carry it very, very rapidly. We cannot see the reason for delay.

In short, I would be very willing to answer any questions the committee may have. Mr. Maressa is here with me. He will certainly be able to answer some of the questions that I can't answer.

THE NEW JERSEY EXPERIENCE

Mr. Louis Scibetta, President, New Jersey Hospital Association

Mr. SCIBETTA. Thank you, Mr. Rinaldo and Mr. Courter. It is a pleasure to have you here.

I am Louis Scibetta, President of the New Jersey Hospital Association. With me is Don Camisi, Senior Vice President and Director of Financial Management Services for the New Jersey Hospital Association. We are pleased to have a chance to present testimony before you today, and I do prefer to read the statement, which we have circulated to you in advance.

The NJHA, which represents all of the hospitals in New Jersey, is testifying today at this field hearing of the House Select Committee on Aging to lend our assistance to this committee on our experiences with New Jersey's prospective payment/DRG experiment. It is our understanding that the primary concern of this hearing is to determine the effects of the DRG prospective payment system on the aged of our state, and to project from these effects their possible implications under the new national Medicare prospective reimbursement law.

We applaud the concerns of this committee for the hospitalized elderly of this nation and we would caution the members of the committee not to be hasty in drawing conclusions from hearsay, misinterpreted or incomplete data. There is too great a temptation to sensationalize speculative effects of the DRG system and we feel it is essential for this committee to understand that the New Jersey experiment is still underway. The conclusion from this demonstration will not be fully examined for some time. Ours is a dramatically new system with volumes of change which, in itself, brings criticism—some justified, some not.

If there is anything we have learned, however, from our experiences, it is that the financial integrity of the individual institution must be preserved. If the Federal Government designs a system which averages all hospitals' costs or diagnoses to a single rate, the catastrophic result will be average care, average services, and average quality.

New Jersey experiences must always be viewed in light of the State's hospital rate setting law. Among other things, this law spreads the costs of uncompensated care among all payers and guarantees the solvency of effectively and efficiently operated hospitals.

The Medicare DRG reimbursement system does not include these features. Official statistics show that costs per any unit of output selected, including both admissions and days, have risen at a slower rate in New Jersey than in the nation as a whole since DRGs were implemented here. However, costs also rose slower in New Jersey before DRGs were implemented.

While conclusions are being drawn to point to savings attained through our system which uses DRGs for reimbursement, unfortunately, most of the savings were realized by the state's suppression of hospital workers' wages.

Since 1980, NJHA pursued a change in the labor component of the annual inflation calculation used in the DRG system. Prior to 1983 the employment cost index of the Northeast was used to calculate the labor component of this economic factor. Finally, in May of this year, a more appropriate measurement of hospital wage increases, the average hourly earnings of hospital workers has been put in place. This new index will enable hospitals to receive a reasonable inflation amount to give in the form of wages to hospital employees.

It is important to note that while using this four year period, while using the ECI, the national inflation factor was 14 percentage points higher than what was allowed by the state. This means that the rate of increase in New Jersey hospital workers' salaries was 14 percentage points below that of their counterparts nationwide over the last four years. It is also important to note that this has nothing to do with whether we use DRGs or another system of reimbursement in New Jersey since this trend began in 1976 under the previously state mandated SHARE system of hospital revenue controls.

Six concerns expressed at the previous hearing of this committee held in Princeton in March 1983 were included by Mr. Rinaldo in remarks in the Congressional Record of May 23, 1983. We feel it is necessary to explore each of these points at this time. These concerns include cost shifting to payers other than Medicare, DRG creep, as a second item, shifting services to circumvent the DRG system, prevalance of outliers, unnecessary readmissions, and premature discharges. The implications of most of these concerns are that hospitals are behaving inappropriately. We find such allegations at the very least to be inaccurate and misleading.

First, as to cost shifting, as Representative Rinaldo said in the Congressional Record, the New Jersey program applies to all payers. Thus, the question of cost shifting from Medicare to other payers is moot in our state.

Second, the Representative also expressed concern about cost shifting to non-covered services. Avoidance of DRG rates in favor of Part B reasonable charge reimbursement has effectively been prohibited.

Third, HCFA now requires that all non-physician inpatient services must be furnished by hospitals, and will be reimbursed to hospitals only through DRG prospective rates.

The next concern addresses the phenomenon referred to as DRG creep which implies that hospitals would take advantage of the system to fraudulently place patients in a DRG with a higher payment rate than the one to which the hospital is entitled. There is absolutely no documented evidence of such behavior.

The DRG system requires proper and accurate coding of medical records when identifying diagnoses and assigning DRGs. The result is a strong trend toward comprehensive identification of all medical problems treated during the course of the hospital stay. Inclusion of additional diagnoses can sometimes alter the payment rate. This in no way constitutes manipulation or perceived system loopholes. Rather, it represents exactly the process of clinically complete medical information anticipated when the DRG system was developed. These activities are overseen by PSROs and audited by payers and fiscal intermediaries, and responsibly reviewed and audited by hospital medical staff review committees.

Additional references concern the perceived high percentage of patients classified as outliers. A patient is not classified as an outlier because of an inability to place the diagnosis in any of the 467 DRGs. Patients are generally classified as outliers because of their unusually long or short lengths of stay. They can also be patients who discharge themselves against medical advice, or who die while hospitalized, or who are admitted and discharged the same day.

In an effort to more closely watch the costs of providing care with the DRG rate, an issue of particular concern to hospitals, third party payers and self-pay patients, the New Jersey system has been repeatedly modified and fine tuned. The result is that up to 30 percent of patients are classified as outliers, and pay controlled charges rather than DRG rates. It must be emphasized that the New Jersey system continues to be an experiment, and it cannot and should not be implied that it can yet be determined whether or not this relatively high outlier rate represents a strength or weakness of the system.

Finally, the suggestion that under New Jersey's DRG reimbursement methodology, patients are discharged from hospitals prematurely, has not been substantiated to exist in any differing degree than before the DRG system was begun. Nor can it be said with certainty that shorter lengths of stay, if they exist, are necessarily undesirable. What has been observed is a critical shortage of nursing home beds as a consequence of restrictions and planning formulas imposed by the New Jersey Department of Health. This shortage restricts the ability of hospitals to transfer their patients to more appropriate levels of care and places unnecessary pressure on admitting physicians.

It is important to note here for clarity that it is the physician, not the hospital who controls the admission and discharge of patients. Many hospitals in New Jersey have conducted independent studies to examine readmissions and the appropriateness of discharges. The hospitals report that generally, the findings of these studies refute the myth of premature discharges, spurred by DRGs and resulting in readmission for more care. Rather, readmissions tend to be characteristic of patients who have chronic disease conditions such as chronic obstructive pulmonary disease and congestive heart failure. These patients will likely continue to be readmitted to hospitals regardless of payment system.

These studies, designed to evaluate the appropriateness of discharge, examined not only the timeliness, but more importantly the preparedness, of the patients for discharge from the hospital.

There are quality assurance mechanisms in hospitals designed to identify and review situations which could compromise the quality of the patient care. This is assured by a sophisticated network of professionals specializing in discharge planning, utilization review and quality assurance which functions to guarantee high quality patient care.

These mechanisms are internally organized and directed by doctors and hospitals. Additionally, there are review organizations, external to the hospital and mandated by the government, to assure that inappropriate admissions, premature discharges and inadequate care do not occur.

In conclusion, New Jersey is a state in which our aged population is increasing in number at almost twice the national rate. The New Jersey

THE NEW JERSEY EXPERIENCE

Hospital Association members are faced daily with the reality of the well established and unfortunate fact that the elderly of our communities consume far more health care resources than does the population as a whole.

As a result, we supported state legislation which created a prospective payment system that eventually adopted the DRG methodology for paying hospitals. We willingly participate in this innovative and challenging experiment but we feel it is necessary at this time to restate our cautionary words to this committee. The New Jersey experiment is still in progress. We warn against premature and ill-founded attempts to draw conslusions, however well meaning, while data remains incomplete.

Horror Stories

Read this section on DRG "horror stories" and you're guaranteed to be the star of the doctors' table in the dining room. The stories were compiled by a doctor who rules on patients' appeals of their bills. They illuminate the personal side of DRGs by showing what happened to individuals who were victims of the inevitable inequities of the system.

The case was known as "The $6,000 Finger," and, as an example of how things could go terribly wrong under DRGs, it was circulated throughout New Jersey and soon became one of the system's legendary horror stories.

This is what happened: In May 1980, a man was in an automobile accident and came to the Emergency Room of Morristown Memorial Hospital in Morristown, NJ, with an injured hand. He was admitted to the hospital and the next day underwent surgery to insert a pin into the broken ring finger of his right hand. The next day he was discharged.

Two nights in the hospital, one relatively simple operation. The bill under Diagnosis Related Groups: $6,313.20. That represented a DRG fee of $4,931.20 and doctors' fees of $1,382.

When the insurance company saw the bill, they naturally balked. Actual hospital charges for the case were approximately $800, they said.

Morristown was one of the first twenty-six hospitals in the state to participate in DRGs, and the system was very new at this point. The hospital explained things this way: The facts of this patient's case were fed into the computer according to a formula mandated by the state. The computer came up with a DRG assignment—No. 348, which deals with fractures with major surgery (amputation, restoration of hip joint, other major).

The charge for DRG No. 348 was $4,931.20. That's the charge for a hip replacement, an amputation, or as in this case, a fractured finger. Although the patient remained in the hospital only

---

This section written by Mendel Silverman, M.D., Department of Family Practice, Hackensack Medical Center, Hackensack, NJ. Dr. Silverman is a member of the Association for Professional Health Care Review, DRG Appeals Panel.

48 hours, that was within the designated length of stay for DRG No. 348—2 to 66 days.

The insurance company questioned the DRG assignment. They contended that the patient should have been assigned to DRG No. 345, which deals with fractures of the arm, hand, foot and shoulder blade. The bill for DRG No. 345 would have been about one-third the bill for DRG No. 348.

But the Department of Health confirmed that the proper DRG assignment had been made. The hospital was thus locked into the bill.

The insurance company had no choice but to pay, because under New Jersey's no fault law, insurance companies must pay all medical expenses for treatment of personal injuries resulting from automobile accidents.

Although both the insurance company and the hospital agreed that the bill seemed excessive, no appeals were filed because the hospital was convinced that it had acted properly under the DRG law, as indeed it had. Since the patient did not have to pay anything out of pocket, he did not pursue the case either.

In fact, under the way DRGs were constituted at the time, everyone had acted properly. Yet it was obvious that something was very wrong with a system that could charge $6,000 for a broken finger—especially a system whose stated purpose is to help contain hospital costs.

The case came to light when the insurance company leaked the story to the press in order, they said, to point up the inequities of the system.

Soon other disturbing cases surfaced, all blatant examples of how DRGs could go seriously awry:

*A man was brought into St. Barnabas Hospital in Livingston with a heart attack. He was treated for four hours and then died. The DRG bill: $4,416.

*A man had a diagnostic procedure performed at Overlook Hospital in Summit in November, before DRGs, and the bill was $530. Six months later he was sent back to the hospital to have the same test repeated. By this time the hospital was under DRGs, and the bill was $2,500.

Less than two months after the famous finger incident, the

Department of Health refined the system by narrowing the ranges for length of stay for various DRGs. The designated length of stay for DRG No. 348 was changed from 2 to 66 days to 16 to 23 days. Any shorter or longer stays would thus be outliers, with the patients billed charges rather than the DRG fee. Under this new refinement the patient with the broken finger who stayed only two days would have been an outlier and would have been billed charges—an amount considerably less than the DRG fee.

Besides tightening the range for length of stay, there was a need to make the DRGs themselves more clinically homogeous. Broken fingers and total hip replacements, obviously, should not be grouped together. In 1982 the DRGs were completely revamped with the help of a panel of New Jersey physicians who expanded the 383 DRGs to 467. These new DRGs were supposed to be more reflective of the actual hospital resources consumed and thus would correlate more closely with costs. Separate categories were established for fingers and for hips, for instance.

Another change mandated that anyone who dies while in the hospital is treated as an outlier. Thus, the estate of the man who died of a heart attack after four hours in the hospital would have been billed charges rather than the $4,000 DRG fee.

Most people agree that the expanded DRGs and the more meaningful length of stay cutoff points, along with refinements in the computer programs for determining DRG assignments, have made for a workable system. Yet the horror stories continue—perhaps not as dramatic as the four-digit finger or the $1,000-an-hour heart attack—but nevertheless disconcerting reminders of the way some cases just don't fit the system. *(It is important to remember though, that these cases represent only a small portion of all the cases handled under DRGs.)*

A visitor from a foreign country had a heart attack at Newark International Airport and was brought to Newark Beth Israel Medical Center. The patient left the hospital to return to his own country after running up charges of about $4,000. His stay, nevertheless, was within the trim points. His DRG bill was $8,000.[5]

---

[5]"Payment by Diagnosis: How the Great Experiment is Going," *Medical Economics*, May 10, 1982.

Insurance companies and other third party payers can put up with the inevitable inequities of the system because they have an opportunity to balance out DRG losses and profits among a large number of cases. They win a few, they lose a few, and it probably evens out in the end.

But for individuals who must pay either all or part of the bill out of their own pockets, inequities can mean a real hardship. Arguments about average costs and "it all evens out in the end" are meaningless to patients who are coping with just one hospitalization. Receiving a bill which shows that actual costs are considerably less than the DRG charge can appear totally unreasonable and be downright infuriating.

Dr. Lawrence Denson, an internist at Hackensack Medical Center, had a patient who was admitted to the hospital with a coronary insufficiency two months after losing his job and his health insurance. Although he was in the hospital for only three days, his bill, because of his DRG assignment, came to several thousand dollars. With no job and no insurance coverage, the bill was a real hardship—a direct result of a DRG system that is supposed to save everyone money.[6]

Despite efforts to educate the public about the new system, patients keep complaining about DRGs: arguments with physicians, angry telephone calls to hospital billing departments, and letters of protest to various state organizations and agencies are commonplace in New Jersey. The following letter to the *Record* from an Oakland, NJ, woman is typical.

Editor, The Record:

Thank you for giving front-page attention to a growing issue of concern—the issue of hospital billing under the system of diagnosis-related groups (DRG) (The Sunday Record, Aug. 14).

After a personal experience in a well-known hospital in our area, I am strongly inclined to agree with the Medical Society of New Jersey

---

[6]"Payment by Diagnosis: How the Great Experiment is Going," *Medical Economics*, May 10, 1982.

that this plan is "fraught with confusion and spun from an illusion and can endanger a hospital patient's health."

While the concept of being charged a "fair price" for my recent surgery seemed on the surface very appealing, I was hardly prepared for the frustration and unnecessary strain that was to follow.

After the operation, I was sent to the recovery room for a one-hour stay. I was in pain and asked for medication to ease it. I was told by a member of the staff that they couldn't give me such medication because they would then have to keep me in the room for more than the DRG-allotted hour.

I lay there in pain for 40 minutes until I was transferred to the day accommodation room (DAR). There, I spent another 15 minutes in agony until I was given an injection of a morphine-based drug. The use of so strong a drug is a measure of the intensity of my post-operative pain and discomfort.

My "rest" was interrupted on two occasions by a DAR attendant who dutifully informed me that I would need to "get up and walk around." Needless to say, I was in no shape to move, let alone walk!

After three hours, I realized that I needed to spend the night in the hospital. I asked the attendant to make the arrangements for me and I was told that under the terms of the DRGs I could not stay overnight, since my "condition" was not dramatic enough to warrant it. Finally, frustrated and in a great deal of pain, I chose to leave the hospital.

For one week after my "routine" surgery, I could not walk. And the only comfort, weak as it was, that I could derive from the entire ordeal was that I had helped to save the hospital, its staff, and my insurance company some money.

While I heartily endorse any plan that can effectively cut hospital costs, I seriously object to a plan that denies the patient proper and precious recuperative time.

Please continue to inform the unsuspecting public about this dangerous health-care program. If enough DRG patients speak up, Trenton *might* make reforms.

Mrs. A.
Oakland

THE NEW JERSEY EXPERIENCE

From my experience in helping to implement DRGs at Hackensack Medical Center, it is clear that part of the problem is that patients are not fully aware of the workings of DRGs when they enter the hospital. Although hospitals provide informational brochures for patients, they are often so distressed about their hospital admission that they either don't read or don't fully comprehend the material. Even when they do basically understand the DRG system, many still have trouble accepting a bill which shows two different figures, especially when they are asked to pay the higher amount.

My experience with DRGs in New Jersey includes membership in the PSRO Committee which audits hospitals in Bergen County, as well as ongoing activity with the Association for Professional Health Care Review, where I sit on a panel that adjudicates DRG appeals and complaints from many sources, including insurance companies, patients and hospitals.

One of the most glaring problems of New Jersey's system is the area of DRG billing for newborn infants. The designated length of stay for this DRG, which is No. 391, is three to six days. When a normal newborn is discharged on the third day, as is often the case, the difference between the DRG charge and the total patient charge (TPC), or actual costs incurred, is difficult to reconcile. The DRG charge may be three times higher, depending on the hospital. At one Bergen County hospital, the DRG for newborn care is $916, while actual charges were $240.

This is especially difficult for patients whose insurance coverage does not include newborn care, such as Blue Cross and Blue Shield of New York State.

This problem is so prevalent that about 30 percent of all the DRG appeals adjudicated by the Professional Health Care Review in New Jersey involve newborn care. No amount of explanation of the DRG rationale can effectively pacify these patients.

Since DRGs began in New Jersey in 1980, the New Jersey Hospital Association in Princeton has received scores of complaints. As expected, many of these deal with the apparent inequity of billing for newborn care.

Consider this complaint from a Farmingdale, N.J. couple:

> We had a hospital stay from Oct. 12 through Oct. 15. The insurance

company paid all bills except for the baby's bill of $531.60. The hospital is billing for time not spent in the hospital. They say that is their policy. We spent three days at $68 a day nursery care, but we were billed for $531.60 because of their DRG program, leaving a balance of approximately $300 for which no services were given.

Similarly, a woman from Nutley, N.J., wrote the following letter to the New Jersey Hospital Association about a newborn care inequity:

I gave birth last March 22 this year by cesarean section at Riverside General Hospital in Secaucus. Last March 28 I went out of the hospital with my baby, but before I was released I was made to pay a deposit and sign a promissory note stating that I will pay the hospital a total of about $700 for baby care since she is not covered by medical insurance. The following week, however, the hospital sent me a bill for $1,129.29. In inquiring about the discrepancy they told me that the charges are based on the final diagnosis under the DRG. I can see no reason why I should be charged almost double of the worth of the services I received just because I fall under the same category as other patients. Could you please explain the logic behind this? You see, I almost collapsed when I received the bill for $1,129.19 because my husband is out of work and I was on disability at that time. At present I have a hard time making both ends meet and I still have the hospital bill and pediatrician's fee to think of.

I hope to hear from you soon and I would appreciate it if you could enlighten me regarding this matter. Thank you.

A patient from Hackettstown went straight to the point in her letter of complaint: "I'd like to appeal the hospital bill recently sent to me. I feel that the hospital's actual charges, which also appear on the bill are most reasonable. The DRG rate is far beyond my means."

Of course, none of the patients seem to mind when things work out the other way—when the DRG fee is lower than the actual charge of the hospital.

Our DRG panel hears an average of thirty cases a month from hospitals throughout Bergen County. Frequently the cases point up problems with the health care system that existed prior to the institution of DRGs but which are brought into sharper focus under the constraints of the new system and the need for hospitals, physicians, insurers and patients to operate in a DRG-like atmosphere.

For instance, "physician failure" is a serious problem in some hospitals, one which impacts directly on how well DRGs work.

In a recent case, a young patient was admitted to the hospital with enlarged cervical glands, fever and splenomegaly. He underwent seven days of tests, including X-rays, chem screens and many others, before being discharged with a diagnosis of infectious mononucleosis. A simple office test would have prevented this admission. Charges were disallowed to the chagrin and consternation of both the hospital and the physician.

Here is a similar case: A patient was admitted because of a fever of undetermined origin. After routine investigation, a hematological consult was ordered. But this did not occur until seven days later, allegedly because the hematologist was unavailable. During this waiting period, a battery of highly specialized tests were performed, including gallium scan, I.V.P., and others, possibly because the physician had to justify in some way the patient's continued hospital stay. The panel disallowed one week's hospital stay. Our files are replete with cases such as these.

Another major source of dispute is erroneously designated DRG assignments. For example, our panel recently heard an appeal involving the admission of a patient for chemotherapy following previous surgery for cancer of the colon. The patient was in the hospital for two days and then discharged without treatment because it was discovered she had anemia. The diagnosis for this patient was cancer, leading to a DRG charge of $2,300.

Several weeks later the patient was readmitted and discharged after two days, having completed a course of chemotherapy. The charge this time was $2,200 (sic). The insurance company, amazingly enough, paid both fees. But the case came to the attention of the panel because the patient's husband, although he did not have to pay any costs himself, was convinced a mistake had been made.

Both times, the diagnosis should have been chemotherapy rather than cancer, since it was the chemotherapy that explained the reason for admission to the hospital. A chemotherapy diagnosis carries a much lower DRG rate than a cancer diagnosis.

Furthermore, the first admission could have been completely avoided if the patient had had pre-admission testing which would have discovered the anemia and postponed admission.

In a similar case a man was admitted for a cardiac catheterization and spent two days in the hospital before his blood test results were returned with an abnormality, which meant that the cardiac cath would have to be delayed. Once again, pre-admission testing would have turned this up and avoided an unnecessary admission.

Still another flaw in the health care system brought into sharper focus by DRGs is a lack of coordination between the social service department and attending physicians when long-term nursing care becomes the ultimate solution. It is not unusual for patients to languish for weeks in acute care hospital settings while waiting for placement in a nursing home facility. Frequently this is not the fault of either the doctor or the hospital, but merely due to the scarcity of nursing home beds.

Sitting on the DRG appeals panel has given me an understanding of one very important factor—the importance of a hospital's utilization review system and its impact on DRGs. There is a definite correlation between the number of appeals we listen to and the efficacy of the utilization review system—the weaker the review system, the more appeals we hear. Utilization review is aimed at more efficient use of hospitals, and, ultimately, cost containment; and since cost contaiment is the guiding force behind DRGs, the connection between the two is obvious.

New Jersey's experience is not unique. The national system can expect the same kind of fall-out during the transition period—cases which fall through the cracks and patients who are confused and frustrated with a system that they perceive as working to their detriment. When considering these patient complaints, it is important to remember that the Medicare system, at this time, has no mechanism to hear them.

How New Jersey's Practicing Physicians Feel About DRGs (Not so Good)

The Medical Society of New Jersey (MSNJ), which represents the majority of practicing physicians in the state, is opposed to DRGs. Its official policy is opposition to the concept, with a resolve to lead the fight against continuation or extension of the program.

It is noteworthy that there is unprecedented unanimity of opinion on this issue. The objections stem from a variety of philosophical, ethical, and economic reasons.

The DRG methodology is the most recent addition to the evergrowing state regulation of the delivery of health care. Most physicians feel that the doctor-patient relationship is adversely affected by intrusion of any third party into the decision making process. This is brought vividly to their attention by the impersonal and often inhumane nature of DRGs' reliance upon averages rather than individual patient needs.

It is important to note that prior to the introduction of DRGs, New Jersey was among the most over-regulated states in the nation. This is significant because comparisons to other states, using statistical data, often show percentage differences which convey a false impression as to the cost-saving aspects of the program.

Undoubtedly the biggest single reason for opposition were the deceitful and highhanded tactics associated with the introduction of the program. MSNJ was led to give conditional approval to the program originally on the basis of its characterization as a *limited, voluntary, experiment*. When it became apparent that it was none of the above, belated efforts to resist the process proved futile, frustrating, and generated far more resentment than anyone might have expected.

Voluntary was the first descriptive term to bite the dust. Of the original twenty-six hospitals which entered the DRG system in

---

This section written by Frank J. Primich, M.D., Co-Chairman, DRG Committee of the Medical Society of New Jersey; Department of Obstetrics and Gynecology and President of the Medical Staff, Riverside General Hospital, Secaucus, NJ.

1980, only ten volunteered. The other sixteen were "selected" to give the proper case-mix.

Limited didn't last much longer. Before the first group was even operational, it was announced that an additional forty hospitals would be added to the program in 1981, with all the remainder scheduled for 1982 induction.

Experiment, in the sense used regarding DRGs, meets none of the moral, ethical, or scientific criteria for experimentation. Even when prisoners are used for experimental purposes, their participation must be voluntary and on a fully informed basis. By definition, experiments must yield a result that can be evaluated before their merit is judged. The Health Research and Education Trust, the presumably impartial organization entrusted with evaluation of the New Jersey "experiment," still characterizes its findings to date as *inconclusive.*

General information regarding DRGs, to the extent that it has been disseminated to the general public and health care providers, has served to spread many misconceptions. It is necessary to review the sequence of events which set the stage for DRGs in New Jersey, and to point out the fact that many who support the program do so for reasons which have nothing to do with the questionable merits of the process. There are many hospital administrators who accept DRGs as a necessary evil, since they have been led to believe that were the program to be unmasked, it would terminate a source of additional income vital to their survival.

New Jersey Public Law 1978, Chapter 83, had a dual purpose. It was designed to rectify perceived inequities in the hospital rates charged to various categories of bill payers. Blue Cross enjoyed a markedly discounted rate. Medicare and Medicaid received a lesser discount. Commercial insurers and self-pay patients paid a disproportionately higher rate in order to make up the difference. The second and more significant purpose was to address the problem of "uncompensated costs." Unpaid hospital bills in New Jersey had reached more than $100 million per year. This problem primarily affected inner-city hospitals and other inefficiently operated institutions.

Chapter 83 proposed to bring the widely varying rates into a closer range, and add to those rates an "uncompensated cost component." In other words, those who were already paying their fair share would be burdened with the additional welfare costs.

To the legislators who glibly promised high quality health care for all, regardless of ability to pay, it appeared to obviate the need for additional taxes or curtailed services. Its appeal to many of those involved in the process need not be addressed here.

Chapter 83 gave broad discretionary powers to the Commission of Health to implement the avowed intent of the legislation. The effect would be to totally regulate hospital reimbursement in the private as well as the public sector. There was no specific methodology mandated.

Since cost containment is an overriding consideration, it could be accomplished, via strict regulation, regardless of whatever reimbursement system was employed. Holding down costs is simple enough, if we do not concern ourselves with such issues as quality and availability of care, and that old American prerogative of freedom of choice.

New Jersey's practicing physicians, as those elsewhere in the country, are genuinely concerned about quality and availability of health care. They want to preserve their patients' freedom of choice, protect their privilege of using their discretion as to how, when, and where to provide care, and use logic rather than force to contain costs.

There are ample examples of extravagant waste in the provision of health care, but they pale by comparison to waste in government. The costs of health care rarely include the costs of the bureaucracy itself. Were it to be calculated, its rate of increase would dwarf the other elements involved. Physicians share the common desire of most productive Americans to get the government off their back.

As relates to the New Jersey program, the State Department of Health repeatedly makes claims of cost savings, and disclaims any evidence of diminished quality of care or restricted availability. They go so far as to claim their program will improve quality.

MSNJ has repeatedly asked for figures to substantiate any cost saving and any evidence of improved quality. There has been no answer. Failure to provide the requested figures is understandable when we note that public statements embody subtle changes. We hear more about slowing the rate of increase, and more recently that results will not be achieved until three or four years from now.

The term high quality care is being replaced by references to standard care. It is a logical progression from there to sub-standard. Many feel that we have already entered that phase. Precise documentation of such charges is difficult because of the libel and malpractice considerations.

As the press has slowly turned its attention from mere transmission of unsupported claims of success from the Department of Health and the Rate Setting Commission to the rising number of complaints from a variety of sources, there is hope that the truth will come out. Unfortunately, DRGs are already being spread to national Medicare hospital reimbursement before sufficient evidence can be accumulated of its inevitable negative impact on patient care.

It is a strange paradox that physicians with decidedly higher credibility than politicians must substantiate their charges before press or media will permit space or time. Meanwhile governmental proclamations are accepted as gospel.

Visiting nurses have been among the first to cite cases which suggest that patients are being prematurely discharged from hospitals. The rate of early readmission is being questioned with good cause. Any decent experiment would have included consideration of that factor, but we are told that only now will there be an effort to study that issue. The most shocking charge to date regarding premature discharge has related to the early demise of discharged patients. Several have already died in the ambulance en route home. It is a shame that gory incidents of this sort will be necessary before there will be public support of the physician's principled resistance to this bureaucratically sponsored abomination.

The lack of awareness on the part of the New Jersey public is readily understandable. What is hard to comprehend is how unknowledgeable many of our own doctors are regarding the subject. Since the majority do not overutilize hospital facilities, they do not realize the growing number of "economies" that are traceable to DRGs. When told that Drug A is not available in the hospital pharmacy, many assume this is an oversight or a supply problem. They fail to comprehend that it has been replaced by Drug B, which is less expensive, and very likely less effective. If cost becomes the prime consideration, devices such as pacemakers may be available on the basis of price rather than utility. Similar examples can be found in every facet of hospital service. While high cost does not insure high quality, it is a reasonable generalization to say that you usually get what you pay for. The patient who wants and can afford the very best no longer has the prerogative to make that decision. Since bills are fixed by regulation, quality of care is necessarily reduced to the common denominator.

The better physicians, as they become aware of these changes, find themselves in confrontation with hospital administrators and purchasing agents. There will be growing adversarial relationships that will be mutually disagreeable.

There has been little meaningful comment regarding the philosophically questionable basic provisions of Chapter 83. Most references to hospital reimbursement in New Jersey refer to the entire package as DRGs. Separation is vital when evaluating the comments of hospital administrators. Those with a history of high uncollectibles praise the system for its "increased" income. When asked specifically regarding DRGs, we get a somewhat different response. Most will concede the need for additional record keeping. Many will cite the complexity involved. Most will deplore the frequent changes in regulations, and the varying and contradictory interpretations by other regulatory agencies, or even within the same department. DRGs, if they had to stand on their own, would probably get a failing grade.

"Prospective" ratesetting is a deceptive, redundant, term. Ratesetting, by definition, must be prospective. In New Jersey, Blue Cross, Medicaid and Medicare negotiated or mandated hospital rates for each upcoming year before the advent of DRGs. What has happened is that rates for all payers are now determined by governmental edict. Those who promulgate the rates are the same people who act as judge and jury regarding appeals. There is no semblance of separation of powers. This mini-version of socialized medicine bodes ill for the rest of the country. Limiting the national extension to Medicare patients assures the justifiable complaints of cost shifting that will ensue, with the predictable "solution" that everyone be included. Were this to happen, the federal government would exercise total control over all hospital provision of care.

Perceptive physicians are alert to the fact that the Department of Health and Human Services has already been mandated to study the feasibility of DRGs for doctors' fees. It becomes critical that the general public realize the long range implications of the present course of action. New Jersey is the place to look, if one wants a chilling view of what the future holds.

In a desperate attempt to show some tangible results from the program, the small fractional decrease in length of stay is often cited. This is essentially irrelevant, since it is primarily attributable to increased intensity of care, which is more expensive. Regarding length of stay, New Jersey is running over 30 percent outliers (cases which fall outside the parameters of this supposedly sophisticated system). The federal version proposes to limit this factor, by fiat, to 5.5 percent. Even in a single payer system this could create havoc. If spread to all payers, the results could be devastating.

In addition to increased intensity of care, this system increases record keeping and billing procedures. Doctors are seeing expansion of record rooms and billing offices, with the hiring of more and better trained personnel. There is no comparable increase in nurses, who must cope with greater demands on their time. There have been few outright firings in the name of economy, but diminution through attrition is a real and present danger. Replacement of RNs with GNs or LPNs, who are in turn replaced by less qualified members of the hierarchy can only hurt patient care. Regulatory requirements tend to ensnarl nurses in the red-tape of paperwork which only they have the authority to complete. The patient population now embodies a higher percentage of more acutely ill or more recently operated cases. More patients and fewer skilled nurses spell decreased quality of care in any language.

With limited reimbursement, if the costs of compliance go up, budget demands must adversely affect the provision of adequate care.

Growing pressures to relinquish traditional professional judgments to cook-book averages which encourage mediocrity are stirring the apathetic majority of physicians to register complaints. Patients, who feel that they have been shortchanged financially or regarding services, tend to blame or question their doctors. Self-preservation may serve to activate many otherwise tranquil individuals. This will all take time to develop. Whether the resistance will be too little, too late, remains to be seen.

Perhaps the most disturbing accusation is that physicians, since they admit, order, and determine date of discharge, are responsible for the escalating cost of health care.

This charge has been fueled by hospital administrators who seek to deflect the blame heaped upon them. There are valid explanations of rising costs in health care being caused by present and previous governmental actions. Costs of compliance with governmental regulations head the list. Labor costs attributable to coercive union pressures, minimum wage laws and broadened fringe benefits have impacted more on health care than elsewhere. First dollar coverage has increased demand. The malpractice climate has led to the high costs of "defensive medicine". Expensive technological advances have added immeasurably to costs.

Most of the flagrant abuse of overutilization has been controlled by voluntary and mandatory peer review. The abusers are relatively few in number and might be weeded out through less traumatic means. The vast majority of physicians practice within the bounds of the contemporary state of the art. With no direct control over the going costs of essential services, they are no more responsible for the costs that they generate than a mother is for the cost of milk!

A volume would be needed to explore all the interacting facets of health care costs. Cosmetic "solutions" by poorly informed legislators do nothing more than create bigger and worse problems for subsequent "saviors" to compound.

In summary it should be noted that the Medical Society of New Jersey, representing organized medicine, which too often tends to compromise, has taken a firm stand against DRGs. Among individual physicians, there is a growing resentment and increasing signs of resistance. The adverse effects, logically projected from the beginning, are coming to pass. Only time is needed to document the damage being done. All that needs to be done is to declare a moratorium on further intrusion until then.

Chapter Seven
Using DRG Data

Corporate business planning. Cost accounting. Product line management.

Not so long ago these words would have had no place in hospital corridors. What, after all, did corporate business planning have to do with a hospital, with caring for sick people?

DRGs have changed all that. DRGs have brought the imperatives of the corporate board room into the hospital environment. Cost accounting, labor productivity and strategic planning have become important aspects of health care. DRGs represent a challenge and an opportunity to hospitals—a challenge because they demand efficient and cost-effective management if hospitals are to survive under this new system which puts them at risk financially for their performance; and an opportunity because one of the most important by-products of the system is a wealth of data which can show—as never before—how, why and exactly where the hospital is succeeding or failing.

The computer systems that are necessary to determine DRGs and billing can also tell hospital management a great deal of other statistical information: how physicians compare to one another in terms of the cost of their treatment of similar patients; how various departments are utilized according to each diagnosis related group; how the hospital compares overall to other hospitals in delivering the same types of service.

Proper utilization of these data is absolutely critical if hospitals are to survive under DRGs. Now for the first time we can pinpoint areas for special study; we can understand exactly why things are happening the way they are and then make important decisions about the direction the hospital must take.

Although in the months ahead it may seem to physicians that the computer's only function is to reveal detailed information about the way they practice medicine within the hospital, the computers are actually doing a great deal more.

1. *One category of information identifies how much of the hospital's resources—laboratory, radiology, respiratory therapy, etc.—is being used for each DRG or DRG grouping.* This information may be broken down in a number of ways. For example, how does the individual physician, the user of the service, compare with other physicians? How does the cost of these services compare to the standard costs per DRG? Which DRGs require the greatest use of which resources?

   Hospitals are now looking at how much of these resources are being used, by whom, and at what cost, especially for the most frequently recorded DRGs.

   This information is intended for use primarily by clinical chiefs within their own departments in order to measure the performance of individual physicians.

   The data may be sent to the clinical chief, who then sets up working committees of physicians within his or her department to review the data and determine the internal mechanisms for sharing this information with the individual doctors.

   The data can readily identify the high and low cost physicians. The ultimate goal is to bring those physicians who may be out of step with the norm back into the system according to whatever policy and enforcement procedures are mandated.

   Having this type of information readily available as soon as DRGs are implemented is a crucial step in understanding and succeeding under the new system. The mechanism must be there; the information must be disseminated to the physicians; policies must be set and carried out by the medical board; and an enforcement system must be in place for those physicians who are out of step.

2. *Another broad category of information deals with program budgeting.* These data give the hospital cost and income information for each clinical program, such as renal dialysis, open-heart surgery, etc. As hospitals learn to live with DRGs, they will be looking at each of those programs just as a business looks at separate divisions within the corporation. How much income per DRG is received from patients who use the service? Is the service profitable? Is it worth being expanded? Should it perhaps be eliminated?

   It is exactly this type of information that will determine the mix of programs offered at your hospital in future years.

   Program budgeting before DRGs appears rudimentary by comparison. Previously management would add up patient days and outpatient procedures to determine in a very rough way what the financial picture would be in the years ahead. With the sophisticated DRG data now available, hospitals can make decisions about various programs based on much more specific information. Your hospital will no longer start a new program simply because a group of doctors want it. Management must take a hard look at the financial implications and marketplace need for each program before making a decision.

3. *Development of financial profiles for clinical programs means looking at clinical programs in terms of the kinds of DRG patients that use the programs, the volume of business, and the cost of running the programs.* These data also tell hospitals the amount of revenue and expenses generated by each physician in each clinical program, giving management another look at how the physician is utilizing the hospital's resources and whether or not that use justifies the continuation of an already existing program or the implementation of a new one.

4. *The last type of data concerns marketing per DRG grouping.* The information shows how much of the market share the hospital is capturing for each DRG. Does the market share justify continuation of the program? Should the hospital expand its market share by aggressive promotion and selection of physicians who bring these DRGs to the hospital?

DRG data reports such as these help hospitals make decisions about their facilities, equipment and supplies. From now on, hospitals will base their construction and remodeling plans on the perceived availability of patient DRGs, and will build those kinds of facilities that will be most efficient in answering patient needs. For instance, as the trend in outpatient services continues to grow, a wise hospital management will put its money into outpatient facilities. As a hospital's patient population becomes older, it will have to respond by providing beds in long-term care units, affiliated nursing homes, hospice programs and home care settings. In these ways, DRGs will have a direct effect on the hospital's physical planning.

Now, once all this information is gathered, it must be disseminated to the appropriate people.

At Hackensack Medical Center, this statistical information is sent directly to department chiefs and key committees of the medical staff so that they may begin to make the connection between quality of care and cost. Among the committees that soon will be receiving this information are utilization review, pharmacy and therapeutics, and medical education. These committees will now be sending reports, based on the data, to the quality assurance committee, which is delegated by the board of governors to assure that the quality of care at the medical center is rendered at the appropriate level and in a cost efficient way.

Hospital management also feeds its own reports, based on DRG data, to the quality assurance committee and the finance committee, which is concerned with the financial welfare of the institution.

Ultimately the quality assurance committee and the finance committee send reports to the board of governors. Based on this information, the board can consider various options: opening or closing a specific program; marketing a new program; asking the medical staff leadership to deal with physicians who fail to respond appropriately to DRG requirements; etc.

As you can see, DRGs have implications for the future of hospitals and physicians far beyond merely placing patients in certain categories and determining how much hospitals will be reimbursed for them. DRGs and DRG-related data have a direct impact on what direction your hospital takes. In this respect, your hospital is no different from any large corporation which utilizes statistical data for strategic planning.

DRGs provide management with a great deal of information which, if properly used, can have a significant impact on the decisions of the board, management and medical staff about the services the hospital will provide. Perhaps even more important for you, DRGs give management a very good overview of physician use of the hospital. Just like the football coach who studies the game films and sees exactly how his quarterback performed, hospital administrators will now be privy to very detailed and significant information about physician performance within the hospital. Each physicians performance can now be analyzed to see how he or she is affecting the financial well-being of the institution.

This information must, of course, be used in a judicious way, but in a way that will have an impact on how physicians utilize the resources of the hospital. All of this represents a very dramatic change in the relationship between the hospital and its medical staff. Whether the change is positive or not depends to a great extent on how willing all participants are to work together for the good of the hospital in its delivery of health care.

PHYSICIAN'S GUIDE TO DRGs

A Look At the Data

As we have just discussed, DRGs give hospitals the ability to study their performance in many different ways and from many different angles. The tables that follow at the end of this section are just a few examples of the kinds of information that will now be readily available to your hospital, and to you. You may find this useful or threatening; but in any case it *will* be readily available.

Table 7.1 is a length of stay analysis report which shows how your hospital compares to other similar hospitals in terms of length of stay for each DRG.

Let's look at DRG No. 110, major reconstructive vascular procedures for patients age 70 or over or who have complications or other conditions. During the year 1982, the hospital treated 57 cases in DRG No. 110 (column A). The standard length of stay (the average length of stay statewide for major teaching hospitals) was 19.9 days (column B). The average length of stay at this hospital for DRG No. 110 was 17.4 days (column C). In other words, on average, this hospital treated patients in DRG No. 110 in 2.5 fewer days (column F) than the statewide standard—a useful piece of information when the hospital is asked to make decisions regarding services involving the treatment of this DRG.

Table 7.2 takes DRG No. 110 and shows how much of the hospital's resources it is using, broken down by departments. This information is available for all the DRGs.

Let's go to the bottom of the list of cost centers and see what's happening with DRG No. 110 in Radiology. Column C shows that the hospital is being reimbursed an average of $222 for radiology services for each case in DRG No. 110. Column D shows that it is actually costing the hospital only $186 in radiology to treat each case in DRG No. 110. Therefore, the hospital is making an average profit of $36 per case for this DRG in Radiology (column E). Totals for the year appear in the last three columns. As you can see from column H, the hospital made a total of $2,079 over the year on DRG No. 110 in Radiology. By looking down column H, you can easily tell which departments are money makers and which are not, for this particular DRG.

The same figures we have just studied also appear in Table 7.3, a cost center incentive DRG analysis report for Radiology. This table shows how Radiology is doing, in terms of cost, reimbursement, and profit or loss, for each DRG. The table is broken down into incentive DRGs—those that are making money—and disincentive DRGs—those that are losing money. With this information in hand, physicians and managers can easily see which cases they are handling efficiently and which they are not, and hopefully they can begin to understand the pattern and make necessary changes.

Table 7.4 shows direct patient care incentive/disincentive by physician for DRG No. 110. This information is available for all the DRGs.

This table takes each physician, lists the number of cases he or she had in DRG No. 110, and compares length of stay to the average.

Physician No. 56 (this number does not represent any actual physician), for instance, had 21 cases in DRG No. 110 (column A). Average length of stay was 19.1 days (column B), which, when compared with the state standard length of stay of 19.9 days, means that, on average, this physician is treating patients in .8 fewer days (column C). For 21 patients in DRG No. 110, the total length of stay variance was 16.8 days (column D).

Column E shows this physician's average cost per case in DRG No. 110, $4,895. By comparing this cost with the DRG payment rate of $4,448.18, you can see that this physician's cases are costing the hospital an average of $433 more to treat (column F). Over the year, this physician's cases in DRG No. 110 have cost the hospital $11,201 more to treat than the hospital was reimbursed. Given the fact that the doctor's length of stay was shorter than the standard, the department chief and the hospital administration might want to know just what is accounting for the added cost and whether it could be avoided.

Table 7.5, DRG case mix by physician, examines how physician No. 56 is doing for all the different DRGs. For DRG No. 110, as we just saw, No. 56's cases are costing the hospital $11,201. By scanning the last column, you can see that this physician's cost-effectiveness varies depending on which DRG is being treated. In all, this physician treated 182 cases in the hospitals which were inliers, and thus subject to DRG rates. Average length of stay was 8.3 days, or 1 day less than the standard.

It is hoped the physician will find this information useful in beginning to understand how his or her practice of medicine within the hospital is affecting the overall picture. In those areas where costs are high, he or she might want to talk to other physicians whose costs are lower, to see why there is a discrepancy.

Table 7.6 takes individual physicians by service, in this case surgery, and examines their lengths of stay and costs. Our friend physician No. 56 had a total of 182 cases during 1982 (column A). For these cases the hospital was reimbursed $325,351 (column B), while the actual cost of treating these patients was $324,635 (column C). The hospital thus recorded a gain of $715 (column D) for these cases, or $4 per case (column E).

Columns F and G compare the standard length of stay (9.3 days) with this physician's length of stay (8.3). So physician No. 56 is treating patients in one day less than the average (column H), which means he or she has saved the hospital 182 patient days (column I) over the course of the year.

These are just a few of the many different reports available as a by-product of DRGs. As you can see, there is very little the computer can't tell you, whether it's which cases are losing money in Radiology to which doctors are treating which types of patients most efficiently. If both hospitals and doctors view this information as an incentive to improving the practice of medicine and the delivery of health care, it should have a very positive effect.

Table 7.1

HOSPITAL MANAGEMENT REPORTING SYSTEM
LENGTH OF STAY ANALYSIS REPORT

    HACKENSACK MEDICAL CENTER

PERIOD ENDING 12/31/82

MDC   DRG   DESCRIPTION

03 DISEASES AND DISORDERS OF THE EAR, NOSE AND THROAT

    057 OTHER TONSIL AND/OR ADENOID O.R. PROCEDURE W AGE 18+
    059 TONSILLECTOMY AND/OR ADENOIDECTOMY ONLY, AGE 18+
    060 TONSILLECTOMY AND/OR ADENOIDECTOMY ONLY, AGE 0-17
    062 MYRINGOTOMY, W AGE 0-17
    064 EAR, NOSE AND THROAT MALIGNANCY, MEDICAL
    065 DISEQUILIBRIUM, MEDICAL
    066 EPISTAXIS, MEDICAL
    069 OTITIS MEDIA AND/OR URI, AGE 18+, WO AGE 70 CC, MED
    070 OTITIS MEDIA AND/OR URI, AGE 0-17, MEDICAL
    071 LARYNGOTRACHEITIS, MEDICAL
    072 NASAL TRAUMA AND DEFORMITY, MEDICAL

    SUB-TOTAL

04 DISEASES AND DISORDERS OF THE RESPIRATORY SYSTEM

    075 MAJOR CHEST O.R. PROCEDURE
    076 MINOR CHEST AND/OR OTHER RESPIRATORY O.R. PROC W CC
    077 MINOR CHEST AND/OR OTHER RESPIRATORY O.R. PROC, WO CC
    078 PULMONARY EMBOLISM, MEDICAL
    080 INFECTION AND/OR INFLAM., W AGE 18+, WO AGE 70 CC, MED
    082 NEOPLASM OF RESPIRATORY SYSTEM, MEDICAL
    083 MAJOR CHEST TRAUMA, W AGE 70 CC, MEDICAL
    084 MAJOR CHEST TRAUMA, WO AGE 70 CC, MEDICAL
    085 PLEURAL EFFUSION, W AGE 70 CC, MEDICAL
    087 PULMONARY EDEMA AND/OR RESPIRATORY FAILURE, MEDICAL
    088 CHRONIC OBSTRUCTIVE PULMONARY DISEASE, MEDICAL
    089 SIMPLE PNEUM. OR PLEURISY, W AGE 18+, W AGE 70CC, MED
    090 SIMPLE PNEUM. OR PLEURISY, W AGE 18+, WO AGE 70CC, MED
    091 SIMPLE PNEUMONIA AND/OR PLEURISY, W AGE 0-17, MEDICAL
    093 INTERSTITIAL LUNG DISEASE, WO AGE 70CC, MEDICAL
    096 BRONCHITIS AND/OR ASTHMA, AGE 18+, W AGE 70CC, MED
    097 BRONCHITIS AND/OR ASTHMA, AGE 18+, WO AGE 70CC, MED
    098 BRONCHITIS AND/OR ASTHMA, AGE 0-17, MEDICAL
    099 SIGNS AND/OR SYMPTOMS, W AGE 70CC, MEDICAL
    100 SIGNS AND/OR SYMPTOMS, WO AGE 70CC, MEDICAL

    SUB-TOTAL

05 DISEASES AND DISORDERS OF THE CIRCULATORY SYSTEM

    110 VASCULAR O.R. PROC. W MAJOR RECONSTRUCTION, W AGE 70CC
    111 VASCULAR O.R. PROC, W MAJOR RECONSTRUCTION, WO AGE 70CC
    112 VASCULAR O.R. PROCEDURE, EXCEPT MAJOR RECONSTRUCTION
    113 AMPUTATION, EXCEPT UPPER LIMB AND/OR TOE

REPORT 2

PAGE 2
WED MAY 11, 1983

A	B	C	D	E	F	G
CASES	STD LOS	LOS	STD DAYS	DAYS	VARIANCE LOS	DAYS
4	2.9	3.8	11.6	15	-0.9	-3.4
87	1.9	1.6	165.3	141	0.3	24.3
134	1.4	1.2	187.6	158	0.2	29.6
108	1.0		108.0	1	1.0	107.0
15	7.5	6.6	112.5	99	0.9	13.5
19	5.3	4.6	100.7	88	0.7	12.7
13	4.6	4.3	59.8	56	0.3	3.8
11	3.9	4.2	42.9	46	-0.3	-3.1
54	3.5	3.4	189.0	182	0.1	7.0
18	3.0	3.2	54.0	57	-0.2	-3.0
23	2.2	1.4	50.6	32	0.8	18.6
983	2.6	2.3	2531.1	2302	0.3	229.1
27	15.7	14.2	423.9	384	1.5	39.9
9	17.0	13.3	153.0	120	3.7	33.0
14	8.1	5.0	113.4	70	3.1	43.4
23	13.9	13.6	319.7	313	0.3	6.7
1	15.1	15.0	15.1	15	0.1	0.1
117	11.2	9.0	1310.4	1055	2.2	255.4
12	8.5	8.8	102.0	105	-0.3	-3.0
2	5.6	6.0	11.2	12	-0.4	-0.8
20	12.5	9.1	250.0	183	3.4	67.0
14	10.3	8.2	144.2	115	2.1	29.2
70	9.4	10.0	658.0	697	-0.6	-39.0
112	11.0	10.7	1232.0	1195	0.3	37.0
37	7.6	7.3	281.2	272	0.3	9.2
47	5.7	5.7	267.9	270		-2.1
5	7.3	6.2	36.5	31	1.1	5.5
59	8.5	8.1	501.5	480	0.4	21.5
64	5.8	5.6	371.2	357	0.2	14.2
120	4.0	3.8	480.0	459	0.2	21.0
13	7.2	6.5	93.6	84	0.7	9.6
26	4.6	4.1	119.6	107	0.5	12.6
792	8.7	8.0	6884.4	6324	0.7	560.4
57	19.9	17.4	1134.3	992	2.5	142.3
19	13.8	12.0	262.2	228	1.8	34.2
27	12.1	12.2	326.7	330	-0.1	-3.3
9	20.0	19.9	180.0	179	0.1	-1.0

Table 7.2

```
              HOSPITAL MANAGEMENT REPORTING SYSTEM
                  DRG COST CENTER ANALYSIS REPORT
                    HACKENSACK MEDICAL CENTER
        PERIOD ENDING: 12/31/82


        DRG: 110
        VASCULAR C.R. PROC.W MAJOR RECONSTRUCTION,W AGE 70CC
        LOW TRIM:  7   HIGH TRIM: 38

        STATE UNEQUAL. STD RATE:    4854.15
        HOSP BASE NON-PHYS RATE:    3850.68
        % OF STATE STD RATE    :      50.96
        NON-PHYS CPC DRG RATE  :    4362.01
        PHYS. COMPONENT CF RATE:      66.17
        TOTAL CPC DRG RATE     :    4448.18
```

	A	B	C	D
	NON-PHYS CPC RATE		
COST	STATE	HOSP	TOTAL	NON-PHYS
CENTER	STD	BASE	RATE	COST/CASE
ACU	1086	856	973	1281
ICU	534	250	395	0
NBN	0	0	0	0
NNI	0	0	0	0
OTH	595	504	550	599
EMR	7	9	8	13
ROUTINE	2222	1619	1926	1893
CCA	16	81	48	10
DEL	0	0	0	0
DIA	46	0	23	0
DRU	342	212	278	295
EDG	37	26	31	22
LAB	519	474	497	537
MSS	534	419	477	99
NMD	0	0	0	0
OPM	0	0	0	0
ORR	668	682	675	1127
PHT	31	7	20	29
RAD	240	203	222	186
RSP	199	131	166	120
THR	0	0	0	0
ANCILLARY	2632	2235	2438	2427
DRG TOTAL	4854	3854	4364	4320

REPORT 4

PAGE 67
WED MAY 11, 1983

	HOSP	STATE	VAR
# CASES:	57		
LCS:	17.4	19.9	2.5

	E	F	G	H
-- AVG INC/CASE ---				
STATE HOSP		---- COST CENTER TOTALS ----		
STD BASE TOTAL		REIMBURSE	COST	INCENTIVE

STATE STD	HOSP BASE	TOTAL	REIMBURSE	COST	INCENTIVE
-99	-208	-308	55476	73007	-17531
272	123	395	22504	0	22504
0	0	0	0	0	0
0	0	0	0	0	0
-2	-47	-49	31378	34164	-2786
-3	-2	-5	434	732	-298
168	-134	33	109793	107904	1889
3	35	38	2727	578	2149
0	0	0	0	0	0
23	0	23	1334	0	1334
24	-41	-17	15866	16838	-973
8	2	10	1786	1240	545
-9	-31	-41	28324	30635	-2311
221	157	378	27206	5665	21541
0	0	0	0	0	0
0	0	0	0	0	0
-234	-218	-453	38460	64266	-25806
1	-11	-10	1118	1676	-558
28	9	36	12656	10577	2079
40	6	46	9465	6848	2617
0	0	0	0	0	0
105	-94	11	138941	138324	618
272	-228	44	248734	246227	2507

Table 7.3
HOSPITAL MANAGEMENT REPORTING SYSTEM

COST CENTER INCENTIVE/DRG ANALYSIS REPORT

HACKENSACK MEDICAL CENTER

COST CENTER - RAE

PERIOD ENDING: 12/31/82

DRG DESCRIPTION

INCENTIVE DRGS:

```
100 SIGNS AND/OR SYMPTOMS, WC AGE 70CC, MEDICAL
363 D&C,CONIZATION,&/OR RADIUM IMPLANT W PR DIAG OF MALIG
300 ENDOCRINE DISORDER, W AGE 70CC, MEDICAL
110 VASCULAR O.R. PROC,W MAJOR RECONSTRUCTION,W AGE 70CC
184 GASTRO-INTESTINAL DISORDER, AGE 0-17, MEDICAL
266 SKIN GRFT WC PRNC DIAG CF SKIN ULCER &/OR CELL.,WC CC
024 SEIZURE AND/OR HEADACHE, AGE 18+, W AGE 70 CC, MED.
262 BREAST PRC,BIOPSY OR LCL EXCIS WC PRNC DIAG OF MALIG.
354 OTHER HYSTERECTOMY, W AGE 70CC
097 BRONCHITIS AND/OR ASTHMA, AGE 18+, WC AGE 70CC,MED
402 LYMPHOMA &/OR LEUKEMIA, W MINOR O.R. PROC,WO AGE 70CC
175 GASTRO-INTESTINAL HEMORRHAGE, WO AGE 70CC, MEDICAL
430 PSYCHOSES, MEDICAL
257 BREAST PRC,> SUB MAST. W PRNC DIAG OF MALIG.,W A 70CC
258 BREAST PRC,> SUB MAST. W PRNC DIAG OF MALIG,WO A 70CC
018 CRANIAL OR PERIPHERAL NERVE DIS., W AGE 70CC, MED.
404 LYMPHOMA &/OR LEUKEMIA, AGE 18+, WO AGE 70CC, MEDICAL
064 EAR, NOSE AND THROAT MALIGNANCY, MEDICAL
112 VASCULAR O.R. PROCEDURE, EXCEPT MAJOR RECONSTRUCTION
001 CRANIOTOMY, AGE 18+, WC PRINICPAL DIAGNOSIS OF TRAUMA
358 UT. OR ADNEXAL PRC,WO PR DIAG OF MALIG,WO TUBAL INTER
162 INGUINAL & FEMORAL HERNIA PROC,W AGE 18+,WC AGE 70CC
198 TOT CHOLECST*MY,WC COMMON BILE DUCT EXPLR,WO AGE 70CC
096 BRONCHITIS AND/OR ASTHMA, AGE 18+, W AGE 70CC,MED
173 DIGESTIVE SYSTEM MALIGNANCY, WO AGE 70CC, MEDICAL
449 POIS. &/OR TOXIC EFF OF DRUGS,AGE 18+,W AGE 70CC,MED
366 FEMALE REPRODUCTIVE SYSTEM MALIGNANCY,W AGE 70CC,MED
090 SIMPLE PNEUM. OR PLEURISY,W AGE 18+,WO AGE 70CC,MED
146 RECTAL RESECTION, W AGE 70CC
268 SKIN, SUBCUTANEOUS TISSUE AND/OR BREAST PLASTIC PROC
381 ABORTION, W D&C
077 MINOR CHEST AND/OR OTHER RESPIRATORY O.R. PROC, WC CC
296 NUTR OR MET DIS NOT INB ERRS OF MET,A 18+,W A 70CC,MD
032 CONCUSSION, AGE 18+, WC AGE 70 CC, MEDICAL
161 INGUINAL AND FEMORAL HERNIA PROC,W AGE 18+,W AGE 70CC
229 HAND PROCEDURE, WC PRINCIPAL DIAGNOSIS OF GANGLION
401 LYMPHOMA &/OR LEUKEMIA, W MINOR O.R. PROC, W AGE 70CC
360 VAGINAL, CERVICAL AND/OR VULVAR PROCEDURE
274 BREAST, MALIGNANCY, W AGE 70CC, MEDICAL
207 DISORDER OF BILIARY TRACT,WC AGE 70CC, MEDICAL
311 TRANSURETHRAL PROCEDURE, WO AGE 70CC
208 DISORDER OF BILIARY TRACT, WC AGE 70CC, MEDICAL
149 MAJOR SMALL AND/OR LARGE BOWEL PROCEDURES,WC AGE 70CC
280 TRMA TO SKN,SUBC TIS &/OR BREAST,W A 18+,W A 70CC,MED
085 PLEURAL EFFUSION, W AGE 70 CC, MEDICAL
367 FEMALE REPRODUCTIVE SYSTEM MALIGNANCY,WC AGE 70CC,MED
```

REPORT 7

PAGE 78
WED MAY 11, 1983

--- CASES ---		DRG	ACTUAL	***** INCENTIVE/DISINCENTIVE ****			
TCTAL	W/CHGS	REIMB.	COST	TCTAL	PCT	BASE	STD
A	B	C	D	E	F		
26	21	3027	743	2285	307.6	932	1353
34	18	3079	850	2228	262.2	894	1334
17	16	4354	2204	2150	97.6	1786	364
57	54	12656	10577	2079	19.7	497	1582
113	25	3391	1398	1993	142.6	1162	831
50	17	2486	533	1954	366.7	1099	855
41	37	6355	4445	1911	43.0	1218	693
157	69	3288	1419	1869	131.8	439	1430
52	42	3832	1967	1865	94.9	513	1352
64	45	2989	1181	1808	153.1	920	888
13	7	2168	365	1803	494.0	870	933
38	31	3871	2125	1747	82.3	788	959
242	156	8013	6303	1709	27.2	-138	1847
16	11	2054	413	1640	397.1	338	1302
16	13	1915	321	1594	496.6	326	1268
17	14	3188	1598	1590	99.5	901	689
31	14	3118	1585	1533	96.8	810	723
15	7	1857	326	1530	469.4	1300	230
27	26	5278	3767	1511	40.2	1155	356
28	27	9497	8001	1496	18.7	582	914
125	52	3746	2263	1484	65.6	150	1334
202	156	4933	3494	1439	41.2	315	1124
113	104	8634	7199	1436	20.0	879	557
59	48	3952	2526	1425	56.5	583	842
16	5	1670	259	1411	544.8	798	613
24	17	2341	933	1408	151.0	1076	332
15	5	1776	396	1380	348.5	744	636
37	36	3281	1913	1368	71.6	743	625
19	19	3623	2289	1333	58.3	214	1119
59	18	2174	849	1325	156.1	710	615
202	13	1889	574	1315	229.1	-26	1341
14	10	2101	802	1300	162.1	499	801
40	35	4959	3668	1291	35.2	897	394
99	71	11787	10500	1287	12.3	1516	-229
95	69	3496	2212	1284	58.1	307	977
101	45	3100	1819	1281	70.5	463	818
5	3	1615	347	1268	365.5	606	662
95	23	1905	718	1186	165.2	101	1085
9	8	1814	628	1185	188.7	782	403
27	27	4679	3520	1159	33.0	322	837
39	33	2885	1769	1115	63.1	478	637
32	30	4232	3126	1107	35.5	296	811
32	26	3109	2004	1106	55.2	213	893
17	11	1947	845	1102	130.5	745	357
20	20	3187	2115	1072	50.7	424	648
12	5	1414	348	1066	306.4	130	936

Table 7.3 (cont.)

HOSPITAL MANAGEMENT REPORTING SYSTEM

COST CENTER INCENTIVE/DRG ANALYSIS REPORT

HACKENSACK MEDICAL CENTER

COST CENTER - RAD

PERIOD ENDING: 12/31/82

DRG DESCRIPTION

DISINCENTIVE DRGS:

```
243 BACK DISORDER, MEDICAL
215 BACK AND/OR NECK PROCEDURE, WO AGE 70CC
319 KIDNEY AND/OR URINARY TRACT NEOPLASM, WO AGE 70CC,MED
210 HIP OR FEMUR PROC NOT MAJ JNT,W AGE 18+,W AGE 70CC
002 CRANIOTOMY, AGE 18+, W PRINCIPAL DIAGNOSIS OF TRAUMA
211 HIP OR FEMUR PROC NOT MAJ JNT,W AGE 18+,WO AGE 70CC
209 MAJOR JOINT PROCEDURE
130 PERIPHERAL VASCULAR DISORDER, W AGE 70CC, MEDICAL
326 SGNS & SYMP OF KDNY/UR. TRCT DIS,W A 18+,WO A 70CC,MD
026 SEIZURE AND/OR HEADACHE, AGE 0-17, MEDICAL
301 ENDOCRINE DISORDER,WO AGE 70CC, MEDICAL
003 CRANIOTOMY, AGE 0-17
453 COMPLICATIONS OF TREATMENT, WO AGE 70CC, MEDICAL
244 BONE DISEASE AND SPECIFIC ARTHROPATHY,W AGE 70CC,MED
029 TR STPR OR COMA,WO COMA>1HR,AGE 18+,WO AGE 70CC,MED
429 ORGANIC DISTURBANCES AND/OR MENTAL RETARDATION,MED
251 FRC,SPR,STR,DIS OF FOREARM,HND,FT,A 18+,WO A 70CC,MED
016 NON SPECIFIC CEREBROVASCULAR DISORDER, W CC, MEDICAL
328 URETHRAL STRICTURE, AGE 18+, W AGE 70CC, MEDICAL
252 FRC,SPR,STR,DIS OF FOREARM,HAND,FT,AGE 0-17,MED
418 POSTOPERATIVE AND POSTRAUMATIC INFECTION, MEDICAL
368 FEMALE REPRODUCTIVE SYSTEM INFECTION, MEDICAL
460 BURN, MEDICAL
009 SPINAL DISORDER AND/OR INJURY, MEDICAL
043 HYPHEMA, MEDICAL
440 WOUND DEBRIDEMENT FOR INJURY
318 KIDNEY AND/OR URINARY TRACT NEOPLASM, W AGE 70CC,MED
228 HAND PROCEDURE, W PRINCIPAL DIAGNOSIS OF GANGLION
038 PRIMARY IRIS O.R. PROCEDURE

 29 LISTED DISINCENTIVE DRGS
 10 OTHER  DISINCENTIVE DRGS
 39 TOTAL  DISINCENTIVE DRGS
```

-- CASES --		DRG	ACTUAL	***** INCENTIVE/DISINCENTIVE ****			
TOTAL	W/CHGS	REIMB.	COST	TOTAL	PCT	BASE	STD
A	B	C	D	E	F		
270	235	25623	35832	-10209	-28.5	-2708	-7501
43	38	5337	7421	-2084	-28.1	-876	-1208
10	7	699	2384	-1684	-70.7	-1077	-607
51	51	8303	9825	-1522	-15.5	-278	-1244
10	10	3437	4595	-1158	-25.3	-429	-729
21	21	2970	3912	-942	-24.1	-412	-530
73	73	8377	9311	-934	-10.1	-150	-784
51	47	7055	7989	-934	-11.7	-380	-554
8	7	775	1576	-801	-50.9	-421	-380
39	25	2282	2978	-696	-23.4	-214	-482
7	6	854	1442	-588	-40.8	-289	-299
9	8	1913	2384	-472	-19.8	-334	-138
16	6	354	822	-468	-57.0	-356	-112
10	10	1521	1970	-449	-22.8	-133	-316
7	5	1000	1443	-442	-30.7	-199	-243
15	12	1177	1615	-438	-27.2	-262	-176
8	6	576	970	-393	-40.6	-205	-188
8	8	1324	1592	-269	-16.9	-153	-116
13	10	775	1025	-250	-24.4	-214	-36
8	8	372	591	-219	-37.1	-90	-129
12	8	285	497	-212	-42.7	-200	-12
19	14	1054	1256	-202	-16.1	27	-229
22	12	342	493	-151	-30.7	-143	-8
1	1	112	232	-119	-51.3	-86	-33
9	7	249	340	-91	-26.8	2	-93
9	8	191	276	-85	-30.8	-90	5
4	3	471	548	-77	-14.1	-75	-2
30	9	480	549	-69	-12.6	-70	1
1	1	15	18	-3	-16.7	0	-3
784	656	77923	103886	-25961	-25.0	-9815	-16146
259	159	12129	12850	-721	-5.7	-409	-312
1043	815	90052	116736	-26682	-22.9	-10224	-16458

187

Table 7.4

HOSPITAL MANAGEMENT REPORTING SYSTEM

DIRECT PATIENT CARE INCENTIVE/DISINCENTIVE BY PHYSICIAN

HACKENSACK MEDICAL CENTER

PERIOD ENDING: 12/31/82

DRG 110
VASCULAR C.R. PROC,W MAJOR RECONSTRUCTION,W AGE 70CC
LOW TRIM: 7   HIGH TRIM: 38
PAYMENT RATE: 4448.18   STATE STD LOS: 15.9

*NUMB. PHYSICIAN NAME	A CASES	B LOS
DISINCENTIVE PHYSICIANS:		
56	21	19.1
57	1	28.0
58	1	27.0
59	1	15.0
4 LISTED DISINCENTIVE PHYSICIANS	24	19.7
0 OTHER DISINCENTIVE PHYSICIANS	0	0.0
4 TOTAL DISINCENTIVE PHYSICIANS	24	19.7
INCENTIVE PHYSICIANS:		
60	21	16.0
61	6	13.7
62	1	14.0
63	1	18.0
64	1	22.0
5 LISTED INCENTIVE PHYSICIANS	32	15.6
1 OTHER INCENTIVE PHYSICIANS	1	21.0
6 TOTAL INCENTIVE PHYSICIANS	33	15.8
10 TOTAL PHYSICIANS	57	17.4

*Physician numbers in this exhibit and in those that follow do not represent actual physicians.

REPORT 8

PAGE 73
WED MAY 11, 1983

C	D	E	F	G
VARIANCES		AVG.	INCENTIVE/DISINCENTIVE	
LOS	DAYS	COST	AVERAGE	TOTAL.
0.8	16.8	4895	-533	-11201
-8.1	-8.1	6107	-1745	-1745
-7.1	-7.1	5475	-1113	-1112
4.9	4.9	5029	-667	-667
0.2	4.8	4976	-614	-14727
0.0	0.0	0	0	0
0.2	4.8	4976	-614	-14727
3.9	81.9	3987	375	7874
6.2	49.6	3481	881	7049
5.9	5.9	3482	880	879
1.9	1.9	3759	603	603
-2.1	-2.1	3839	523	522
4.3	137.6	3833	529	16929
-1.1	-1.1	4158	204	204
4.1	135.3	3843	519	17133
2.5	142.5	4320	42	2406

Table 7.5
HOSPITAL MANAGEMENT REPORTING SYSTEM
DRG CASE MIX BY PHYSICIAN

HACKENSACK MEDICAL CENTER

PERIOD ENDING 12/31/82

PHYS NO. 66

DRG DESCRIPTION

```
015 SPEC CV DIS., W PRINC DIAG OF TRANS ISCHMC ATTK, MED
019 CRANIAL OR PERIPHERAL NERVE DIS., WO AGE 70CC, MED.
032 CONCUSSION, AGE 18+, WO AGE 70 CC, MEDICAL
110 VASCULAR O.R. PROC, W MAJOR RECONSTRUCTION, W AGE 70CC
111 VASCULAR O.R. PROC, W MAJOR RECONSTRUCTION, WO AGE 70CC
112 VASCULAR O.R. PROCEDURE, EXCEPT MAJOR RECONSTRUCTION
119 VEIN LIGATION AND STRIPPING
128 DEEP VEIN THROMBOPHLEBITIS, MEDICAL
130 PERIPHERAL VASCULAR DISORDER, W AGE 70CC, MEDICAL
131 PERIPHERAL VASCULAR DISORDER, WO AGE 70CC, MEDICAL
146 RECTAL RESECTION, W AGE 70CC
148 MAJOR SMALL AND/OR LARGE BOWEL PROCEDURES, W AGE 70CC
149 MAJOR SMALL AND/OR LARGE BOWEL PROCEDURES, WO AGE 70CC
153 MINOR SMALL AND/OR LARGE BOWEL PROCEDURES, WO AGE 70CC
158 ANAL AND PERIANAL PROCEDURES, WO AGE 70CC
161 INGUINAL AND FEMORAL HERNIA PROC, W AGE 18+, W AGE 70CC
162 INGUINAL & FEMORAL HERNIA PROC, W AGE 18+, WO AGE 70CC
165 APPENDECTOMY, W COMPLICATED PRINC DIAG, WO AGE 70CC
167 APPENDECTOMY, WO COMPLICATED PRINC DIAG, WO AGE 70CC
174 GASTRO-INTESTINAL HEMORRHAGE, W AGE 70CC, MEDICAL
181 INTESTINAL OBSTRUCTION, WO AGE 70CC, MEDICAL
182 GASTRO-INTESTINAL DISORDER, AGE 18+, W AGE 70CC, MED
183 GASTRO-INTESTINAL DISORDER, AGE 18+, WO AGE 70CC, MED
197 TOT CHOLECST'MY, WO COMMON BILE DUCT EXPLOR, W AGE 70CC
198 TOT CHOLECST'MY, WO COMMON BILE DUCT EXPLR, WO AGE 70CC
204 DISORDER OF PANCREAS OTHER THAN MALIGNANCY, MEDICAL
206 DIS OF LIV. NOT MALIG.,CIRR.,AL. HEP.,WO AGE 70CC,MED
207 DISORDER OF BILIARY TRACT, WO AGE 70CC, MEDICAL
208 DISORDER OF BILIARY TRACT, WO AGE 70CC, MEDICAL
211 HIP OR FEMUR PROC NOT MAJ JNT, W AGE 18+, WO AGE 70CC
225 FOOT PROCEDURE
258 BREAST PRC,> SUB MAST. W PRNC DIAG OF MALIG,WO A 70CC
262 BREAST PRC,BIOPSY OR LCL EXCIS WO PRNC DIAG OF MALIG.
267 PERIANAL AND PILONIDAL PROCEDURE
268 SKIN, SUBCUTANEOUS TISSUE AND/OR BREAST PLASTIC PROC
281 TRMA TO SKN,SUBC TIS &/OR BREAST, W A 18+, WO A 70CC,MD
284 MINOR SKIN DISORDER, WO AGE 70CC, MEDICAL
300 ENDOCRINE DISORDER, W AGE 70CC, MEDICAL
304 KDNY,URTR, MAJ BLAD PRC,WO PR DIAG OF NEPL.,W A 70CC
305 KDNY,URTR, MAJ BLAD PRC,WO PR DIAG OF NEPL.,WO A 70CC
312 URETHRAL PROCEDURE, W AGE 18+, W AGE 70CC
348 BENIGN PROSTATIC HYPERTROPHY, W AGE 70CC, MEDICAL
364 D&C, CONIZATION, WO PRINCIPAL DIAGNOSIS OF MALIGNANCY
369 MENSTRUAL & OTHER FEMALE REPRODUCTIVE SYSTEM DIAG,MED
378 ECTOPIC PREGNANCY
418 POSTOPERATIVE AND POSTRAUMATIC INFECTION, MEDICAL
```

REPORT 9

PAGE 156
WED MAY 11, 1983

SERVICE: SURGERY

A	B	C	D	E	F	G	H	I
CASES	STD LOS	LOS	VARIANCE LOS	VARIANCE DAYS	ORG RATE	COST/ CASE	INCENTIVE AVG	INCENTIVE TOTAL
2	7.8	5.5	2.3	4.6	1213	1100	112	224
1	7.9	2.0	5.9	5.9	1064	442	621	621
1	3.6	5.0	-1.4	-1.4	561	882	-321	-321
21	19.9	19.1	0.8	15.9	4362	4895	-533	-11201
7	13.8	14.1	-0.3	-2.4	3311	3259	50	356
13	12.1	11.2	0.9	12.3	2736	2544	192	2496
8	5.3	5.7	-0.4	-3.6	988	1255	-267	-2140
6	11.1	10.0	1.1	6.6	1541	1341	199	1196
11	9.4	3.7	5.7	62.4	1299	789	509	5605
8	8.2	5.4	2.8	22.6	1098	854	243	1949
1	21.3	30.0	-8.7	-8.7	4676	5355	-679	-679
5	18.9	16.2	2.7	13.5	3874	3011	862	4312
1	13.1	12.0	1.1	1.1	2640	2412	227	227
2	8.7	8.0	0.7	1.4	1718	1452	264	529
8	4.5	4.0	0.5	4.0	803	871	-68	-547
9	6.6	5.7	0.9	8.4	1102	1088	13	125
6	4.6	5.7	-1.1	-6.4	862	1129	-268	-1610
3	9.1	6.0	3.1	9.3	1745	1170	574	1722
2	4.7	4.5	0.2	0.4	951	1009	-58	-117
1	9.0	16.0	-7.0	-7.0	1566	2736	-1170	-1170
1	6.0	5.0	1.0	1.0	1028	747	280	280
2	7.4	6.5	0.9	1.8	1129	1110	17	35
7	5.7	3.3	2.4	16.9	869	505	363	2543
2	11.4	9.5	1.9	3.8	2165	2091	73	146
7	8.6	10.1	-1.5	-10.8	1613	1987	-374	-2624
1	8.1	5.0	3.1	3.1	1284	898	384	384
1	7.5	2.0	5.5	5.5	1086	507	578	578
2	8.1	6.0	2.1	4.2	1278	985	292	585
1	5.4	8.0	-2.6	-2.6	889	1264	-375	-375
2	17.8	18.5	-0.7	-1.4	2992	4204	-1211	-2423
1	5.6	9.0	-3.4	-3.4	1040	1392	-352	-352
1	9.2	9.0	0.2	0.2	1764	1707	55	55
9	2.5	1.8	0.7	6.5	591	562	28	255
4	4.6	6.7	-2.1	-8.6	820	1107	-287	-1151
1	2.7	1.0	1.7	1.7	661	232	428	428
2	3.3	1.5	1.8	3.6	613	280	332	664
6	2.6	0.0	2.6	15.6	539	304	235	1410
1	10.7	2.0	8.7	8.7	1853	450	1402	1402
1	16.0	12.0	4.0	4.0	2810	1960	849	849
1	11.4	12.0	-0.6	-0.6	1942	2622	-681	-681
1	5.4	5.0	0.4	0.4	713	922	-209	-209
1	4.7	11.0	-6.3	-6.3	833	2144	-1311	-1311
1	2.1	2.0	0.1	0.1	506	523	-17	-17
1	2.8	4.0	-1.2	-1.2	464	641	-176	-176
1	6.2	4.0	2.2	2.2	1222	975	246	246
5	7.6	7.6	0.0	0.0	966	1056	-91	-457

Table 7.5 (cont.)

HOSPITAL MANAGEMENT REPORTING SYSTEM
DRG CASE MIX BY PHYSICIAN

HACKENSACK MEDICAL CENTER

PERIOD ENDING 12/31/82

PHYS NO. 56

DRG DESCRIPTION

441 HAND PROCEDURE FOR INJURY
453 COMPLICATIONS OF TREATMENT, WO AGE 70CC, MEDICAL

TOTAL INLIERS

REPORT 9

PAGE 157
WED MAY 11, 1983

SERVICE: SURGERY

A	B	C	D	E	F	G	H	I
	STD		VARIANCE		DRG	COST/	INCENTIVE	
CASES	LOS	LOS	LOS	DAYS	RATE	CASE	AVG	TOTAL
1	3.3	4.0	-0.7	-0.7	749	1588	-839	-839
2	3.7	4.5	-0.8	-1.6	582	638	-55	-111
182	9.3	8.3	1.0	181.0	1787	1783	4	716

Table 7.6

HOSPITAL MANAGEMENT REPORTING SYSTEM

PHYSICIAN DRG INCENTIVE AND LENGTH OF STAY REPORT

HACKENSACK MEDICAL CENTER

SERVICE - SURGERY

PERIOD ENDING: 12/31/82

*PHYS. NUMB.	PHYSICIAN NAME	A CASES	B INLIER REIMBURS.
51		690	833208
52		303	408797
53		225	236037
54		191	120112
55		190	297691
56		182	325351
57		174	178417
58		161	136983
59		149	164625
60		134	181257
61		109	83934
62		79	76346
63		70	91849
64		54	69473
65		47	54148
66		18	11483
67		12	8717
	INCENTIVE PHYSICIANS	2257	2832938
6	DISINCENTIVE PHYSICIANS	531	445493
1	OTHER PHYSICIANS	4	7898
18	TOTAL PHYSICIANS	2792	3286329

REPORT 10

PAGE 4
WED MAY 11, 1983

C	D	E	F	G	H	I
TOTAL	***** INC/DIS ****		STD		** VARIANCE **	
COST	TOTAL	AVG.	LOS	LOS	LOS	DAYS
736907	96300	140	6.3	5.4	0.9	621.0
355804	52992	175	7.1	5.6	1.5	454.5
198989	37048	165	5.6	3.9	1.7	382.5
123827	-3715	-19	2.8	2.2	0.6	114.6
270781	26909	142	8.1	6.4	1.7	323.0
324635	715	4	9.3	8.3	1.0	182.0
176768	1648	9	5.6	4.5	1.1	191.4
141463	-4480	-28	4.3	4.0	0.3	48.3
150054	14570	98	6.7	5.8	0.9	134.1
179947	1309	10	7.1	6.1	1.0	134.0
81201	2732	25	3.6	2.6	1.0	109.0
81001	-4654	-59	6.2	5.4	0.8	63.2
94697	-2847	-41	7.2	6.6	0.6	42.0
59849	9624	178	6.6	7.5	-0.9	-48.6
51704	2444	52	6.1	5.2	0.9	42.3
11684	-200	-11	2.9	2.2	0.7	12.6
9881	-1164	-97	3.2	2.5	0.7	8.4
2586639	246296	109	6.6	5.5	1.1	2482.7
462555	-17062	-32	4.4	3.8	0.6	318.6
7026	871	218	5.9	2.0	3.9	15.6
3056220	230104	82	6.2	5.2	1.0	2792.0

Technology Appeals: A Case Study

So far in this book, we have been talking about cost containment and belt-tightening. We have been telling you how to be more efficient and warning you that only those new programs that can pay for themselves will be approved by hospitals in this new DRG mentality.

But the system can also work to your advantage, as it did in the case study you are about to read. Hackensack Medical Center purchased a new Dyna Camera, an advanced piece of diagnostic technology, which, in many cases, obviated the need for surgery. Patients were benefiting and so was the system, but the hospital found that the decrease in surgical cases meant a drop in reimbursement that was not matched by an equal drop in costs. So the hospital appealed to the New Jersey Hospital Rate Setting Commission for the cost of the Dyna Camera—and won.

Using DRG data, the hospital substantiated its claims of revenue loss and was able to show a correlation between that revenue loss and the Dyna Camera by using statistics that were never before available. Previously, hospitals had to rely on presumptions and anectodotal evidence ("our cases are more difficult;" "we have an unusual case mix;" "we're getting our patients out more quickly.") Now, for the first time, the hospital had the statistics to substantiate its claims. The appeal was won—a direct result of using the DRG data.

The following article was written by Michael J. Kalison, and if you can't guess by the language, Mr. Kalison is a lawyer. He handled the appeal for the medical center, and also was one of the authors of New Jersey's DRG regulations.

In 1980, Hackensack Medical Center petitioned the New Jersey Hospital Rate Setting Commission for rate relief in connection with the acquisition of a new piece of diagnostic technology—a Dyna Camera. Ultimately, the Commission awarded HMC the capital cost associated with this piece of major moveable equip-

---

This section written by Michael J. Kalison, partner in the law firm of Manger, Kalison, Murphy and McBride, Morristown, NJ. Mr. Kalison specializes in the field of health care and hospital reimbursement. The appeal was prepared with the assistance of Cosmo Mongiello, Vice President—Finance, Hackensack Medical Center, and Jim Hull of Network, Inc.

ment. To understand the significance of the appeal, however, it is important to review the matter in the context of the regulatory structure within which the Commission functions. The prospective payment system for New Jersey hospitals based on patient case-mix—Diagnosis Related Groups ("DRG")—was implemented in 1980.

Under a waiver from the Health Care Financing Administration, various states, including New Jersey, were involved in conducting demonstrations and experiments in prospective rate-setting—i.e., developing rates of payment, "fixed in advance". Like most other prospective systems, such rates are developed using costs and statistics from a historic base year. Various adjustments are then made to these data, including an adjustment for realized and projected inflation. Among other things, this reflected an underlying philosophy that management should be held accountable only for factors within its control—general economic inflation being beyond the control of an institution.

Adjusting for inflation is, of course, only one element involved in the development of prospective rates. Among other things, the hospital and regulatory communities had worked jointly over a three year period to develop adjustments to account for: geographic differences in the cost of labor; significant changes in volume; the extra responsibilities assumed by teaching hospitals; fixed/variable; the extraordinary inflation of certain items, such as medical malpractice; the non-comparability of certain items, such as physician contractual arrangements; and imperfections in certain patient categories within the system of classification itself—i.e., DRG. Thus, for example, concerning the latter, hospital rates of payment are composed utilizing a statistic (the coefficient of variation) which takes into account the relative predictive strengths of each DRG. This prevents arbitrariness.

The distinguishing feature of the New Jersey system is, of course, that the application of all of these various elements ultimately results in the determination of prospective prices per DRG. This reflected a belief shared by both the hospitals and the regulators that the performance of such institutions could not be fairly compared without taking into account patient case-mix—patients being the business of the health care industry. In other words, it was considered important to understand the real cost differences between treating cancer patients, as contrasted with delivering babies.

The responsibilities of the regulatory process did not end with the determination of prices per case. In order to identify the remaining task, it is helpful to consider all of the adjustments discussed to this point—e.g., inflation, volume, wage equalization—as general rules which are applied in order to develop prospective rates. All rules, however, have exceptions. In the case of the New Jersey system, great efforts were made to develop detailed rules which resolved a myriad of issues, such as inflation, in order to guide the parties toward a single, primary focus—medical practice. Indeed, one way to judge the quality of a regulatory system is to consider the effectiveness of the balance between rules and exceptions—i.e., does it crystallize the right kinds of questions? In this regard, a major objective of the New Jersey system was to involve physicians in the deliberation of the economic issues which affect health care.

Understanding the Dyna Camera issue involves relating three of the issues just discussed—the general rules regarding historic data and inflation, and the exception involving medical practice. Among the historical cost elements used to develop prospective rates is depreciation on major moveable equipment. Recognizing that, like labor and supplies, such equipment is affected by inflation, a technique was developed to "price-level" major moveable equipment. Although indices were successfully developed to account for various kinds of equipment that a hospital utilizes (e.g., business equipment), it was recognized that fully anticipating the impact of totally new technology was probably not possible. Among other things, the cost effect would vary directly with the kind of technology.

The Dyna Camera is an advanced piece of diagnostic technology which was purchased by the hospital *after* the close of the historic base year utilized to develop rates. It followed, therefore, that the costs of the equipment were not accounted for in the prospective rates. In developing its appeal, the hospital began by isolating the cost impact of the camera: Under the guidance of the hospital's radiologists, the procedures commonly performed by the Dyna Camera were identified (Table 7.7). On Table 7.7, the high volume procedures (which account for almost 80% of the equipment's utilization) were linked to those DRGs likely to consume the service. Noting that the hospital already compared favorably, case-mix adjusted (see Table 7.9, Column 9), the hospital then advanced the following caution: " . . . it is important to note that the Dyna Camera is only one element in the course of treatment for these cases which generally involves the consumption of resources, different in kind and amount, from various cost centers."

The appeal continued:

> Heretofore we have been highlighting the issue of relative *cost* performance on both a cost center and DRG specific basis; however, the data tends to reveal a potentially significant *revenue* effect, as well. Column 7 of Table 7.9 shows the projected 1980 case-mix based on six months of actual figures. (In reading the table, it should be noted that non-surgical and surgical DRGs have been paired, with the non-surgical appearing first.) Column 8 show the distribution of non-surgical and surgical cases based on the assumption that the proportions displayed in base year, 1978, were repeated. A comparison of these two columns shows the emergence of a significant shift from surgical to non-surgical over this period of time.
>
> Once again, we stress that the Dyna Camera is only one element in the course of treatment. Given this caution, it is interesting to observe that the introduction of enhanced diagnostic capability, which allows the physician to be more secure in his diagnosis, may in fact have obviated the need for "exploratory" surgery in a certain percentage of cases. Although the results are by no means conclusive, the comparison also tends to show, as one would expect, that real dissemination involves a "rate of acceptance"; i.e., it takes a reasonable period of time for physicians to understand, to utilize, and to feel confident in the results obtained through the use of new technology.
>
> The potential revenue effect of the phenomenon described above is important. Since, as column 2 shows, surgical cases tend to be more expensive than non-surgical, the net effect of a switch from the former to the latter, however desirable from a patient point of view, produces a loss of potential revenue, $130,613. This is shown in the final column. Although of great interest, it is simply not possible to track the 1980

cost behavior of these DRGs at this time in order to determine how much the hospital might be able to save as a result of the switch to non-surgical. Thus, at this point, we are not able to determine whether or not the likely significant loss of revenue exceeds the potential savings. Moreover, as we have said, it would be inappropriate to attribute the entire effect to the Dyna Camera because of the complex interrelationships involved.

Given our cautions, the exercise does tend to reveal that the institution *will suffer* a revenue penalty because of enhanced diagnostic capability. Under a system where patient care revenue is 100% variable, the institution will be able to avoid a net loss only if it is able to reduce costs at the same rate at which its revenue is failing. Assuming, however, that promoting non-surgical treatment is a desirable goal, the more important immediate objective may be to preserve an environment in which the development of this kind of pattern is not discouraged. While we do not suggest putting a bounty on non-surgical DRGs, it would seem not inappropriate to pay for the cost of introducing the kind of technological improvements likely to produce this kind of patient benefit. And, although we may be equipped to deal only with incentives and signals at the front end, all of the above tends to underscore the importance of sensitivity to detail in isolating, over time, the kinds of trends which may be important to future DRG appeals.

From a financial point of view, the Dyna Camera appeal was not particularly significant; Hackensack Medical Center has brought and won appeals involving much higher awards. Nevertheless, it is important for other reasons because it caused the hospital to link financial data to medical data (patient cases) in order to establish its argument. In so doing, it developed an understanding of the economic impact of a certain kind of new technology—a perspective important to the institution, its physicians and patients, as well as to the rate system. Among other things, it is also the kind of cost/benefit analysis necessary to guide prudent investments in future technology.

The importance of the Dyna Camera Appeal is not, however, limited to Hackensack Medical Center, or to the New Jersey system. The Medicare prospective payment system and the New Jersey system are not identical. Nevertheless, it is quite clear that of all the waivered state demonstrations and experiments, New Jersey had the greatest impact on federal thinking. There is, of course, the obvious—prices per DRG, established prospectively. However, Medicare has also established a Prospective Payment Assessment Commission charged, among other things, with evaluating the impact of new technology on DRGs. The approach to the Dyna Camera Appeal must be varied, depending on the kind of new technology under scrutiny. But it is a valuable precedent which can be profitably studied by other members of the health care community.

TABLE 7.7
Six Month Period from September 1979 to February 1980
Total Number of Procedures Performed = 2250

SCAN	NUMBER PERFORMED	PERCENTAGE
BRAIN SCAN	120	5.3
BRAIN FLOW	144	6.4
BONE SCAN	473	21.0
LIVER SCAN	366	16.3
SPLEEN SCAN	100	4.4
LIVER/LUNG SCAN	1	—
LUNG PERF.	164	7.3
LUNG VENT.	151	6.7
THYROID SCAN	139	6.2
THYROID UPT.	154	6.8
GALLIUM SCAN	65	2.9
THALLIUM R/S	138	6.1
PYROPHOSPHATE	41	1.8
R.A.C.	91	4.0
RENAL FLOW	10	0.4
RENAL SCAN	16	0.7
RENOGRAM	4	0.2
CISTERNOGRAM	13	0.6
VENOGRAM	2	0.1
TC-THYROID	3	0.1
RADIOANGIOGRAMS	15	0.7
131 I THERAPY	9	0.4
TESTICULAR SCAN	3	0.1
VOIDING CYSTO	8	0.4
PIPIDA	15	0.7
G.I. BLEED	1	—
MECKELS	3	0.1
LEVEEN SHUNT	1	—

Table 7.8

Procedure/Diagnosis	DRG #	1978 No. of Cases	1980 Cases Dist. on 1978 Ratio	Est. 1980 Cases
Brain Scan:				
Cerebral Infarction	141	35	65	74
″ ″ w/Surgery	145	32	59	50
		67	124	124
Brain Tumor	40	36	42	52
″ ″ w/Surgery	44	39	46	36
		75	88	88
Liver Scan:				
Carcinoma Liver (primary site)	7	18	22	26
″ ″ w/Surgery	11	111	136	132
		129	158	158
Carcinoma Liver (metastatic)	40			
″ ″ w/Surgery	44			
Thallium Scan:				
Coronary Artery Disease	122	92	117	128
″ ″ ″ w/Surgery	126	29	37	26
		121	154	154
Thyroid Scan:				
Thyroid Nodule	69	17	18	14
Hyperthyroidism	70	5	5	6
″ w/Surgery	71	42	43	46
		64	66	66
Lung Perfusion & Ventilation Scan				
Pulmonary Embolus	154	27	30	16
Chronic Obst. Lung Disease	176	48	52	60
″ ″ ″ ″ w/Surgery	180	20	22	28
		95	104	104
Bone Scan:				
Pagets Dis. & Osteomyelitis	298	39	36	32
″ ″ ″ ″ w/Surgery	300	22	20	24
		61	56	56

Table 7.9

Procedure/Diagnosis	(1) DRG #	(2) Rate	(3) Non-Phys. Cost per Case	(4) Equalized Non-Phys. Standard	(5) Variance (4 less 3)
Brain Scan:					
Cerebral Infarction	141	2,191	1,191.58	1,091.88	(99.70)
" " w/Surgery	145	5,010	2,590.72	3,623.06	1,032.34
Brain Tumor	40	1,830	974.91	1,101.55	126.64
" " w/Surgery	44	5,750	3,100.74	3,166.96	66.22
Liver Scan:					
Carcinoma Liver (primary site)	7	1,443	775.72	951.96	176.24
" " w/Surgery	11	5,969	3,204.25	3,318.90	114.65
Carcinoma Liver (metastatic)	40	1,830	974.91	1,101.55	126.64
" " w/Surgery	44	5,750	3,100.74	3,166.96	62.22
Thallium Scan:					
Coronary Artery Disease	122	1,647	881.38	738.27	(143.11)
" " " w/Surgery	126	4,645	2,535.51	2,231.22	(304.29)
Thyroid Scan:					
Thyroid Nodule	69	1,578	856.29	746.04	(110.25)
Hyperthyroidism	70	2,290	1,322.86	811.93	(510.93)
" w/Surgery	71	1,578	859.17	844.59	(14.58)
Lung Perfusion & Ventilation Scan:					
Pulmonary Embolus	154	3,504	1,928.38	1,632.58	(296.30)
Chronic Obst. Lung Disease	176	2,140	1,190.52	1,027.76	(162.76)
" " " " w/Surgery	80	2,808	1,448.84	1,985.52	536.68
Bone Scan:					
Pagets Dis. + Osteomyelitis	298	2,248	1,211.63	1,275.78	64.15
" " " " w/Surgery	⁻]0	2,102	1,148.48	1,084.18	(64.30)

(6) 1978 No. of Cases	(7) Est. 1980 Cases	(8) 1980 Cases Dist. on 1978 Ratio	(9) 1978 DRG Variance (5 x 6)	(10) 1980 Rev. at 1980 Actual Case-Mix (7 x 2)	(11) 1980 Revenue at 1978 Case-Mix (8 x 2)	(12) Increase (Decrease) Due to Case-Mix Change
35	74	65	(3,490)	162,134	142,415	19,719
32	50	59	33,035	250,500	295,590	(45,090)
67	124	124	29,545	412,634	438,005	(25,371)
36	52	42	4,559	95,160	76,860	18,300
39	36	46	2,583	207,000	264,500	(57,500)
75	88	88	7,142	302,160	341,360	(39,200)
18	26	22	3,172	37,518	31,746	5,772
111	132	136	12,726	787,908	811,784	(23,876)
129	158	158	15,898	825,426	843,530	(18,104)
92	128	117	(13,166)	210,816	192,699	18,117
29	26	37	(8,824)	120,770	171,865	(51,095)
121	154	154	(21,990)	331,586	364,564	(32,978)
17	14	18	(1,874)	22,092	28,404	(6,312)
5	6	5	(2,555)	13,740	11,450	2,290
42	46	43	(612)	72,588	67,854	4,734
64	66	66	(5,041)	108,420	107,708	712
27	16	30	(8,000)	56,064	105,120	(49,056)
48	60	52	(7,812)	128,400	111,280	17,120
20	28	22	10,734	78,624	61,776	16,848
95	104	104	(5,078)	263,088	278,176	(15,088)
39	32	36	2,502	71,936	80,928	(8,992)
22	24	20	(1,415)	50,448	42,040	8,408
61	56	56	1,087	122,384	122,968	(584)
	TOTAL		21,563	2,365,698	2,496,311	(130,613)

Chapter Eight
Looking Ahead

This book takes the general position that prospective price-setting using DRGs is a new approach to thinking about hospital decisions. Physicians need to be informed about and involved with this new system because they, and the very content of medical practice, will be affected. It represents a major and significant change in both the reimbursement system and the incentives and disincentives facing hospitals and hospital administrators. Not since the implementation of Medicare and Medicaid in 1965 has so fundamental a change occurred.

At that time there were deep ideological divisions within the medical fraternity—fear of "socialized medicine" and of government intrusion into the prerogatives of medicine on the one hand and, on the other, recognition that these programs would improve access for the old and the poor and make available funds to cover the costs of caring for them which had not previously been available.

A similar ideological spectrum within the medical community regarding prospective price-setting using DRGs is represented by the physician contributors to this book. Both Dr. Todd and Dr. Passaglia see the system as a challenge and an opportunity—to increase physician sensitivity to hospital costs, to improve physician/hospital cooperation, and to cause physicians to participate

---

This chapter was written by Joel May, President, Health Research and Educational Trust of New Jersey, Princeton, NJ.

more actively in decisions regarding new equipment, staffing, programs, and hospital operations which directly affect them.

Dr. Alessi, while styled as "one of the most outspoken critics of the DRG system," demonstrates what seems to me to be a wait and see attitude. He accurately states some of the problems in the system, urges further evaluation, and generally argues the official position of the Medical Society of New Jersey that implementation should be delayed until we know more about effects of the system on hospitals, patients, and medical practice.

Dr. Silverman takes the position that the system is seriously flawed (due primarily to an intrinsic lack of precision in the scheme for classification of patients), but his "horror stories" also point up some aspects of medical decision-making which may result, for example, in inappropriate admissions. Under the DRG prospective pricing system, these will be much more visible and, therefore, can be more readily addressed.

At the opposite end of the ideological spectrum from Drs. Todd and Passaglia is Dr. Primich. Rather than a challenge and an opportunity, he sees the DRG system as a "bureaucratically sponsored abomination" which will reduce physicians' prerogatives and intrude into their practices. He simply wants it to go away.

This range of attitudes, I believe, reflects accurately the sort of reactions that physicians around the country have or will have when they become aware of the new approach. As I talk to hospital medical staffs around the country, I find physicians who are eager to understand and use the system for a wide variety of reasons: to improve the utilization review process; to get a handle on what they perceive as wide variations in the way cases are handled by colleagues; to help them to convince administration that a particular piece of equipment, or a particular change in staffing, is a good idea; and many others. I also find physicians who are convinced that the kind of visibility that such a system brings to how particular cases are handled and how this may vary across physicians, coupled with the financial incentives to do "less," will homogenize medical practice and force them into a mold within which they may not feel comfortable. This group also feels strongly that the next step will be the extension of this sort of system to payment for physicians' services (and, indeed, there is in the legislation a Congressional mandate to explore ways of doing just that). Some in this group are merely wary and concerned, but many have the deep fear and strength of conviction of Dr. Primich. Finally, there is a group of physicians not (for obvious reasons) represented in this book, who do not understand or even care about the changes in the making and who choose to remain oblivious to them.

It is probably appropriate that there be so many viewpoints concerning a system as new and as complicated as this one. The system is flawed and, in the manifestation chosen by HCFA, potentially grossly unfair to some hospitals because of its lack of fine-tuning to the differences between various classes of hospitals (and even differences between individual institutions). The data produced by the system will make much more visible the ways in which individual physicians practice medicine (ways which are more "efficient") and may very well cause administration and medical staff leadership to bring to bear pressures to move in the direction of perceived efficiency. In the future, hospital decisions concerning new programs, investments in new equipment, staffing, and granting of privileges may very well be made in the context of the contributions to net revenue of the particular DRG, type of patient, or individual physician involved. They will be run more like businesses and this will not be as comfortable for many physicians, administrators, or trustees as the current approach.

Whether these changes are good or bad depends on the particular point of view of the individual. There are those who take the position that "it is the law" and attempt to gear up to function as well as possible under it. Some see the possibilities for better management and increased opportunities for cost containment under the system and leap at the chance to take advantage of them. Others see opportunity in the expanded capability of peer review and the educational possibilities it offers. On the other hand, there are those who do not want others to have access to information on how they care for patients, who are bothered by the need to take cost into consideration when planning and carrying out a regimen of care, or who believe that no corners can or should be cut in patient care regardless of the cost.

By using this system as a means for reimbursing hospitals,

Medicare hopes to be a "prudent buyer" of hospital care. But, as indicated earlier in this book, if Medicare is too "prudent" the result will be significant cost-shifting to other payers. The law encourages experimentation with all-payer systems at the state level. Several states already have started a movement to extend the system to all payers and, by definition, all patients. I expect to see many more such initiatives around the country and this will increase both the impact of the system and the likelihood that changes such as those discussed here will occur.

No system is all good or all bad, and no system will please everybody. But we have been living, for the past two decades at least, with a reimbursement system for hospital care that virtually guaranteed that if we spent a dollar we would subsequently be paid a dollar—regardless of how much we really needed the care that the dollar was spent for. This encouraged waste, casual spending, a feeling that nothing was too good for the patient, and, in general, an attitude about quality and quantity of care that has a counterpart nowhere else in the economy.

Of course the reimbursement system is not alone to blame. Large medical malpractice suits have led to defensive medicine, increasing the number of tests and procedures performed. Technological advances, leading to a better ability to treat patients, have almost universally cost more than did the previous technology. Manufacturers and venders of hospital supplies and equipment and the labor unions with which hospitals dealt understood the reimbursement system well enough to know that a price or wage increase would be easier to take knowing that the dollar spent would retroactively be added to the reimbursement.

All of this led to an inflation rate, specifically for the hospital industry and generally for the medical care industry, so far above that for the rest of the economy that something had to be done. What Congress did was totally reverse the incentives facing hospital management. Where before, under a retrospective cost-based per diem reimbursement, the more hospitals spent, the longer the patient stayed, and the more lavish the equipment and staff, the more hospitals were paid; under the new prospective price per case system, hospitals will hope to discharge patients as soon as possible, to provide only those services that are absolutely necessary, and to staff and equip as minimally as they can consonant with patient safety.

This will change the hospital world in which physicians spend much of their time and it will change the ways in which physicians and hospitals work together. I would expect a much closer working relationship between medical staff leadership and hospital management and increased expectations on the part of the trustees with regard to the peer review process. I would expect more full-time chiefs of service who would be charged with the responsibility of managing the "production process" in their department, taking responsibility for the costs incurred in the patient care process. In short, most of the changes at Hackensack Medical Center which you read about in this book will occur in your institution as well. And for your well-being and that of your institution, you must participate in planning for the system and operating under it.

But you must also recognize that, if this new approach doesn't "work," which means that it doesn't reduce the rate of cost increase, preserve the financial viability of the Medicare Trust Fund, and ease the economic pressure on the major payers, then it will be replaced by something else which might. The Commissioner of Health of New Jersey has been quoted as saying that if the system doesn't work, the alternative is "socialized medicine." It is my view that socialized medicine is not a viable alternative since it would still have to deal with the problems of reimbursement without having much to say about the quantity of care used. In fact, most governmentally operated health care systems around the world are perceived as "entitling" citizens to care—certainly not an effective way to reduce costs.

I'm afraid that the only really effective way to hold costs down (and therefore make the system affordable) is to somehow restrict the quantity of care available. The DRG-based prospective pricing system attempts to do this by providing incentives to hospitals and to physicians to do only what is medically necessary. But it leaves control over the decision at the local level and allows decisions to be made with respect to the needs of individual patients. If it doesn't work as expected—and it won't without the full and open cooperation of all concerned—the only other way that I can think of to restrict the quantity of care is to ration it. I hope that by working together to make the best of the current situation we can avoid that eventuality.

Appendix A

I. Twenty-Seven Suggestions for a Smooth Transition

Attitude is all important as hospitals begin to cope with DRGs. As one chief financial officer in New Jersey advised: "Stay loose, be flexible, don't panic." Those are words of wisdom not only for finance departments that will be grappling with the technicalities of DRG financing, but also for administrators seeking to placate diverse elements within the hospital and physicians who may be utterly confused.

The detailed and specific changes required by DRGs may at first seem overwhelming, and the implications frightening. But if everyone involved is at least willing to accept the changes required, the process should go much more smoothly.

Some of New Jersey's hospitals have already had more than three years' experience with DRGs. Hospitals in other parts of the country have the benefit of our hindsight. The following suggestions, some quite general and others specific, are offered in the hope that your hospital can benefit from our experience. Although some of these suggestions relate to specific individuals and departments of the hospital, it is essential that doctors be aware of the total game plan, as well as the specific strategies involved in implementing DRGs.

1. **Thoroughly educate *everyone* to the DRG system.**

    The board of governors, managers, physicians, employees,

patients and the community—everyone should learn about the system.

2. **Develop programs to educate, indoctrinate and prepare the medical staff leadership for DRGs.**

   Physicians must direct and monitor other physicians so that the hospital and its management are put in the position of dictating to physicians how to practice medicine. Medical staff leadership, who will be implementing and monitoring this program on a day-to-day basis, must be well prepared and thoroughly committed to working closely with the hospital management and staff.

3. **Have the data processing system up and running as soon as possible.**

   An effective DRG information system can be produced only by the computer. This is essential for DRG assignments, billing and for monitoring the performance of the hospital under DRGs.

4. **Establish a chain of command for monitoring the DRG system.**

   Be sure everyone understands how the information in the DRG reports will be used, who is accountable to whom, and what is expected of everyone once the system begins.

5. **Prepare your public information early.**

   Have your public affairs office prepare information explaining the DRG system to your patients and the community. Have brochures ready to distribute with the patient information kits and patient bills, and have knowledgeable, trained staff ready to answer questions. This will not *eliminate* confusion on the part of the public, but it may help head off at least some of the complaints and questions.

6. **Be sure the business office is prepared to issue DRG bills accurately and quickly.**

   The key here is a close working relationship between Medical

Records and the billing department. DRG information must flow quickly and accurately from medical records, where DRG assignments are made, to the business office, where the bills are produced so that you will maintain a positive cash flow.

7. **Make sure your Medical Record Department is fully trained and geared up for DRGs.**

    It must be ready and willing to assist the medical staff in making appropriate DRG assignments. Medical Records must make every effort to minimize coding errors by hiring and/or reassigning personnel if necessary.

8. **Be sure doctors have access to information about the system.**

    Establish a DRG "hotline" in Medical Records with a trained staff person available to assist in recording the final diagnosis and to answer other physician questions. Distribute wallet-sized cards to physicians listing important DRG terminology: principal diagnosis, secondary diagnosis, etc.

9. **Encourage medical staff to cooperate with Medical Records.**

    Since Medical Records personnel know more about the intricacies of DRG coding than physicians do, doctors should avail themselves of the services Medical Records is prepared to offer. This will relieve some of the burden from physicians and help ensure accurate reimbursement to the hospital.

10. **Assign special staff to assist the physicians with the DRG system.**

    If it seems appropriate, hire and/or assign administrative/clerical assistance to the medical staff as it implements, controls and monitors the DRG system on behalf of the hospital.

11. **Let the medical staff know the hospital is depending on them.**

    Now more than ever, a hospital's success is largely dependent upon the cooperation of its medical staff. Doctors must be given adequate information and brought into management decision-making since they are now a much more integral part of the financial well being of the institution.

12. **Create a DRG workgroup composed of representatives of Finance, Medical Records, Utilization Review, Administration, Data Processing, Admitting, and Social Services, as well as key members of the medical staff.**

   The group should meet regularly to monitor the implementation of DRG within the hospital, and it should deal with the different aspects of DRG implementation: data and personnel requirements, procedures and methods of communicating DRG information to physicians, departments and the public. The group should arrange meetings with medical administrative departments and educational seminars for physicians.

13. **Create an inservice education team to discuss DRGs with physicians in each department.**

   Members of the team should include the chief financial officer, the director of medical records, the chairman of the utilization review committee and other key people.

14. **Offer DRG educational programs for the nursing staff.**

   Nursing notes on patient charts are very important in helping to determine DRGs, and nurses must be made a part of the team.

15. **Continually reevaluate how the DRG implementation is working.**

   DRGs can't be learned overnight. Be sure the medical staff leadership, the board, and the administration discuss the DRG issue as a regular agenda item. Constant monitoring will produce better results.

16. **Prepare the finance department for major changes.**

   Finance personnel must be fully trained and prepared to change the hospital's billing system to accommodate DRGs. This may require major accounting changes, and you may want to use your auditing firm to help you make the necessary changes. Make sure the cashier and any other financial staff who deal with the public are fully knowledgeable.

17. **Use outside help if necessary.**

    You may want to hire a consulting firm to help you with the initial implementation of DRGs. Use their expertise, but don't become overly dependent on consultants. Use them only until you can fly on your own.

18. **Acquire computer systems.**

    Management information is the key to survival, so the importance of a computer system cannot be stressed enough. Be certain you have the leadership as well as the computer hardware and software programs needed to broaden the base of information that will be given to the management and the medical staff.

19. **Stress the need for medical staff leadership.**

    Medical staff leadership must serve as a buffer between the administration and physicians in guiding the medical staff through DRGs, monitoring their performance and enforcing policy.

20. **Set internal deadlines and keep to them.**

    For instance, the final diagnosis must be on the patient's medical record within 72 hours of discharge or the physician's admitting privileges will be withdrawn. Likewise, the discharge summary must be completed within 10 days of discharge. The medical record should be on its way to billing within five to seven days. The bill must be prepared and in the mail two days after the medical record is received.

21. **Set a policy that prohibits medical records from being signed out of the Medical Record Department until they are processed.**

22. **Establish a program of concurrent medical record analysis.**

    An analyst from the department should visit the unit while the patient is still hospitalized to review the medical record and make sure it is complete. Anticipate problems by drawing the physician's attention to incomplete areas of the record. Color-coded flags may be used for quick identification by various departments.

23. **Clinical department directors must play a key role.**

    Clinical department directors should create review mechanisms within each department to ensure proper monitoring of physicians' behavior under DRGs. If your hospital is not departmentalized, then a DRG steering committee or coordinating committee should be formed to fulfill this function.

24. **Include your house staff in the DRG system.**

    The house staff in teaching hospitals must be made an integral part of the mechanism of implementing DRGs. They often complete patient charts (under the supervision of an attending physician) and therefore have an important role in the DRG assignment. They also have a direct bearing on the use of the hospital's resources, so be certain that their behavior conforms to the standards of your institution and that there is active monitoring of the services they request on behalf of the attending medical staff.

25. **Involve doctors in planning for the future.**

    Now that physicians are being looked to by management and the board as active participants in holding down costs, they have a responsibility and a right to participate in overall hospital planning.

26. **Hire a physician or physicians to direct and monitor the DRG system if private practitioners cannot afford to take the time.**

    If this move helps the medical staff and hospital cope with DRGs, don't hesitate to do it.

27. **Obtain total commitment throughout the hospital to making DRGs work.**

    Whether or not individuals agree or disagree with the system, hospitals cannot afford to be less than assiduous in striving for success.

II. Thirteen Dangers to Avoid

Some mistakes, obvious to us after three years of DRGs, can be avoided if you are careful. Be aware of these DRG hazards and pitfalls, and your transition to the new system should go more smoothly.

1. **Medical staff should assume responsibility for implementing and monitoring the DRG system.**

   Otherwise hospital management will be in the position of telling physicians what to do—how they should practice medicine in the hospital. This must be avoided as it will place doctors and hospital management in an adversarial position, which will doom the hospital to failure under DRGs.

2. **Even though your average length of stay is low, don't assume that there isn't room for improvement.**

   A careful review of individual practitioners' performance may reveal a surprise. Utilization review is more important than ever, as a low length of stay is critical under DRGs.

3. **Scrutinize patient services carefully with an eye toward greater efficiency.**

   There is always room for improvement—more outpatient services, better discharge planning, etc. Doctors and hospitals can't afford to rest on past achievements. You must continue to ask whether there isn't a better way for your hospital to deliver health care services.

4. **Don't think DRGs aren't your problem or that they will simply go away if you ignore them.**

   DRGs are here and you must learn how to cope with them. The more you know about them, the better for you and for your hospital.

5. **Don't think the hospital's problems can all be solved by the other guy.**

Physicians and administration must work together, as there is a distinct interdependence of both in the delivery of service. For instance, improved scheduling of services and increased availability of physicians in the hospital can have a dramatic impact on length of stay. But this takes a combined effort with both parties working together for the same goal.

6. **Physicians must not be so inflexible and defensive about the realm of patient care that they are unwilling to give Medical Records the latitude it needs in determining and recording the proper DRG classification.**

    Physicians must allow Medical Records to review the information, ask questions and make the appropriate DRG assignment, which will maximize the hospital's reimbursement. Physicians must not view Medical Records' involvement as interference in their right to practice medicine. Medical Record personnel are the *experts* in DRG classification, and physicians must utilize rather than spurn their expertise.

7. **Physicians should not leave the whole business of DRG assignment to Medical Records.**

    Tempting as that might be, doctors still record the diagnosis and the more they know about DRGs, the more they will become active participants in the new system.

8. **The medical staff should not be threatened by the hospital's increased reliance on computer systems.**

    The information supplied by these new systems will be as vital to the individual physician as it is to the hospital administration. The medical staff leadership must demand access to this information and take appropriate action before the task is usurped by hospital management.

9. **Once the DRG system is implemented, physicians must not think their job is done.**

    Communication with administration and active physician monitoring of the system must continue. It is obviously to the physician's advantage to remain knowledgeable about the hospital's financial status, what the problems are, and what role the medical staff should have in resolving them.

10. **The medical staff should not hesitate to establish procedures and mechanisms for disciplining physicians who fail to cooperate with the system.**

    Delay can only cause further problems. The Board of Governors, the medical staff leadership and the administration should all know how the medical staff intends to deal with physicians who do not comply.

11. **The medical staff must not fail to communicate their feelings about the DRG system, as well as their plans for implementing and monitoring it, to the board of governors.**

    The medical staff must therefore make DRGs a subject of discussion at the joint conference committee, the medical executive committee, the executive committee of the board of trustees and other appropriate settings. Such discussions provide an opportunity to enhance communication among the medical staff, the administration and the board.

12. **Don't think you can keep on practicing medicine the way you have been, convinced that is the only way to provide quality health care.**

    That would be as dangerous as for the hospital to believe it can go on spending as usual, convinced the reimbursement will ultimately be forthcoming. It is impractical to assume that either rates will be rebased (a newer, more expensive base year) or that the system will revert to a cost-based system. This thinking on the part of physicians and/or administrators is likely to be costly, as regulators devised the current approach specifically to prevent this from happening.

13. **Don't pride yourselves on the fact that you're not a business, that no one can put a price tag on health care.**

    Sorry, but that's exactly what DRGs have done, and telling yourself otherwise is a "head in the sand" approach. The system must be met with positive, aggressive action by physi-

APPENDIX A

cians and all others in health care as well. If you think DRGs are awful, set out to prove it. Don't wrap yourself in medical chauvinism and try to talk the system to death; help change it!

III. Fourteen Suggestions to Improve Efficiency

As this book suggests, one very important outcome of the DRG system is that it has forced management and medical staffs to look at the care they deliver in a new way—to take cost into serious consideration. It has been very tempting in the past to operate the hospital without sufficient consideration of cost-effectiveness.

DRGs have taught hospitals in a compelling fashion that they have to live within a budget, and that they must learn to make choices.

DRGs have forced hospitals and physicians to be innovative in our planning for the future of hospitals.

It may seem at times that the entire burden of living with DRGs is on the physician, that hospital management is issuing an ultimatum to doctors. Hospitals are all too aware that they must clean house also; they must cast aside old ways of thinking about the delivery of health care and come up with innovative methods that will balance quality care with efficiency.

Below is a list of changes that Hackensack Medical Center has already implemented or is considering. In some cases, we are benefiting by lessons learned from industry, which has had a head start on cost-efficiency. Other ideas grow out of the specific needs of a hospital setting. Perhaps these changes can serve as a checklist for other physicians and hospitals as they proceed with implementation of the DRG system.

1. **Hospitals may now have to consider functioning on a full seven-day-a-week schedule for maximum utilization of existing resources.**

    Hospitals have traditionally operated at full capacity for only five days of the week. Weekends are generally marked by lower service, with many departments functioning at reduced capacity or not at all. For example, operating rooms frequently do not function for a full day or on weekends. A seven-day schedule throughout the hospital would mean the costs associated with the physical plant would be spread over the fullest utilization; there would be an increased volume of patients and services with only the added variable costs of staff, supplies, etc.

2. **Pre-admission screening saves patient days and makes more beds available for other patients.**

   Pre-admission testing has always been an important program at Hackensack Medical Center. The day before DRGs went into effect here, on May 1, 1980, a memo was sent to all the attending staff emphasizing the importance of full utilization of pre-admission testing because of its critical importance under DRGs. It can cut days off a hospital stay and sometimes the result of these tests will show that the patient should not be admitted at all at that particular time. How much better to find that out before the patient is admitted!

3. **Efficiency must be an important criterion as the hospital evaluates many different areas.**

   Capital purchases should be reviewed for effectiveness, cost and necessity by both the medical staff and management, and hospitals should evaluate their existing resources before deciding on new purchases.

   Similarly, operating systems should be studied with an eye toward increased efficiency, such as improved scheduling of services between departments. Delays in patient care that could be tolerated under the old system now may mean financial losses, so the entire system should be analyzed to see if there is room for improvement.

   Productivity-based merit pay for employees may act as an incentive toward increased efficiency, and this also should be studied.

   These are all methods which have been used effectively by

industry; now it is health care's turn to follow industry's example.

4. **Staffing patterns should be reviewed and variable staffing systems instituted in order to minimize overtime and maximize use of the hospital's facilities in response to patient demand.**

   Split shifts and flex time, utilized by industry for some time now for the same reasons, should become available alternatives to the regular 9-to-5 day. Staff forecasting should become routine.

5. **Nurses comprise the largest single group of hospital employees, so the cost of nursing should be carefully studied with an eye toward maximizing service and minimizing cost.**

   Studies should be made of the various types of nursing care delivery, such as primary care, team care, etc., with a view toward finding the most efficient mix of nursing and non-nursing support personnel. Without jeopardizing patient care, it is important to use non-nursing staff for duties that do not require the care of a professional nurse. In this way, the hospital will get the most efficient use of its professional nursing staff.

6. **The hospital of the future will be the place where only the sickest patients are housed, those truly needing acute care.**

   Just as it would be wasteful to have all patients in the intensive care unit, it is just as wasteful to have certain types of patients in the hospital at all—those patients who do not require the intensive medical care associated with an acute hospital setting. That means hospitals must begin to develop other modes of delivering care which are more suited to their patients' individual needs, and therefore are most cost-efficient. These alternatives to traditional hospital care include self-care units, hospice programs, home care programs, and a whole range of preventive care, ambulatory care and outpatient services.

   Self-care units, where a family member stays with the patient during the hospital stay, can result in a tremendous saving of nursing time. Affiliated nursing homes would ensure a bed for those patients who no longer need to be hospitalized but cannot be discharged to a home and have no place else to go. Each day a patient spends in the hospital waiting for a nursing home bed can mean a great financial loss to your hospital and is an inappropriate use of hospital beds, besides. Hospice programs treat patients in a much less costly manner at home than in a hospital bed, and they are an alternative that is vastly preferred by both patients and their families. In general, there is a need for a much wider variety of health care settings, and if these settings are not available, hospitals must begin to provide them.

7. **Continual monitoring of the appropriateness of requests for such services as laboratory, pharmacy, respiratory therapy, physical therapy, diagnostic and therapeutic radiology, and other high-cost areas is essential.**

Ancillary services must be used as needed, and not simply because they are available. This is an excellent opportunity for physicians to become involved through the establishment of more specific guidelines for use of these services, as well as improved scheduling—more hours per day and more days per week.

Ancillary services such as these represent 20 percent of our hospital's budget and their proper utilization is crucial under DRGs. For instance, with the cost of antibiotics soaring (up 21 percent in 1982), Hackensack Medical Center brought in an Infectious Disease Fellow to monitor and guide physicians on the proper ordering of antibiotics. It is important for doctors to use the lowest cost drugs at the lowest possible dose for the shortest possible time, and for them to understand why. Physicians were given a comparison sheet showing the cost of various drugs. For example, four cephalosporins range in cost from $117 to $400 for a ten-day treatment. Once physicians realize the financial consequences of their ordering practices, they should become more careful about them.

8. **If your hospital does not have a single day surgery unit, it should look into establishing one for those surgical procedures deemed appropriate by the medical staff.**

   Whether there is a need for local or general anesthetic, many types of procedures may be performed on an outpatient basis. At Hackensack Medical Center, more than 60 different types of procedures are performed through the Day Accommodation Room, where patients are admitted, undergo surgery and leave the hospital the same day. The cost-saving is obvious to both the patient and the hospital, and many patients vastly prefer the convenience of not having to spend a night in the hospital. Some hospitals even give patients the option of having babies as a same day procedure.

9. **No matter what your outpatient service is like, you can probably expand it.**

   For many individuals, outpatient care entirely obviates the need for a hospital admission. For others, it means they may be discharged from the hospital sooner. In any case, outpatient services free hospital beds for patients who truly need them, and, from the hospital's viewpoint, allow a quicker turnover of patients. The formula for success under DRGs is more admissions and shorter lengths of stay. Any appropriate alternative care which promotes this aim is good for the hospital.

10. **For the system to work, patients must be made to view health care in a new way, too.**

    When patients are admitted, they should be advised that the hospital will be working closely with them and with their physician to provide services in the shortest possible time so they may be discharged as soon as possible. Patients should be made to realize that some services which have been associated with hospitals in the past will now be provided in other settings.

11. **All clinical programs should be looked at carefully and cost accounted on a profit and loss basis.**

DRGs have taught us in New Jersey that every hospital can no longer have every new piece of equipment and provide every service possible. Decisions about whether a specific service should be initiated, continued, expanded or dropped must be made after a bottom line evaluation of whether or not there is a real demand for that service. Careful consideration must be given to whether the service duplicates a similar service at a nearby hospital. If it is determined that the other hospital is providing the service more efficiently and has a greater market share, your hospital should consider very carefully whether it is worth competing.

Just like in business, hospitals should concentrate on those services it performs best—whether they are cardiac catherization, dialysis, inpatient psychiatry or any other. On the other hand, hospitals might be wise to eliminate those services in which they cannot successfully compete.

12. **Computers are an absolutely essential tool for hospitals as they attempt to deal with DRGs in the years ahead.**

    Hospitals should immediately begin planning for the purchase and implementation of computer systems. Such systems are crucial for management decisions regarding hospital efficiency and productivity. DRGs and computers can provide a wealth of information that the hospital will be able to use in making a whole series of important management decisions: what types of services to expand, how to increase utilization of the laboratory, what kinds of patients it is best able to care for, which doctors are using the hospital most efficiently, and many others.

13. **Consider very carefully the benefits of expanding facilities versus remodeling the existing plant.**

    New construction may not always be in the hospital's best interests. There may be other alternatives to meet physical plant limitations such as developing relationships with other institutions including nursing homes and rehabilitation facilities.

14. **Because shorter lengths of stay are a must under DRGs, discharge planning is crucial.**

    Discharge coordinators might be hired to oversee plans for patients so that they may leave the hospital sooner, secure in the knowledge that a continuum of care will be provided once they leave, whether that continuum is a home care program, a nursing home or placement in a long-term care facility. Representatives from nursing, social service, home care and other allied specialties should work together with the physician to find other sources of care for patients who no longer need to stay in the hospital.

Appendix B

How to Speak the DRG Language

DRGs carry with them a whole new jargon that you'll need to learn in order to sound like you know what you're talking about. This list will get you started.

GLOSSARY

AUTOGRP: Automated grouper, the computer program used to determine DRG classifications. The AUTOGRP partitions patients' hospital discharge information into homogeneous groups according to specific variables such as medical diagnoses, surgical procedures, and age.

Case mix: The types of patients, defined by diagnosis, age, acuity, etc., treated in a hospital. Hospital case mix varies slightly but generally remains fairly constant.

Charge-based reimbursement: Prior to DRGs in New Jersey, this represented the amount reimbursed to a hospital, based on the actual charges incurred during the hospital stay. This was applicable to commercial insurance and self pay patients. (See cost-based reimbursement.)

Clinical outlier: Patients assigned to DRGs with poorly defined clinical characteristics, precluding valid comparisons of patients within the DRG. Also, patients with surgery unrelated to the principal diagnosis.

Comorbidity: A pre-existing condition, that will, because of its presence with a specific principal diagnosis, affect the treatment received and/or length of stay.

Complication: A condition that develops after admission to the hospital which affects the treatment received and/or length of stay. (You already knew that one, didn't you?)

Concurrent analysis: Ongoing quantitative and qualitative review of medical records during the patient's hospitalization.

Controlled charges: The actual cost of care plus a mark-up component to cover the cost of indigent care, indirect costs, and a prompt pay discount. Controlled charges are subject to limitations by the state and are a part of New Jersey's DRG system.

Cost-based reimbursement: Prior to DRGs in New Jersey, this represented the amount of reimbursement based on a hospital's approved cost per patient day. This was applicable to Medicare, Medicaid, and Blue Cross. (See charge-based reimbursement.)

Cost-per-case: The cost to the hospital to treat a patient; what the hospital spends on a patient's care.

Data base: Collection of information.

DRG: Diagnosis Related Group; one of 467 categories of diagnoses or procedures which relate to hospital inpatients. Patients are grouped into DRGs according to characteristics such as principal diagnosis, secondary diagnosis, sex, age, surgical procedure, and other complications. Each classification exhibits a consistent amount of resource consumption as measured by some unit (e.g., patient days, dollars, etc.).

Discharge abstract: A summary description about the patient's hospitalization, prepared upon discharge.

Grouper: A computer program that assigns patients to DRG categories using medical abstract data.

HCFA: Health Care Financing Administration.

ICD-9-CM: International Classification of Diseases, 9th Revision, Clinical Modification. A codification of diseases and procedures, used as a basis for determining DRGs.

MDC: Major diagnostic category; one of 23 major groupings of DRGs, based on the area or system of the body affected.

Major secondary diagnosis: A complication or associated condition which requires treatment during the patient's hospital stay.

Outliers: Patients displaying atypical characteristics relative to other patients in a DRG. In the Medicare system, outliers are currently defined as patients with atypically long or atypically expensive hospital stays, who are billed charges rather than DRG rates. (In New Jersey, outliers include atypically long and short stays, as well as patients who die in the hospital, leave against medical advice, or are admitted and discharged the same day.)

Principal diagnosis: The condition responsible for the patient's admission to the hospital; the major factor in determining the DRG classification.

Principal procedure: A procedure performed for definitive treatment rather than one peformed for diagnostic or exploratory purposes, or one that was necessary to take care of a complication.

Prospective payment system: A method of reimbursing hospitals which determines "reasonable" expenses for the year ahead and sets a fixed payment rate based on this projection.

Secondary diagnosis: Conditions that coexist at the time of admission, or that develop subsequently, and which affect the treatment received and/or length of stay.

Secondary procedures: Other therapeutic and diagnostic procedures performed during a patient stay.

Trim points: Low and high lengths of stay. Patients who fall outside the high trim point for a particular DRG are outliers under the Medicare system.

Index

Appeals of DRG charges, 123–125, 136

Base year, 10, 101–103, 108

Case mix by physician: sample report, 190–193
Comorbidity and complications, 10, 45, 70
defined, 229
Cost-shifting, 7, 21, 37, 56, 124, 164
"Creep", DRG, 21, 79

Development of DRGs, 6–7, 9–10
Diagnosis
final, 20, 54, 62
major (not the equivalent of principal), 77
and medical records, 63–64, 71–75, 77–82, 86–89, 118–120
primary (principal) and secondary, 9–10, 54, 59, 230
Discharge status, 10, 62, 64
DRG defined, 2–3, 229

Fees, private physicians', and DRGs, 54–55

Glossary, 228–230

Home health care, 46–47, 54, 130

ICD-9-CM explained, 61–62
Implementation costs, 109–110
"Incentive/disincentive" sample reports, 188–189, 194–195
Inflation and DRGs, 101–103
Insurance (non-Medicare), 37, 56, 112–113, 120

Length-of-stay sample report, 180–181

"Market share" per DRG, 173
Medicare: cost to federal budget, 7–8, 14–15, 138

Nursing-home care, 117, 161

"Outliers", 11–12, 84–85, 115, 136, 155; see also definitions in glossary, 228–230
Outpatient procedures and services, 26, 46, 54, 114

Pre-admission testing, 54

231

Procedure, primary and secondary surgical, 9–10, 230
Prospective payment system
 defined, 2, 230
 extension beyond Medicare, 54–56, 100–101, 116–117, 120, 136, 209
PSROs, 40, 49, 123, 158

"Ratcheting", 20
Rates, methods of calculating for DRGs *(see also* base year), 10–13, 24, 104–15, 108–110, 113–114

Regionalization of hospital services, 50, 98–99, 109

Services used per DRG, 172, 182–187 (sample reports)
Social Security Amendments of 1983: Title VI, 8

Teaching hospitals, 11–12, 110
Technological advances and equipment, 6, 25, 108–109, 196–205

Underutilization, 47–49